WILDLIFE MANAGEMENT IN INDIA

WILDLIFE MANAGEMENT IN INDIA

N.K. Bose

CYBER TECH PUBLICATIONS
4264/3, Ansari Road, Daryaganj, New Delhi-110002 (India)
Ph.: 011-23244078. Fax: 011-23280028
E-Mail: cyberpublicationsdelhi@yahoo.com

WILDLIFE MANAGEMENT IN INDIA

N.K. Bose

First Edition 2009

Published by

G.S. Rawat for **Cyber Tech Publications**
4264/3, Ansari Road, Daryaganj, New Delhi-110002 (India)
Ph.: 011-23244078. Fax: 011-23280028
E-Mail: cyberpublicationsdelhi@yahoo.com

Printed at : **Amit Enterprises**, Maujpur, Delhi, (9810878184)

Preface

The rapid growth of human and livestock populations coupled with urbanization and industrialization in the 19th century and consequent pressures of land hunger and development have taken an increasingly heavy toll of the country's wilderness. Conservation measures to mitigate the impacts of these pressures, however, have largely been slow and inadequate. The first few wildlife Protected Areas (PAs) were set up some fifty years ago, but it was only in the late 1960s that growing concern at the scale of environmental degradation allowed the development of PAs in many parts of the country. Accordingly, in 1983 the Government of India decided that the rational planning and implementation of a comprehensive network of PAs would be the keystone of the National Wildlife Action Plan. In 1984 the then Department of Environment appointed the Wildlife Institute of India to formulate plans for such a network. Consultants were asked to gather data from the States, and their information was compiled at the Institute. A draft report was produced in 1988. Four main subject areas were covered: (a) the preparation of a biogeographic classification of India designed to facilitate conservation planning, (b) a consideration of important areas, (c) a review of existing protected areas, and (d) the recommendation of new protected areas to ensure an adequate network covering the range of biological diversity in the country.

—*Author*

CONTENTS

1

Wildlife Management in India: Policies, Practices and Future Needs

India's forests and wildlife are currently the subject of a variety of suggestions for their management in view of the ever increasing human and livestock population pressures in and around the forests. The main thrusts in the suggested new approaches revolve around the premise that people living in and around the forests should be coopted in the management of forests to meet their basic sustenance needs so that they come forward to protect the forests and wildlife. Perspectives in the relationships between people and natural resources have changed rapidly over the past few decades, but not necessarily in the forms in which these are being perceived by different strata of human society. Hence there is no unanimity about the approach to be adopted in management of forest areas and there is uncertainty about the achievement of desired conservation goals.

Traditional forestry had been providing the very benefits to the people that are currently being sought through the recent suggestions for forest and wildlife management in India.

A review of the perceived and achieved impacts of practices in wildlife management, ecodevelopment and people's participatory approach in the management of forested areas brings out the need for reorientation of the approach for forestry on purely ecological principles if sustainability of production potential in natural ecosystems is to be ensured for sharing the benefits of conservation with the people on a longterm basis.

INDIA'S ACHIEVEMENTS

Post economic reforms, the gross development product (GNP) improved from an average of about 5.7 per cent in the 1980s to an average of about 6.5 per cent in the Eighth and Ninth Plan periods, making India one of the ten fastest growing developing countries, where the dismantling of the industrial licensing system, free investments by foreign companies, lowering of import tariffs on capital goods all contributed.

Encouraging progress was also made in other sectors. The percentage of the population in poverty continued to decline, even if not as much as was targeted. Population growth decelerated below 2 per cent for the first time in four decades. Literacy increased from 52 per cent in 1991 to 65 per cent in 2001 with improvement evident in all states. Software services, entertainment and information technology-enabled services emerged as new sources of strength, creating confidence about India's potential to be competitive in the world economy.

THE OTHER SIDE

However, the picture is not all rosy and are clouded by other features which give cause for concern. The economy is currently in a decelerating phase and urgent steps are needed to arrest the deceleration and restore momentum. Although employment growth has almost kept pace with labour force growth, the incidence of unemployment on current daily status basis is relatively high, at above 7 per cent.

More than half of the children between 1-5 years in rural areas are under-nourished, with girl children suffering even more severe malnutrition. The infant mortality rate has stagnated at 72 per 1000 for the last several years. As many as 60 per cent of rural households and 20 per cent urban households do not have power connection. Only 60 per cent of urban households have taps within their homes, and far fewer have latrines inside the house. The decline in the juvenile sex ratio over the last decade, visible in the data from Census 2001, is an indication that the Constitutional assurance of freedom and equality for women is still far from being fulfilled.

Environmental Costs

This development has also come at a price. Rapid population growth coupled with rapid industrialisation has caused severe environmental degradation and pollution with local, national, regional and global impacts. According to a World Bank study, between 1975 and 1995, as India's GDP doubled, industrial and vehicular pollution load went up between 4 and 8 times respectively.

Deterioration in urban environment, increase in slum population, and in air, river, and water pollution has vastly affected the quality of life of the urban poor. The air quality of major cities indicate that ambient levels of nitrous oxides, sulphur dioxide, lead and suspended particulate matter are often higher than World Health Organisation and Indian standards. Other harmful substances like ozone are not even monitored. Land and forest degradation in the rural areas, and overexploitation of groundwater is seriously threatening sustainability of food production.

ENVIRONMENTAL DEGRADATION, POVERTY AND ECONOMIC DEVELOPMENT

The strong linkage between environment degradation, poverty and economic development is now an established fact. It has been more or less accepted now that it is not always the poor who are the greatest polluters responsible for a degraded environment. Urbanisation and industrialisation and unsustainable use of natural resources have all contributed to serious environmental problems (See Box: The Small Industries Pollution Problem).

Conventional thinking on environment blamed the poor for overexploitation of natural resources, as poverty and environment were considered linked in a 'downward spiral,' in which poor people, forced to overuse the environmental resources for their daily survival, are further impoverished by the degradation of these resources. Population growth and economic change (which often bypasses the poor, or reduces their access to natural resources) were also seen to contribute to this process.

It was therefore believed that poverty needs to be eradicated in developing countries before they can turn their attention to environmental protection.

The perception of the 'vicious circle' as characterising the environmental degradation and poverty in countries is vulnerable to criticism on several counts. It is a simplistic, exaggerated and misleading thesis. In the past, when poverty levels were much higher in developing countries, there was not much environmental degradation. Now that poverty levels are declining significantly, it does not seem plausible to attribute environmental degradation to poverty. Evidently other factors play a more important role.

The poor should be viewed as the victims rather than the perpetrators of environment damage. As they are dependent on nature for livelihood, they are very vulnerable to natural calamities, environmental degradation and ecological disasters, which are often humanmade, such as Bhopal Gas Tragedy, and pollution caused in the river Yamuna by industries and upstream rich farmers. Thus the belief that all economic development alleviates poverty is not entirely true. There are cases of destructive development which aggravate poverty and contribute to environmental degradation at the same time.

Probably the first victim of any environmental degradation are the women among the poor. A fuelwood crisis as a result of deforestation, for example, forces village women to travel for miles in search of wood. This involves waste of energy and time which women could have devoted to more remunerative work. They have to bring water for cooking and washing from great distances. Fodder scarcity also affects women first: the care of livestock is their responsibility. This burden on women in turn has an impact on girl children. When the mothers' time is spent on fetching fuel food and drinking water, girl children are kept at home and discouraged from attending school. They have to look after younger children, sweep the house and do the household chores.

There is enough empirical evidence to establish that environmental conservation must go hand in hand with economic development because any economic development which destroys the environment will create more poverty, unemployment and diseases and thus cannot be called even economic development. It may just be transfer of resources from the poor to the rich. Environmentally destructive economic development will impoverish the poor even further and destroy their livelihood resource base. Therefore the environmental concern in the developing world must go 'beyond pretty trees and tigers' and must link it with peoples' lives and well being.

Urban Utopia?

While rural populations suffer from an increasingly degrading natural resource base, in urban areas, populations face environmental challenges of a different kind. There is mounting evidence that increasing pressures on urban environments is taking its toll on the quality of life of urban population. Although economic deprivation may be less acute in urban areas than in the rural, the deleterious effects of non-economic factors may indeed be more pervasive. Urban population growth is much higher thanthe rate of population growth, and already about 29 per cent of India's population lives in urban areas, frequently in deplorable conditions.

HUMAN SECURITY

Human security and better quality of life depends on several factors, all of them linked to the environment. These include:

Water security for consumption and livelihood purposes;

Food and nutrition security;

Health security;

Livelihood security;

Ecological security; and,

Social security

These linkages make the issue of environment protection all the more serious in India. The environmental problems facing India are different from those facing the affluent countries and are more immediate. Air and water pollution, soil degradation, deforestation, desertification, shrinking wetlands, inadequate public health and sanitation, indoor pollution in rural areas, growing water scarcity, falling groundwater tables, the lack of minimum flow in rivers, and overextraction of water for irrigation purposes are some of the environmental problems that need to be addressed first before any poverty alleviation programme can meet with success or human security achieved.

Thus environmental management and economic development are mutually supportive aspects of same agenda, indeed two sides of the same coin. A poor environment undermines development, while inadequate development results in lack of resources for environmental protection.

ENVIRONMENT PROTECTION IN INDIA

The regulatory and institutional decision-making framework for environmental protection in India is embodied in nine major acts of the Indian Parliament. These are: the Water (Prevention and Control of Pollution) Act of 1974 which established the Central Pollution Control Board (CPCB) and State Pollution Control Boards (SPCBs); the Air (Prevention and Control of Pollution) Act of 1977 which added the monitoring of air emissions to the responsibilities of the various Boards; the Environment (Protection) Act of 1986; the Forest (Conservation) Act of 1980, amended in 1988; the Motor Vehicle Act of 1938, amended in 1988; the Public Liability Insurance Act of 1991; and Notifications on the Coastal Regulation Zone, 1991; and Environmental Impact Assessment of Development Projects, in 1994, the National Environment Appellate Authority Act, 1997.

Most of the above Acts and Notifications are aimed at strengthening the command-and-control regime. New initiatives, especially in the form of a mix of regulations and legislation, fiscal incentives for technology acquisition, voluntary agreements, educational programs and information campaigns are required. Although the government has introduced some of these measures, more is required because the regulatory structure of a central authority, the ministry of environment and forests (and other ministries) and the Central Pollution Control Board linked to state-level implementation agencies have proved to be largely unsuccessful in effectively managing the protection of the environment.

An assessment of India's environmental management system suggests that weaknesses are evident at every administrative level at the center, state and district. Further, despite aid under specific investment projects, more needs to be done in the area of industrial pollution, particularly air emissions, coastal zone management, urban land use including the citing of industries, and mitigating environmental degradation in the mining sector.

Tightening Up Belts

In 1993, the government, through the ministry of environment and forests issued the Environment Action Program - India (EAP), developed after consultations with other ministries, states and NGOs. The EAP identified seven environmental priorities for India:

(a) conservation and sustainable utilisation of biodiversity in selected ecosystems including forests, mangroves, wetland, coral reefs, mountain ecosystems;

(b) afforestation, wastelands development and conservation of soil and moisture and ensuring that water sources are not polluted;

(c) control of industrial and related pollution with an accent on the reduction and or **management** of wastes, particularly hazardous wastes;

(d) improving access to clean technologies;

(e) tackling urban environmental issues;

(f) an alternative energy plan; and,

(g) strengthening scientific understanding of environmental issues, as well as strengthening structures for training at different levels, orientation and creating environmental awareness.

A1996 study indicated that (a) despite a strong legal framework and various ministries at the center, departments and boards at the state level; and local agencies involved in environmental management, implementation remains weak. Institutional capacity building to strengthen monitoring, enforcement, and compliance with existing laws can have a high payoff; and (b) the government alone cannot be responsible for environmental management, stronger efforts have to be made to involve the large non-governmental organisation community in programs ranging from biodiversity conservation to alternative energy programs.

The study also recognised that this cooperation will require transparent policies and practices such as early involvement in the environmental impact assessment process, access to information, and actions to increase involvement through public participatory processes.

MOVING AHEAD

In the Approach Paper to the Tenth Five Year Plan for the period 2002-2007, the government has recognised that mere economic growth is not enough and that development must be defined in broader terms of human being enhancement. The Tenth Plan has thus outlined a set of monitorable targets to achieve its objectives:

- Reduction of poverty ratio by 5 percentage points by 2007 and by 15 percentage points by 2012;
- Providing gainful high-quality employment to the labour force over the tenth Plan period;
- All children in school by 2003; all children to complete 5 years of schooling by 2007;
- Reduction of gender gaps in literacy and wages rates by at least 50 per cent by 2007.
- Reduction in decadal rate of population growth between 2001 and 2011 to 16.2 per cent
- Increase in literacy rate to 75 per cent with in the Plan period;
- Reduction of Infant Mortality Rate (IMR) to 45 per 1000 live births by 2007 and to 28 by 2012.

- Increase in forest and tree cover to 25 per cent by 2007 and 33 per cent by 2012.
- All villages to have sustained access to portable drinking water within the Plan period.
- Cleaning of major polluted rivers by 2007 and other notified stretches by 2012.

As indicated, these targets relate to good environmental performance and governance,highlighting how cross-cutting environment management issues are.

Approach to the Tenth Plan

The basic objective of the Tenth Plan is to bring about all round enhancement of human well being by eradicating poverty through adopting well conceived development strategies in which environmental concerns are posited as the vital aspects. environmental management and economic development are mutually supportive aspects of the same agenda. A poor environment undermines development, while inadequate developmentresults in a lack of resources for environmental protection.

Environmental conservation must go hand in hand with economic development because any economic development which destroys the environment will create more poverty, unemployment and disease. Environmentally destructive economic development will impoverish the poor even further and destroy their livelihood resource base. Environmental concern must be linked to people's lives and well being, impact as these do various aspects of human existence that include health and livelihood amongst others. Air pollution, soil degradation, deforestation, desertification, shrinking wetlands.

Inadequate public health and sanitation, indoor pollution in rural areas, growing water scarcity, falling ground water tables, the lack of minimum flow in the rivers and over extraction of water for irrigation purposes are some of the environmental problems that need to be addressed first before any poverty alleviation programme can meet with success.

Based on the objectives of the *Approach Paper To The Tenth Five Year plan 2002-2007*, the ministry of environment and forests prepared a strategy for the period and for the year 2002-2003.

MINISTRY OF ENVIRONMENT AND FORESTS

The ministry of environment and forests is charged with the responsibility of planning, promoting, coordination and overseeing the implementation of various environmental and forestry programmes. Responsibilities include environmental management to promote health considerations, focus on poverty alleviation by enhancing access of the poor to natural resources for livelihood and heightening awareness regarding environmentally sound living process by focusing on nature-human synergy. The ministry has been designated as the nodal agency in the country for the United Nations Environment Programme (UNEP), International Centre for Integrated Mountain development (ICIMOD) and looks after the follow-up of the United Nations' Conference on Environment and Development (UNCED).

The objectives are supported by a set of legislative and regulatory measures aiming at preservation, conservation and protection of environment as indicated above. The activities of this ministry can be broadly divided into four sub-sectors namely environment, forestry and wildlife, National Afforestation and Ecodevelopment Board (NAEB) and the National River Conservation Directorate (NRCD).

Strategy for the Tenth Five Year Plan

The ministry has identified the following strategy to meet the objectives of the Tenth Plan:

(a) To promote 'sustainable development' by emphasising the intrinsic linkage between environment management and socio- economic development of the people, through increased access to natural capital which is an essential component of reducing poverty. The emphasis will be on creating an enabling environment in terms of policies, institutions which support the over-arching objective of poverty reduction

(b) To mainstream environment issues in the developmental strategy, a multi-pronged approach will be followed which will include the incorporation of environment in the curriculum, sharpening the mechanism for the environmental auditing of the development activities, creating heightened awareness, broad-basing community involvement and to forging a coordinated effort with corporate and public sector in environmental management

(c) To input environmental concerns in the developmental scenarios by treating environment as a cross-sectoral issue

(d) To take concrete steps for increasing forest/tree cover from the existing level of 19.37 per cent to 25 per cent by 2007 and 33 per cent by 2012. While striving for this goal the thrust will be given to:

   (1) increasing productivity;

   (2) efficient management of resources; and,

   (3) focus on the local needs and location specific strategies in terms of species selection and management of resources.

(e) Cleaning of major polluted rivers by 2007 and other notified stretches by 2012. In order to have efficient, smooth and time bound attainment of the goal, a holistic and integrated approach of addressing not only the intercepting sewers and sewage treatment plants which currently constituted the core of the Plan, but also other components as internal sewage, solid waste management and toilets with the participation of states, public and local bodies. The focus will on be treating the town as a unit by way of convergence of various schemes.

(f) Major changes in the institutional framework with a view to make it responsive and accountable to perceived needs of people

(g) Involvment of youth in environmental education, through a National Green Corps scheme to be implemented in all educational institutions covering class 8th to 12th class.(13)

Thrust Areas

The thrust areas under the environmental sector for the Tenth Plan will be environmental impact assessment and abatement of pollution; ecological survey; conservation and eco-regeneration; environmental education, awareness and people's participation; environmental research and training; and, national river conservation.

Under forestry, the thrust on sustainable management of forestry resources with people's participation initiated during the Eighth Plan and carried through the Ninth Plan will be further strengthen during the Tenth Plan period.

The programmes/schemes will focus on farm forestry, measures to sustain joint forest management, take care of the rights and interests of the tribal population living in an around the forests, review of the subsidies in the sale of non timber forest produce (NTFP) and promote bamboo cultivation and coastal shelter belt plantations for prevention of natural calamities.

The wildlife programmes/schemes will focus on strengthening and enhancing the protective area networking through suitable policy framework and management plans; settlement of right and relocation of villages; promotion of eco-development by giving priority to national parks and sanctuaries having higher biodiversity and high threats; timely payments of compensation against the depredation by wildlife; control of poaching; taxidermy and illegal trade in wildlife species; and, promotion of wildlife tourism.

The Tenth Plan thrusts for research and education segment will be on watershed management, desert development, medicinal plants, coastal areas, bamboos and agro forestry and biodiversity conservation. Added emphasis will be given to educational and training programmes.

Activity Profile

The principal objective of environment sector for the Tenth Five Year Plan is to integrate the objectives of the policies stressed by the Planning Commission and to take cognizance of long term developmental perspectives related to industrialisation, power generation, transportation, agriculture, irrigation and other economic activities. Some of these goals have been identified as indicated below.

Environment

Industrial Pollution Control

It is proposed to ensure that large and medium polluting industrial units and stand alone polluting small scale industrial units (SSIs) install and operate pollution control devices and meet the norms. It will be ensured that small industries located in clusters and in industrial estates are covered under common effluent treatment plants (CETPs). Siting of pollution industries will be insisted to conform to the zoning plan which would be integrated with state industrial policy. Action plans will be effectively implemented to reduce pollution in all the critically polluted areas.

Water Pollution Control

Most of the rivers, streams, and large stretches of the coastal marine environment in India are highly polluted with municipal waste, waste generated from industry, chemical agents from fertilisers, pesticides from crop protection, and silt from degraded catchments. Untreated sewage and other non-industrial wastes account for four times as much pollution as industrial effluent. In the major cities, less than 50 per cent of the total wastewater generated is collected and less than one-fourth is treated. The consequence of such pollution is high levels of waterborne diseases which account for two-thirds of all illnesses in India with a significant loss in productivity. Although there is a Coastal Regulation Zone Notification designed to protect the coastal marine ecosystems, implementation is weak and marine pollution continues largely unabated. Close monitoring of the discharge of industrial effluents into waterbodies will be enforced. A comprehensive plan is proposed to be prepared for setting up of sewage treatment facilities in 1.591 towns having populations more than 20,000). Overextraction of groundwater will be regulated. Areas of groundwater pollution will be identified and a plan will be implemented to contain this.

Air Pollution Control

Air quality in India's major cities indicate that ambient levels of nitrous oxides, sulphur dioxide, lead and suspended particulate matter are often higher than World Health Organization and Indian standards. Sulfur dioxide levels in nine of the country's major cities exceed national standards. Other harmful substances such as ozone are not monitored. Major contributors to air pollution problems in India include thermal power stations, industrial factories, vehicles, and the use of non-commercial fuels such as coal briquettes, animal dung and trash by large sections of the population. The negative environmental effects from increased fossil fuel use will likely increase as India seeks to meet the energy demands of its expanding economy. Coal will play a predominant role in this expansion. The major pollutants from coal exploitation include the principal green house gases (GHGs), particulate air emissions, coal mining runoff and wastes, and coal ash solid wastes which pose a large-scale disposal problem.

In view of the fact that cooperation of the state government is an essential factor in successfully implementing pollution control programmes, it is proposed to work with the state government for preparing location specific plans for reducing automobile pollution, and prevention of burning of biomass/ garbage or any other material (except approved fuel) in the cities and towns to reduce secondary sources of air pollution. It is also proposed to set up a national network of air pollution monitoring stations for the parameters notified in respect of ambient air quality standards and for parameters for which standards have been prescribed for various sources. A database of pollutants releases into the air from different sources will be built up.

Strengthening of central and state pollution controls board

The board targets/activities proposed under the above are the training of officers, up-gradation of laboratories, capacity building in state pollution control boards / pollution control centres of the Northeast and in the new states of Uttranchal, Chattisgarh and Jharkhand.

Economic instruments for prevention and control of pollution will be evolved. To implement the various economic instruments, specific proposals will be formulated keeping in view the relevant considerations which may require a separate set up.

Environmental impact of human health

Environmental studies will be initiated to assess the impact of various pollutants on human health. Measures will be taken to control/eliminate major source of pollutants which have an adverse effect on human health. Phasing out of highly polluting obsolete technologies is also envisaged during the Tenth Plan period.

Hazardous substance management

Comprehensive national chemical profiles are proposed to be prepared. Emergency response centers will be established in all industrial pockets with a large number of accident hazards units as also inventorisation of isolated storage of hazardous chemicals. Some of the other goals set for the Tenth Plan include effective implementation of the Public Liability Insurance Act; preparation of database on risk-prone areas; setting up of hard hazardous-based disposal facilities in all states where significant quantities of hazardous waste are being generated; establishment of sub-regional training centres for implementation of the Basel Convention, setting up of custom laboratories and capacity building of custom officers for checking contraband trade in hazardous chemicals/waste; implementation of environmentally sound practices in ship dismantling and proper management of biomedical wastes; municipal solid waste; plastic waste; and, chemical waste.

Soil contamination and environmental degradation

Contaminated sites are proposed to be identified and soil remediation plans will be prepared. Reclamation of degraded areas is another programme envisaged.

Environmental impact assessmen (EIA)

Capacity building will be undertaken for decentralised EIA of projects and monitoring of compliance of clearance condition. Detailed shoreline management plans and Coastal Zone Management plans are proposed to be prepared as also strengthening of state coastal zone management authorities. Plans for conservation of sensitive ecosystems will be prepared and implemented. Scoping of mega projects and strategic EIA for specific sectors will be undertaken.

Ecological survey, conservation and ecogeneration

Ongoing programmes are proposed to be strengthened and a status paper on achievement indicating the extent to which efforts have yielded the results will be brought out. Added efforts will be made to conserve biodiversity for ecological security including proper evaluation of environmental risks associated with transgenic crops. The overall objective will be to set an example/model highlighting India's achievement in conserving ecologically sensitive area such as mangroves, coral reefs, wetlands and representative ecosystems through biosphere reserves.

Awareness, education, training and research

Comprehensive packages are proposed to be developed on critical issues making them effective so that messages reach citizens like the pulse polio programme. Schools and colleges are proposed to be covered for participation in environmental programmes. On-the-job trainings are proposed. Sustainable relationships with R and D institutions and academia will be developed for programme formulation and execution.

Environmental law and policy

The main theme will be revamping of environmental laws for ensuring their effective implementation, training of judicial officers in environmental laws and strengthening of enforcement mechanism.

Forestry

Forests are natural assets and provide a variety of benefits to the economy. Though the recorded forest area is about 23 per cent of the geographical area of the country much of this is degraded. There forests are therefore unable to play an important role in environmental sustainability and in meeting the forest produce needs of the people, industry and other sectors.

The problem and constraints in forestry development include lack of awareness about multiple roles and benefits of forests; especially its role in drought-proofing and prevention of soil and water runoff; no linkage between management and livelihood security of the people; low level of technology; inadequate research and extension; weak planning capability, wastage in harvesting an processing; market imperfections; overemphasis on government involvement and control; low level of people's participation and NGOs involvement; lack of private sector participation; unwanted restrictions on felling, transport and marketing of forest produce grown by the people; lack of inter-sectoral coordination; and, conflicting roles of public forest administration.Existing policy, laws, rules, regulations and executive orders should be reviewed for removing constraints in holistic development of forestry with people's participation.Areas where action by government is needed and where the government programmes have not been up to the mark include:

- Focus on farm forestry which has been surprisingly diluted since 1991 despite its enormous potential, especially in agriculturally backward areas.
- Measures to sustain JFM beyond the project period have not been conceptualised. These relate to: building one-to-one correspondence between user groups and forest patch through a new forest settlement, recognisation of JFM groups in law and linking them with statutory panchayats, and integrating the activities

of such groups with other income generating programmes such as watersheds and marketing of NTFPs.

- Protecting women's traditional usufruct rights and enabling women's group to collect and market NTFPs has been proved to be viable and cost effective strategy not only for women's empowerment but also for renewal of forests. It is important to acknowledge and recognise women as managers, food gatherers, wage earners and producers. Forestry development policies must be developed accordingly.
- Continuing subsidies on government auctions of wood and bamboo to industries, which act as a disincentive to industry to pay a remunerative price to farmers. Governments need to examine the pattern of subsidy to forest based industries and wipe out that subsidy in a time-bound manner so as to improve valuation of forests.
- The tariff structure on forest-based products such as timber and pulp keeping in view the incentive effect on farmers.
- Poor understanding ofthe social implications of technology; old style plantations still continue to be funded despite the 1988 policy. Forest technology should be changed by shifting attention from timber to floor **management** and production of more gatherable biomass.
- Classification of bamboo as NTFP thereby providing rights to tribal population and other forest dwellers over this resource. Bamboo harvesting policy systematically maximises dry bamboo output for paper mills rather than green bamboo output for artisans. Infact the present practices ban felling of green bamboo. Streamlining the procedure for making green bamboo available directly to artisans.
- Gregarious flowering of bamboo is expected from 2003 onwards. This will result in mass mortality of bamboo, fire, increase of rodents, famines and unrest in tribal

areas. Emergency plan should be formulated to face the calamity.

- Forest fire prevention and control should be given top priority to reduce losses and emission of greenhouse gases.
- Conservation and development of medicinal plants should be given priority to meet the local crude drug requirements and for export.
- Agroforestry, mountain, watershed development, river valleys, arid areas, wastelands afforestation programme should be given priority.
- Research and technological development must increase productivity, production of new products, value addition, improved marketing, export and productive employment generation.
- Promotion of coastal shelterbelts plantations for prevention of natural calamities.
- An integrated system for addressing issues of animal welfare, including ecology, safety and commercial exploitation will need to be evolved. Targets to bring greater areas under forest protection have been set for the five year periods 2002-2007 and 2007-2012. It has been proposed that the forest cover of the country should be increased to 25 per cent by 2007 and 33 per cent by 2012. This would mean bringing up extensive tracts of land under tree cover which would require a substantial investment both by the government and private sector.The main elements of the strategy for 10thplan will include convergence of afforestation schemes to avoid duplicity and canalise smooth flow of funds; introduction of multi cropping system and promotion of agro forestry/ farm forestry; increased role and involvement of private sector in plantation; removing of bottlenecks and reviewing felling and transit rules and standardisation of cost norms under afforestation schemes. It also includes provision of quality planting material, infusion of improved and innovative

technologies in nursery plantation, suitable protection against forest fires, pest attack and other diseases, strengthening of JFM net work for greater involvement of people and sustaining such programmes, strengthening of monitoring mechanism through establishment of IT network, development and sustainable management of NTFPs including medicinal plants, review of state monopoly on NTFPs, revival of working plans, strengthening of human resource planning and management and evolving Sustainable Forest Management (SFM) instrumentations.

Wildlife

Security of soil, sustenance of water regimes and activation of weather regimes as well as moderation of environmental adversities of modern age depend upon the health of natural ecosystems. The benefits from conservation of natural areas are not readily quantifiable as they flow to the local communities and the country somewhat intangibly and are often taken for granted.

The value of effective conservation of natural areas must hence not be linked with direct fiscal benefits. Environmental well-being and food security cannot be ensured in the long run without the care of natural areas. Efforts and initiatives from the side of the communities for revival of natural areas thus need to be supported.

Challenges of wildlife conservation arise from population pressure, adverse impact of industrialisation as well as the lately increasing threats from illegal wildlife trade. Conservation of wildlife and its habitat outside the protected areas particularly in the context of critically endangered species is a challenge which the conservation efforts must address. Such efforts are equally needed for long ranging mega-herbivores like elephants and major predators like tiger and leopard.

For the protection and conserving the wildlife, people's support has an important role. Therefore bio-resource ameliorative and livelihood supplementing participatory eco-development measures are required for local communities with a view to reducing their dependence upon protected areas. The problem of wildlife damage to human life and property need to be effectively mitigated by special management measures and expeditions and reasonable *ex-gratia* financial relief. Also, it is necessary to settle expeditiously the rights of local communities including voluntary relocation of habitations to alternative sites outside the protected areas. Such measures would ensure the participatory support of the people for conservation.

To fructify this objective, larger investments backed by attitudinal change would be essential. Poaching of wild animals due to lucrative clandestine trade in wildlife produce has become a major threat to wildlife conservation. Steps to be undertaken in this regard include filling up of vacant posts in the wildlife sector; reorganisation of field information in and around the protected areas; provision of infrastructure; capacity building; and, intelligence work. Education and awareness building measures as well as research and training have great role to play in making the conservation measures more effective.

The following thrust areas need high priority and enhanced allocation during the Tenth Plan:

Mitigation of human wildlife conflict

As regards settlement of rights and relocation of an estimated number of 10 million people living inside protected areas, it is not possible to the shift entire population, both, on account of resource requirement and unwillingness of the people to move out. For the time being relocation would be on voluntary basis with greater priority being given to national parks and important sanctuaries.

Eco-development

Eco-development process in atleast 15,000 villages under the Tenth Plan period will be initiated. Priority will be given to national parks and sanctuaries having higher bio-diversities and higher threats.

Depredation of Wildlife

Wildlife depredation on human life and property is a major factor of alienation of local community from wildlife conservation. In 1999-2000 alone, 179 human deaths have been caused by elephants. The situation in mountainous regions is very grave. Timely payment of compensation against depredation by wildlife will go a long way in eliciting local support.

Habitat improvement

One of the most important part of the successful wildlife management is habitat improvement and its orientation as per the needs of wildlife along with strict fire control measures and devices in the protected areas. This has been identified as a priority item in the Tenth Plan.

Control of poaching

Poaching of wild animals and its lucrative clandestine trade has become a major threat for conservation of wildlife. In the year 2000-2001 only, about 74, 270 and 41 cases of tiger, panther and elephant poaching respectively have beenreported. The actual number of poached animals may be even higher as all the cases poaching are not reported. The important steps to be undertaken in this regard are filling up of vacant posts in wildlife sector, reorganisation of field formations in an around protected areas, capacity building and intelligence network, development of wildlife forensic system, establishment of wildlife crime unit, provision of essential equipment and amenities to staff and provision for anti-poaching camps and strike forces.

Education and awareness

Considering the crucial role of education, awareness and publicity in wildlife conservation, it is essential to provide adequate funds for these programs in the Tenth Plan.

Research and training

Research and training inputs need to be strengthened in the wildlife sector. The Wildlife Institute of India is proposed to be strengthened during the Tenth Plan period.

Research and Education

Under the environment research programme, the focus will be on the identified thrustareas which include alternatives to chemical pesticides and fertilisers; biotechnologies/ microbiologies for treatment of industrial effluents; development of pollution related instrument; waste minimization and reuse; development of biodegradable plastics; and health and toxicology, amongst others.In the ecosystem research scheme, it is proposed to take up studies relating to conservation, assessment of the impact of human activities on the biosphere, climate change and interrelationships between humans and biological resources. Under the Eastern and Western ghats scheme emphasis will be on location-specific and problem solving research. Efforts will be made to conserve, protect and enhance the biodiversity in Eastern and Western Ghats. Endeavors will be made for tackling the hotspots of pollution by development of biological and other interventions for prevention and control of pollution including waste recycling. Special attention is proposed to be given on human-animal interaction on the boundaries of wildlife sanctuaries, national parks, biosphere reserves and world heritage cites. Attention will also be given to rehabilitation of mixed areas and over burdened dumps in the Eastern and Western ghats as also on strengthening of R&D on endemic fauna and climate change.

The Ministry had identified about 21 thrust areas which will guide the selection of research projects during the Tenth Plan period. Some of the important areas of thrust are development of biological and other interventions for pollution preventing and control including waste recycling; development of strategies for prevention and/or of pollution; clean technologies for sustainable production patterns; restoration of degraded ecosystems; conservation and enhancement of biological diversity; climate change; health and toxicology; research on landuse and landuse changes; mining; impact of developmental activities on drinking water; river conservation and maintenance of their pristine state; research on mountain ecosystem, islands and coastal zones; research on environmental legislation; socio-economic issues.

National River Conservation Directorate (NRCD)

With a view of improving the sustainability of the river and lake cleaning programmes, a number of initiatives are proposed to be taken up in an integrated and holistic approach. The focus will be on large towns and include a decentralised approach for sewage interception, development of demonstration level models in small colonies for the total treatment of sewage and its disposal, promotion of root zone treatment / formulation of wetland technology, tackling more aggressively the non-point source of pollution, utilisation of treated sewage after disinfecting, adoption of a more effective river front development approach involving universities and colleges in the monitoring of water quality in rivers and lakes, approval of projects only after firm commitment from local bodies/state Governments for meeting the operation and maintenance costs.

Strengthening of state Level institutional arrangements for effective and timely implementation of the programmes, assessment of minimum floor requirements in different rivers to ensure minimum floor regimes in critical structures of all rivers and formulation of a legislation for River Regulation Zone on the lines of Coastal Regulation Zones, are some of the important elements of the proposed strategy.

The ministry has also identified capacity building in environmental economics as one of the priority areas of environmental management. It is currently implementing the 'India *Environmental* Management *Capacity Building Technical Assistance Project'* with World Bank assistance. The objective of this programme is to increase the capacity for the application ofeconomic principles and tools to environmental management in India across the full range of issues such as priority setting, cost-benefit analysis of alternative policies for pollution control, resources management, and biodiversity conservation. To achieve these objectives this programme is being implemented through selected core institutions like Madras School of Economics, Chennai; Indira Gandhi Institute of Development Research, Mumbai; Indian Statistical Institute Calcutta; and Institute of Economic Growth, New Delhi.

The Environmental Economics Research Committee (EERC) formed to identify research themes has identified several themes which will stress on the application of economic principles. The areas identified include

1. Environment and natural resource management
   (a) Land Use and Management
   (b) Environmental Aspects of Air
   (c) Water Resource Management
   (d) Biodiversity
2. Environmental pollution and policy design for control
   (a) Air, water and solid waste
   (b) Valuation of damages
   (c) Methods and costs of control
   (d) Economic and Fiscal Incentives
3. Economics of Green Initiative
   (a) Pollution Reduction at Source.

DONOR PRIORITIES IN ENVIRONMENTAL RESEARCH AND MANAGEMENT

Several environment-related programmes have been funded by donors on the basis of priorities identified by them. Some of these include the United Nations Development Programme, Asian Development Bank, the International Human Development Programme and Winrock International India.

The United Nations Development Programme (UNDP)

The UNDP addresses the challenge of protection and regeneration of the environment, vital for sustainable human development by focusing on local priorities as well as global environmental issues. It supports such measures like mobilising and building the capacities of local communities and other stakeholders, and development and promotion of technologies that help conserve use of natural resources. The focus of UNDP-supported programmes is natural resources management, environment and energy, multi-level capacity building for decision-making, mainstreaming environment into the development process, and information dissemination and advocacy. UNDP's environment strategy targets three types of interventions: biodiversity conservation, natural resources management and clean energy technology promotion.

1. For biodiversity conservation, the UNDP supports the setting up of management models for protected areas in which the development rights of communities receive as much attention as the process of conservation. The medicinal plants sub-programme demonstrates the conservation and sustainable utilisation of medicinal plants through the revitalisation of traditional practices for primary health care within local communities. For forest conservation, the UNDP has been supporting the government's forest development programme including community forest management.
2. In water management, UNDP supports interventions and campaigns through its Small Grants Facility to promote appropriate techniques, methods and practices for sustainable use of water. Integrated management of water resources involving participatory planning and management of water is the key aspect of these endeavours. Successful examples of micro-watersheds in Rajasthan illustrate the efficacy of this approach.
3. Providing clean energy services in remote rural areas using renewable energy technologies such as solar with civil society partners and biomass is a major focus area.
4. Management of environment-related development problems which include air and water pollution, and domestic and industrial waste management. The UNDP is also involved in rating different industrial sectors for their environmental performance.
5. Capacity building at various levels - government, private sector, women's groups, NGOs, all associated with decision-making processes in the area of natural resources and in environmental education.

6. Sustainable Development Network Programme (SDNP) to make relevant information on sustainable development readily available to decision-makers.
7. Helping the ministry to meet the control measures as specified in the Montreal Protocol, which has set out a time schedule for freeze and reduction of ozone depleting substances.
8. UNDP is the lead implementing agency for the Global Environment Facility (GEF) in India. With nearly 15 ongoing projects, India is the second largest recipient of GEF funding. Biodiversity and climate change are the key focal areas for UNDP-GEF with an emphasis mainly on technical assistance and capacity building. Apart from global environmental considerations, GEF projects strongly reflect national priorities, and are implemented in close collaboration with the Government. Some of the important UNDP- GEF projects include:
   - Optimising development of small hydel resources in the hilly regions of India
   - National Biodiversity Strategy and Action Plan, one of the world's largest environment planning exercises that aims to develop a series of plans and programmes relating to ecological security and livelihoods of people most dependent on natural resources
   - *National Communication*, a mandatory report to be submitted to the UN Framework Convention on Climate Change (UNFCCC) (24).

The Asian Development Bank (ADB)

ADB's environment strategy supports:

(i) improving the urban environment by focusing on air pollution programs, solid waste management, water supply, and sanitation services;

(ii) awareness raising;

(iii) energy efficiency with concomitant environmental benefits; and,

(iv) natural resource management and biodiversity conservation.

The International Human Development Programme (IHDP)

IHDP is an international, interdisciplinary and non-governmental research programme, aiming at "the development and integration of research on the human dimensions of global environmental change.

The Indian National Scientific Committee of the IHDP has identified several priority areas for research. These include:

(i) Impacts of tourism on natural resources in ecologically fragile cultural landscape in the Ganga watershed of the Garhwal Himalaya

(ii) Climate change and food security: human adaptive strategies

(iii) Natural resource **management** and sustainable livelihood concerns of traditional societies in the mangrove ecosystem of the Sunderbans

(iv) Climate change mitigation through alternate renewable energy sources: societal dimensions

(v) Case study on impacts of urbanisation and industrial transformation.

Winrock International India

In India, the Climate Change (CLC) Program at Winrock International India is addressing this critical issue by working at the intersections clean energy and environment and natural resources management programs. Winrock is working to find solutions that can address various local and global climate change concerns while simultaneously contributing to environment-friendly economic growth and sustainable development of the poor. Activities include preparing Greenhouse Gas (GHG) emissions inventories, examining financing options and mechanisms for implementing GHG mitigation projects, designing abatement strategies and policies, developing mitigation projects, analyzing climate change impacts, and assessing adaptation strategies.

NGO'S PRIORITIES IN THE ENVIRONMENT SECTOR

There are several leading non-governmental organisations in India working on different issues in environment, identified on the basis of perceived need, and where they have developed expertise. Given below are just a sample of many.

Centre for Science and Environment (CSE), New Delhi

The Centre for Science and Environment is one of India's leading environmental NGOs with a deep interest in sustainable natural resource management. CSE's strategy is one of 'knowledge based activism.'

Today when India faces double environmental threat – of 'ecological poverty' and extensive land degradation, on one hand, and rapidly growing toxification and pollution arising out of industrialisation and economic growth, on the other – the centre is trying to advocate solutions to deal with both the problems. Apart from its work on natural resource management issues, it has major campaigns on air and water pollution, on the threats posed to public health by the changing environment, and a project to bring about transparency in the industrial sector by rating the environmental performance of Indian firms. The project is expected to lead not only to increased transparency but also to reduction of corruption in pollution control inspection. CSE is currently working on the following policy-related issues:

(a) Policies dealing with pollution control and prevention

(b) Policies for sustainable and participatory natural resource management (issues that lie at the interface of natural resource management and people's participation, particularly in the areas of water management, wildlife, biodiversity conservation and forests); issues that lie at the interface of poverty and environment

(c) Policies for an equitable framework to manage the global environmental resources;

(d) Policies dealing with issues that lie at the interface of environment and health (the programme includes a plan to set up a laboratory to monitor air, water and pesticide pollution); and,

(e) Policies for sustainable industrialisation.

Underlying these priority areas, CSE has been strongly advocating for science for ecological security' (Anil Agarwal, mimeo). CSE feels strongly that while India has emphasised science for food and defence security, there is a need to address ecological issues through better science.

Development Alternatives (DA)

DA, a New Delhi-based NGO is committed to the research, development and implementation of appropriate technology for agriculture, building, paper making and handlooms which support the principles of sustainable development.

The Indira Gandhi Institute of Development Research (IGIDR)

IGIDR is an advanced research institute established by the Reserve Bank of India for carrying out research on development issues from a multi-disciplinary points of view. The aims and objectives of the Institute are to promote and conduct research on development (in its economic, technological, social, political and ecological aspects) from a broad inter- disciplinary perspective; to gain insights into the process of development and alternative policy options and to disseminate the knowledge so gained. The broad areas of research relating to the environment include:

- Economic reforms and macroeconomic policies
- International trade and exchange rates
- Agricultural economics, food policy
- Poverty, safety nets, public distribution systems, rural development
- Energy and infrastructure
- Environmental studies

- Climate change issues
- Rural pollution and health.

Foundation for the Revitalisation of Local Health Traditions

Based in Banglaore, this organisation is committed towards revitalisating of Indian traditional medicine systems so as to utilise the best traditional knowledge and practices related to prevention, simple cures and promotive health in millions of rural and urban homes; promote effective national programmes for conservation and sustainable utilisation of medicinal plants and other natural resources; promote effective community-based enterprises that can provide income and employment to thousands of rural women and men through cultivation and sustainable collection of medicinal plants as well as manufacture of herbal products based on our medical heritage; undertake effective research programmes that help India make original contributions to the world of medicine from the knowledge base of indigenous medical systems and make effective interventions, which help invigorate institutions as well as social traditions, and people- to-people processes that transmit traditional medical wisdom The focus of the work is (a) conservation of medicinal plants, and, (b) revitalisation of local health traditions.

Tata Energy Research Institute (TERI), New Delhi

TERI, based in New Delhi is an organisation that believes that efficient utilisation of energy, sustainable use of natural resources, large-scale adoption of renewable energy technologies and reduction of all forms of waste will move the process of development towards sustainability

Some of the areas of focus of the organisation include the following:

(a) Issues of national and international environmental governance and urban local governance.

(b) Environmental and energy policy research to ensure efficient and sustainable management of, and equitable access to, resources. The key thematic areas of research include local and global environmental studies; energy economics, modeling and policy analysis; special analysis using geographical information systems; natural resource accounting; and urban infrastructure and transport systems.

(c) To study the environmental dimensions of various economic activities and resource- use patterns and explore strategies to mitigate the adverse effects on the environment. To study the relations between energy and environment in urban, industrial, and rural settings through field service, experiments, quantitative modeling, and economic analysis. The organsiation is also engaged in regional and urban environmental management plans, environmental impact assessment studies, corporate environmental initiatives and an environmental rating system for the municipal sector, human exposure and health studies, environmental management of the mining and power sectors, waste management, and dissemination of environmental information.

(d) The organisation is also undertaking research and outlining policy initiatives to promote effective and equitable solutions to global and environmental challenges, taking into account the concerns of developing countries. In the field of global climate change, the centre prepares GHG (Greenhouse gas) inventories, assesses the impact of climate change, analysis mitigation options, examines national and international policy, and helps build capacity among government, industry, and civil society to address global environmental issues.

(e) To identify, analyse, and prioritise policy options with regard to energy and the environment by quantitative modeling of energy-economy-environment linkages, economic and statistical analysis of energy and related data, and the use of geographical information systems.

(f) Research in environmental security issues that pose potential social and economic threats at local and regional levels.

(g) Integration of the long-term goal of sustainable natural resource management with the immediate objectives of rapid economic growth and poverty alleviation, looking into the dynamic interaction between socioeconomic processes and natural resources.

(h) To draw a sustainable and environmentally sound transport system.

(i) To facilitate wider diffusion of energy-efficient and environmentally sound technologies.

(j) Areas of activities in the Northeast include identification of the factors responsible for the degradation of natural resources in the region and evolve measures to arrest them; preparation of a comprehensive database on natural resources; study of the demand and supply of commercial and non-commercial fuels especially in the domestic sector; development and implementation of interventions that lead to efficient use of natural resources and check the process of degradation; infrastructural development including R&D and training facilities for sustainable utilisation of natural resources; capacity and network building.

Box: The Small Industries Pollution Problem

The role of small industries in the economy is significant. But despite their importance, small industries pollute and are faced with numerous problems including technical and financial issues, and legislative and regulative compliance

In India, industrial pollution is regarded the worst among the many environmental impacts that are causing damage through excessive exploitation of resources and degradation of the environment. The Bhopal tragedy clearly demonstrated one of the world's worst industrial accidents. The significance of this accident, however, extends well beyond avoiding such a disaster and a need to move beyond just polluting the environment. Since the legacy of Bhopal, large manufacturing houses in India have all committed themselves to the environmental movement. However, the crux of the problem is the pollution generated by small and medium industries. Although they are promoted in a large way by the Indian government and play an important role within the economy with their prime role and vast scope in employment, the unsafe environmental practices of these industries for a long time have gone unnoticed, even when research has indicated that they are the worst polluters.

Industrialisation is the central dynamic force for most countries and has been a key growth objective of India's planned economy, with heavy investments being made in this sector. Labour productivity is highest in manufacturing industries; this has assisted in raising national income at a faster pace. Small units play an important role in the Indian economy, as they are labour intensive and create job opportunities. A 1999 report indicates that about 3 million SSI units employing nearly 16.7 million persons account for 35 per cent of India's total exports and about 40 per cent of industrial manufacture The importance of industrialisation in economic development is crucial for a growing economy with a large population like India, so prosperity through industrialisation has been a long-term strategy for the Indian government.

As industrialisation gathered momentum so did the increase in small-scale industries. Small companies are defined as those with less than US $180,000 in capital equipment. They offer a higher productivity of capital than capital intensive enterprises, as they have low investment per worker. They help in dispersal of industries, rural development, and the decentralisation of economic power. All this is required to increase and disperse economic growth.

Several policy initiatives and procedural simplifications have been undertaken by the government to support this sector, not only for employment generation but also to enhance their competitive strength. The government has also provided measures such as greater infrastructural support, more and easier availability of credit, lower rates of duty, technology up-gradation, assistance to build entrepreneurial talent, facilities for quality improvement, and export incentives.

The government's prime role has been to encourage growth of these industries, often neglecting environmental considerations. Industrial effluent largely comes from the three million small - and medium-sized units that are scattered throughout the country, particularly in the production of paper, sugar, leather, and chemicals. Unfortunately, only about half the medium- to large-scale industries have partial or complete effluent treatment. Fourfold industrial growth from 1963 to 1991 resulted in six-fold growth in toxic releases. Heavy industries like iron and steel producers contribute nearly 70 percent of the toxic wastes released but only 20 per cent of industrial output. Industrial disposal of polluted effluent occurs via open drains into streams and reservoirs or through underground injection. Most industrial estates lack wastewater treatment systems.

Small industries lack environmental commitment, technical expertise in environmental management, and the financial capabilities to address environmental problems. Nor do they have standards or effective treatment opportunities and services. Small industries also lack additional space for pollution control facilities. There are difficulties in obtaining the technical assistance of knowledgeable consultants. Since most of the units are dispersed, they find it difficult to come together for a joint or common treatment plant. The concern of depressed profit margins and decline in competitiveness prevents these units from using pollution control measures. More emphasis is laid on new investments, production, and other return oriented opportunities. Soft loans for pollution control measures are not lucrative. There are subsidies offered for investments in pollution control as incentives, but the impact of these incentives on these units is little or nothing, for they do not alter the cost-benefit analysis in favour of pollution control investments.

Regulatorycompliance has been a major issue for these units. Environmental legislation in India, although seemingly as tough as that in major developed nations, is not well enforced. High levels of pollution elicit a formal regulatory response in the form of inspections, but these inspections appear to have no impact on the emissions. Inspections are probably ineffective in bringing about desired changes in behaviour because of bureaucratic or other problems, including the probability that enforcement is low and that the penalty for non-compliance is not stringent enough to act as a deterrent. A point worth noting is that the mandate of the Central Pollution Control Board (CPCB) is to set environmental standards for all plants in India, lay down ambient standards, and coordinate the activities of the State Pollution Control Boards (SPCBs). Unfortunately, the implementation of environmental laws and their enforcement are decentralized and so is the responsibility of the SPCBs. This is another haphazard method of addressing the issue. In addition, pollution laws have achieved little success. The courts have been slow to respond to enforcement actions sought by state pollution boards. The boards themselves have been poorly funded and charges of corruption have been regular and widespread.

2

The Water (Prevention and Control of Pollution) Cess Act, 1977

No. 36 of 1977

[7th December, 1977]

MINISTRY OF LAW, JUSTICE AND COMPANY AFFAIRS

(Legislative Department)

New Delhi, the 7th December, 1977

The foltowing Act of Parliament received the assent of the President on the 7th December, 1977, and is hereby published for general information:—

An Act to provide for the levy and collection of a cess on water consumed by persons carrying on certain industries and by local authorities, with a view to augment the resources of the Central Board and the State Boards for the prevention and control of water pollution constituted under the Water (Prevention and Control of Pollution) Act, 1974.

Be it enacted by Parliament in the Twenty-eighth Year of the Republic of India as foltows :—

SHORT TITLE, EXTENT, APPLICATION AND COMMENCEMENT

(1) This Act may be called the Water (Prevention and Control of Pollution) Cess Act, 1977.

(2) It extends to the whole of India except the State of Jammu and Kashmir.

(3) Subject to the provisions of sub-section (2), it applies to all the States to which the Water (Prevention and Control of Pollution) Act, 1974 applies and the Union territories.

(4) **It shall come into force on such date as the Central Government may, by notification in the Official Gazette, appoint.**

DEFINITIONS

In this Act, unless the context otherwise requires:—

(a) "local authority" means a municipal corporation or a municipal council (by whatever name called) or a cantonment board or any other body, entrusted with the duty of supplying the water under the law by or under which it is constituted;

(b) "prescribed" means prescribed by rules made under the Act;

(c) "specified industry" means any industry specified in Schedule I;

(d) words and expressions used but not defined in this Act and defined in the Water (Prevention and Control of Pollution) Act, 1974 (6 of 1974) shall have the meanings respectively assigned to them in that Act.

LEVY AND COLLECTION OF CESS

(1) There shall be levied and collected a cess for the purpose of the Water (Prevention and Control of Pollution) Act, 1974 (6 of 1974) and utilisation thereunder.

(2) The cess under sub-section (1) shall be payable by—

(a) every person carrying on any specified industry; and

(b) every local authority, and shall be calculated on the basis of water consumed by such person or local authority, as the case may be, for any of the purposes specified in column (1) of Schedule II, at such rate, not exceeding the rate specified in the corresponding entry in column (2) thereof, as the Central Government may, by notification in the Official Gazette, from time to time, specify.

(2A) Where any person carrying on any specified industry or any local authority consuming water for domestic purpose liable to pay cess fails to comply with any of the provisions of section 25 of the Water (Prevention and Control of Pollution) Act, 1974 (6 of 1974) or an of the standards laid so down by the Central Government under the Environment (Protection) Act, 1986, cess shall be and payable at such rate, not exceeding the rate specified in column (3) of Schedule II, as the Central Government may, by notification in the Official Gazette, from time to time specify.

(3) Where any local authority supplies water to any person carrying on any specified industry or to any other local authority and such person or other local authority is liable to pay cess under sub-section (2) or sub-section (2A) in respect of the water so supplied, then, notwithstanding anything contained in that sub-section, the local authority first mentioned shall not be liable to pay such cess in respect of such water.

Explanation—For the purpose of this section and section 4, "consumption of water" includes supply of water.

Affixing of Meters

(1) For the purpose of measuring and recording the quantity of water consumed, every person carrying on any specified industry and every local authority shall affix meters of such standards and at such places as may be prescribed and it shall be presumed that the quantity indicated by the meter has been consumed by such person or local authority, as the case may be, until the contrary is proved.

(2) Where any person or local authority fails to affix any

meter as required by sub-section (1), the Central Government shall after notice to such person or local authority, as the case may be, cause such meter to be affixed and the cost of such meter together with the cost for affixing the meter may be recovered from such person or local authority by the Central Government in the same manner as an arrear of land revenue.

FURNISHING OF RETURNS

(1) Every person carrying on any specified industry and every local authority, liable to pay the cess under section 3, shall furnish such returns, in such form at such intervals and containing such particulars to such officer or authority, as may be prescribed.

(2) If a person carrying on any specified industry or a local authority, liable to pay the cess under section 3, fails to furnish any return under sub-section (1), the officer or the authority shall give a notice requiring such person or local authority to furnish such return before such date as may be specified in the notice.

ASSESSMENT OF CESS

(1) The officer of authority to whom or which the return has been furnished under section 5 shall, after making or causing to be made such inquiry as he or it thinks fit and after satisfying himself or itself that the particulars stated in the return are correct, by order, assess the amount of cess payable by the concerned person carrying or any specified industry or local authority, as the case may be.

(1A) If the return has not been furnished to the officer or authority under sub-section (2) of section 5, he or it shall, after making or causing to be made such inquiry as he or it thinks fit, by order, assess the amount of cess payable by the concerned person carrying on any specified industry or local authority, as the case may be.

(2) An order of assessment made under sub-section (1) or sub-section (1A) shall specify the date within which the

cess shall be paid to the State Government.

(3) A copy each of the order of assessment made under sub-section (1) or sub-section (1A) shall be sent to the person or, as the case may be, to the local authority concerned and to the State Government.

(4) The State government shall, through such of its officers or authorities as may be specified by it in this behalf by notification in the Official Gazette, collect the cess from the person or local authority liable to pay the same and pay the amount so collected to the Central Government in such manner and within such time as may be prescribed.

REBATE

Where any person or local authority, liable to pay the cess under this Act, instals any plant for the treatment of sewage or trade effluent, such person or local authority shall from such date as may be prescribed, be entitled to a rebate of twenty five per cent of the cess payable by such person or, as the case may be, local authority.

[Provided that a person or local authority shall not be entitled to a rebate, if he or it—

(a) consumes water in excess of the maximum quantity as may be prescribed in this behalf for any specified industry or local authority; or

(b) fails to eompty with any of the provisions of section 25 of the Water (Prevention and Control of Pollution) Act, 1974 (6 of 1974) or any of the standards laid down by the Central Government under the Environment (Protection) Act, 1986 (29 of 1986).]

CREDITING PROCEEDS OF CESS TO CONSOLIDATED FUNDS OF INDIA AND APPLICATION THEREOF

The proeeeds of the cess levied under section 3 shall first be credited tO the Consolidated Fund of India and the Central Government may, if Parliament by appropriation made by law in this behalf, so provides, pay to the Central Board and every State Board, from time to time, from out of such proceeds, after deducting the expenses on collection, such sums of money as it may think fit for being utilised under the Water (Prevention and Control of Pollution) Act, 1974 (6 of 1974)

Provided that while determining the sum of money to be paid to any State Board under this section, the Central Government shall have regard to the amount of cess collected by the State Government concerned under sub-section (4) of section 6.

Explanation-For the purpose of this section, "Slate Board" includes a Joint Board, if any, constituted under section 13 of the Water (Prevention and Control of Pollution) Act, 1974 (6 of 19743.

POWER OF ENTRY

Any officer or authority of the State Government specially empowered in this behalf by that Government may,-

(a) with such assistance, if any, as he or it may think fit, enter at an) reasonable time any place which he or it considers it necessary to enter for carrying out the purposes of this Act including the testing of the correctness of the meters affixed under section 4;

(b) do within such place anything necessary for the proper discharge of his or its duties under this Act; and

(c) exercise such other powers as may be prescribed.

INTEREST PAYABLE FOR DELAY IN PAYMENT OF CESS

If any person carrying on any specified industry or any local authority fails to pay any amount of cess payable under section 3 to the State government within the date specified in the order of assessment made under section 6, such person or local authority, as the case may be, shall be liable to pay [7][interest on the amount to be paid at the rate of two per cent for every month or part of a month comprised in the period from the date on which such payment is due till such amount is actually paid.

PENALTY OF AMOUNT DUE UNDER THE ACT

If any amount of cess payable by any person carrying on any specified industry or any Local authority under section 3 is not paid to the State (government within the date specified in the order of assessment made under section 6, it shall be deemed to be in arrears and the authority prescribed in this behalf may, after such inquiry as it deems fit, impose on such person Of, as the case may be, Local authority, a penalty not exceeding the amount of cess in arrears: Provided that before imposing any such penalty, such person or, as the case may be, the local authority shall be given a reasonable opportunity of being heard and if after such hearing the said authority is satisfied that the default was for any good and sufficient reason, no penalty shall be imposed under this section.

RECOVERY OF AMOUNT DUE UNDER THE ACT

Any amount due under this Act (including any interest or penalty payable under section 10 or section 11, as the case may be) from any person carrying on any specified industry or from any local authority may be recovered by the Central Government in the same manner as an arrear of land revenue.

APPEALS

(1) Any person or local authority aggrieved by an order of assessment made under section 6 or by an order imposing penalty made under section 11 may, within such time as may be prescribed, appeal to such authority in such form and in such manner as may be prescribed.

(2) Every appeal preferred under sub-section (I) shall be accompanied by such fees as may be prescribed.

(3) After the receipt of an appeal under sub-section (1), the appellate authority shall, after giving the appellant an opportunity of being heard in the matter, dispose of the appeal as expeditiously as possible.

(4) Every order passed in appeal under this section shall be final and shall not be called in question in any court of law.

PENALTY

(1) Whoever, being under an obligation to furnish a return under this Act, furnishes any return knowing, or having reason to believe, the same to be false shall be punishable with imprisonment which may extend to six months or with fine which may extend to one thousand rupees or with both.

(2) Whoever, being liable to pay cess under this Act willfully or intentionally evades or attempts to evade the payment of such cess shall be punishable with imprisonment which may extend to six months or with fine which may extend to one thousand rupees or with both.

(3) No court shall take cognizance of an offence punishable under this section save on a complaint made by or under the authority of the Central Government.

OFFENCES BY COMPANIES

(1) Where an offence under this Act has been committed by a company, every person who, at the time the offence was committed, was in charge of and was responsible to, the company for the conduct of the business of the company as well as the company, shall be deemed to be guilty of the offence and shall be liable to be proceeded against and punished accordingly:

Provided that nothing contained in this sub-section shall render any such person liable to any punishment, if he proves that the offence was committed without his knowledge or that he exercised all due diligence to prevent the commission of such offence.

(2) Notwithstanding anything contained in sub-section (1), where an offence under this Act has been committed by a company and it is proved that the offence has been committed with the consent or connivance of, or is attributable to any neglect on the part of, any director,

manager, secretary or other officer of the company, such director, manager, secretary or other officer shall also bc deemed to be guilty of that offence and shall be liable to be proceeded against and punished accordingly.

Explanation-For the purpose of this section,-

(a) "company" means any body corporate and includes a firm or other association of individuals; and

(b) "director", in relation to firm, means a partner in the firm.

POWER TO AMEND SCHEDULE-I

(1) The Central Government may, by notification in the Official Gazette, add to Schedule I any industry having regard to the consumption of water in the carrying on of such industry and the consequent discharge thereof resulting in pollution of any stream and thereupon Schedule I shall, subject to the provisions of sub-section (2), be deemed to be amended accordingly.

(2) Every such notification shall be laid before each House of Parliament, if it is sitting, as soon as may be after the issue of the notification and is it is not sitting, within seven days of its re-assembly and the Central Government shall seek the approval of Parliament to notification by a resolution moved within a period of fifteen days beginning with the day on which the notification is so laid before the House of the People, and if Parliament makes any modification in the notification or directs that the notification should cease to have effect, the notification shall thereafter have effect only in such modified form pr be of no effect, as the case may be, but without prejudice to the validity of anything previously done thereunder.

POWER TO MAKE RULES

(1) The Central Government-may make rules for carrying out the purposes of this Act.

(2) Without prejudice to the generality of the foregoing power, such rules may provide for all or any of the following matters, namely:-

(a) the standards of the meters to be affixed and the places at which such meters are to be affixed under sub-section (I) of section 4;

(b) the returns to be furnished under section 5, the form in which and the intervals at which such returns are to be furnished, the particulars which such returns contain and the officer or authority to who or which such returns shall be furnished;

(c) the manner in which and the time within which the cess collected shall be paid to the Central Government under sub-section (4) of section 6;

(d) the date from which any person or local authority liable to pay cess shall be entitled to the rebate [8][and the maximum quantity of water in excess of consumption whereof any person or local authority shall not be entitled to the rebate] under section 7.

(e) the powers which may be exercised by the officer or authority under section 9;

(f) the authority which may impose penalty under section 11;

(g) the authority to which an appeal may be filed under sub-section (I) of section 13 and the time within which and the form and manner in which such appeal may be filed;

(h) the fees which shall accompany an appeal under sub-section (2) of section 13; and

(i) any other matter which has to be or may be prescribed.

(3) Every rule made under this Act shall be laid, as soon as may be after it is made, before each House of Parliament while it is in session for a total period of thirty days which may be comprised in one session or

in two successive sessions and if, before the expiry of the session immediately following the session or the successive sessions aforesaid, both Houses agree in making any modification in the rule or both Houses agree that the rule should not be made, the rule shall thereafter have effect only in such modified form or be of no effect, as the case may be; so, however, that any such modification or annulment shall be without prejudice to the validity of anything previously done under that rule.

SCHEDULE I

[See sectwn 2(c)]

1. Ferrous metallurgical industry.
2. Non-ferrous metallurgical industry.
3. Mining industry.
4. Ore processing industry.
5. Petroleum industry.
6. Petro-chemical industry
7. Chemical industry.
8. Ceramic industry.
9. Cement industry.
10. Textile industry. [9][including cotton synthetic and semi-synthetic fibres manufactured from these fibres];
11. Paper industry.
12. Fertilizer industry.
13. Coal (including coke) industry.
14. Power (thermal, diesel) and [10][Hydel] generating industry
15. Processing of animal or vegetable products industry [11][including processing of milk, meat, hides and skins, all agricultural products and their wastes].

3

WATER (PREVENTION AND CONTROL OF POLLUTION) ACT, 1974

An Act to provide for the prevention and control of water pollution and the maintaining or restoring of wholesomeness of water, for the establishment, with a view to carrying out the purposes aforesaid, of Boards for the prevention and control of water pollution, for conferring on and assigning to such Boards Powers and functions relating thereto and for matters connected therewith.

WHEREAS it is expedient to provide for the prevention and control of water pollution and the maintaining or restoring of wholesomeness of water, for the establishment, with a view to carrying out the purposes aforesaid, of Boards for the prevention and control of water pollution and for conferring on and assigning to such Boards powers and functions relating thereto;

AND WHEREAS Parliament has no power to make laws for the States with respect to any of the matters aforesaid except as provided in articles 249 and 250 of the Constitution;

AND WHEREAS in pursuance of clause (1) of article 252 of the Constitution resolutions have been passed by all the Houses of the Legislatures of the States of Assam, Bihar, Gujrat, Haryana, Himachal Pradesh, Jammu and Kashmir, Karnataka, Kerala, Madhya Pradesh, Rajasthan, Tripura and West Bengal to the effect that the matters aforesaid should be regulated in those States by Parliament by law; BE it enacted by Parliament in the Twenty-fifth Year of the Republic of India as follows:-

PRELIMINARY

Short Title, Application and Commencement

(1) Short title, application and commencement. This Act may be called the Water (Prevention and Control of s Pollution) Act, 1974.

(2) It applies in the first instance to the whole of the States of Assam, Bihar, Gujarat, Haryana, Himachal Pradesh, Jammu and Kashmir, Karnataka, Kerala, Madhya Pradesh, Rajasthan, Tripura and West Bengal and the Union territories; and it shall apply to such other State which adopts this Act by resolution passed in that behalf under clause (1) of article 252 of the Constitution.

(3) It shall come into force, at once in the States of Bihar, Gujarat, Haryana, Himachal Pradesh, Jammu and Kashmir, Karnataka, Kerala, Madhya Pradesh, Rajasthan, Tripura and West Bengal and in the Union territories, and in any other State which adopts this Act under clause (1) of article 252 of the Constitution on the date of such adoption and any reference in this Act to the commencement of this Act shall, in relation to any State or Union territory, mean the date on which this Act comes into force in such State or Union territory.

Definitions

In this Act, unless the context otherwise requires,-

(a) "Board" means the Central Board or State Board;

[(b) " Central Board" means the Central Pollution Control Board Constituted under section3;]

(c) "members" means a member of a Board and includes the chairman thereof;

[(d) "occupier", in relation to any factory or premises, means the person who has control over the affairs of the factory or the premises, and includes, in relation to any substance, the person in possession of the substance.]

[(dd) "outlet" includes any conduit pipe or channel, open or closed carrying sewage or trade effluent or any other holding arrangement which causes, or is likely to cause, pollution;]

(e) "pollution" means such contamination of water or such alteration of the physical, chemical or biological properties of water or such discharge of any sewage or trade effluent or of any other liquid, gaseous or solid substance into water (whether directly or indirectly) as may, or is likely to, create a nuisance or render such water harmful or injurious to public health or safety, or to domestic, commercial, industrial, agricultural or other legitimate uses, or to the life and health of animals or plants or of aquatic organisers;

(f) "prescribed" means prescribed by rules made under this Act by the Central Government or, as the case may be, the State Government,

(g) "sewage effluent" means effluent from any sewerage system or sewage disposal works and includes sullage from open drains;

(i) "State Government" in relation to a Union territory means the Administrator thereof appointed under article 239 of the Constitution;

(j)"stream" includes-

(i) river;

(ii) Water course (whether flowing or for the time] being dry);

(iii) inland water (whether natural or artificial);]

(iv) subterranean waters;

(v) sea or tidal waters to such extent or, as the case may be, to such point as the State Government may, by notification in the Official Gazette, specify in this behalf ;

(k) "trade effluent" includes any liquid, gaseous or solid substance which is discharged from any premises used for carrying on any ["Industry, operation or process, or treatment and disposal system" other than domestic sewage.

THE CENTRAL & STATE BOARDS FOR PREVENTION & CONTROL OF WATER POLLUTION

Constitution of Central Board

(1) The Central Government shall, with effect from such date (being a date not later than six months of the commencement of this Act is the States of Assam, Bihar, Gujarat, Haryana, Himachal Pradesh, Jammu and Kashmir, Karnataka, Kerala, Madhya Pradesh, Rajasthan, Tripura and West Bengal and in the Union territories) as it may, by notification in the Official Gazette, appoint, constitute a Central Board to be called the [1][Central Pollution Control Board] to exercise the powers conferred on and perform the functions assigned to that Board under this Act.

(2) The Central Board shall consist of the following members, namely:-

(a) a full-time chairman, being a person having special knowledge or practical experience in respect of [matters relating to environmental protection] or a person having knowledge and experience in administering institutions dealing with the matters aforesaid, to be nominated by the Central Government;

(b) [such number of officials, not exceeding five] to be nominated by the Central Government to represent that Government;

(c) such number of persons, not exceeding five to be nominated by the Central Government, from amongst the members of the State Boards, of whom no exceeding two shall be from those referred to in clause (c) of sub-section (2) of section 4;

(d) [such number of non-officials, not exceeding three] to be nominated by the Central Government, to represent the interests of agriculture, fishery or industry or trade or any other interest which, in the opinion of the Central Government, ought to be represented;

(e) two persons to represent the companies or corporations owned, controlled or managed by the Central Government, to be nominated by that Government;

[(f) a full-time member-secretary, possessing qualifications, knowledge and experience of scientific, engineering or management aspects of pollution control, to be appointed by the Central Government]

(3) The Central Board shall be a body corporate with the name aforesaid having perpetual succession and a common seal with power, subject to the provisions of this Act, to acquire, hold and dispose of property and to contract, and may, by the aforesaid name, sue or be sued.

CONSTITUTION OF STATE BOARDS

(1) The State Government shall, with effect from such date as it may, by notification in the Official Gazette, appoint, constitute a [7][State Pollution Control Board], under such name as may be specified in the notification, to exercise the powers conferred on the perform the functions assigned to that Board under this Act.

(2) A State Board shall consist of the following members, namely:-

(a) a chairman, being a person having special knowledge or practical experience in respect of [9][matters relating to environmental protection] or a person having knowledge and experience in administering institutions dealing with the matters aforesaid, to be nominated by the State Government.

[Provided that the chairman may be either whole-time or part-time as the State Government may think fit;]

(b) [such number of officials, not exceeding five,] to be nominated by the State Government to represent that Government;

(c) [such number of persons, not exceeding five] to be nominated by the State Government from amongst the members of the local authorities functioning within the State;

(d) [such number of non-officials, not exceeding three] to be nominated by the State Government to represent the interest of agriculture, fishery or industry or trade or any other interest which, in the opinion of the State Government, ought to be represented;

(e) two persons to represent the companies or corporations owned, controlled or managed by the State Government, to be nominated by that Government;

[(f) a full-time member-secretary, possessing qualifications, knowledge and experience of scientific, engineering or management aspects of pollution control, to be appointed by the State Government]

(3) Every State Board shall be a body corporate with the name specified by the State Government in the notification under sub-section (1), having perpetual succession and a common seal with power, subject to the provisions of this Act, to acquire, hold and dispose of property and to contract, and may, by the said name, sue or be sued.

(4) Notwithstanding anything contained in this section, no State Board shall be constituted for a Union territory and in relation to a Union territory, the Central Board shall exercise the powers and perform the functions of a State Board for that Union territory:

Provided that in relation to a Union territory the Central Board may delegate all of any of its powers and functions under this sub-section to such person or body of persons as the Central Government may specify.

TERMS AND CONDITIONS OF SERVICE OF MEMBERS

(1) Save as otherwise provided by or under this Act, a member of a Board, other than, a member-secretary, shall hold office for a term of three years from the date of this nomination:

Provided that a member shall, notwithstanding the expiration of his term, continue to hold office until his successor enters upon his office.

[(2) The term of office of a member of a Board nominated under clause (b) or clause (e) of sub-section (2) of Section 3 or clause (b) or clause (e) of sub-section (2) of section 4 shall come to an end as soon as he ceases to hold the office under the Central Government or the State Government or, as the case may be, the company or corporation owned, controlled or managed by the Central Government or the State Government, by virtue of which he was nominated]

(3) The Central Government or, as the case may be, the State Government may, if it thinks fit, remove any member of a Board before the expiry of his term of office, after giving him a reasonable opportunity of showing cause against the same.

(4) A member of a Board, other than the member-secretary, may at any time resign his office by writing under his hand addressed—

(a) in the case of chairman, tot he Central Government or, as the case may be, the State Government; and

(b) in any other case, to the chairman of the Board; and the seat of the chairman or such member shall thereupon become vacant.

(5) A member of a Board, other than the member-secretary, shall be deemed to have vacated his seat if he is absent without reason, sufficient in the opinion of the Board, from three consecutive meetings of the Board, [or where he is nominated under clause (c) or clause (e) of sub-section (2) of section (3) or under clause (c) or clause (e) of sub-section (2) of section 4, if he ceases to be a member of the State Board or of the local authority or, as the case may be, of the company or corporation owned, controlled or managed by the Central Government or the State Government and such vacation of seat shall, in either case, take effect from such date as the Central Government or, as the case may be, the State Government may, by notification in the Official Gazette, specify]

(6) A casual vacancy in a Board shall be filled by a fresh nomination and the person nominated to fill the vacancy shall hold office only for the remainder of the term for which the member in a whose place he was nominated.

(7) A member of a Board [shall be eligible for renomination].

(8) The other terms and conditions of service of a member of a Board, other than the chairman and member-secretary, shall be such as may be prescribed.

(9) The other terms and conditions of service of the chairman shall be such as may be prescribed.

DISQUALIFICATIONS

(1) No person shall be a member of a Board, who—

(a) is, or at any time has been adjudged insolvent or has suspended payment of his debts or has compounded with his creditors, or

(b) is of unsound mind and stands so declared by a competent court, or

(c) is, or has been, convicted of an offence which, in the opinion of the Central Government or, as the case may be, of the State Government, involves moral turpitude, or

(d) is, or at any time has been, convicted of an offence under this Act, or

(e) has directly or indirectly by himself or by any partner, any share or interest in any firm or company carrying on the business of manufacture, sale or hire of machinery, plant, equipment, apparatus or fittings for the treatment of sewage or trade effluents, or

(f) is a director or a secretary, manager or other salaried officer or employee of any company or firm having any contract with the Board, or with the Government constituting the Board, or with a local authority in the State, or with a company or corporation owned, controlled or managed by the Government, for the carrying out of sewerage schemes or for the installation of plants for the treatment of sewage or trade effluents, or

(g) has so abused, in the opinion of the Central Government or as the case may be, of the State Government, his position as a member, as to render his continuance on the Board detrimental to the interest of the general public.

(2) No order of removal shall be made by the Central Government or the State Government, as the case may be, under this section unless the member concerned has been given a reasonable opportunity of showing cause against the same.

(3) Notwithstanding anything contained in sub-section (1) and (7) of section 5, a member who has been removed under this section shall not be eligible for renomination as a member.

VACATION OF SEAT BY MEMBERS

If a member of a Board becomes subject to any of the disqualifications specified in section 6, his seat shall become vacant.

MEETINGS OF BOARDS

A Board shall meet at least once in every three months and shall observe such rules of procedure in regard to the transaction of business at its meetings as may be prescribed:

Provided that if, in the opinion of the chairman, any business of an urgent nature is to be transacted, he may convene a meeting of the Board at such time as he thinks fit for the aforesaid purpose.

CONSTITUTION OF COMMITTEES

(1) A Board may constitute as many committees consisting wholly of members or wholly of other persons or partly of members and partly of other persons, and for such purpose or purposes as it may think fit.

(2) A committee constituted under this section shall meet at such time and at such place, and shall observe such rules of procedure in regard to the transaction of business at its meetings, as may be prescribed.

(3) The members of a committee (other than the members of Board) shall be paid such fees and allowances, for attending its meetings and for attending to any other work of the Board as may be prescribed.

TEMPORARY ASSOCIATION OF PERSONS WITH BOARD FOR PARTICULAR PURPOSES

(1) A Board may associate with itself in such manner, and for such purposes, as may be prescribed any person whose assistance or advice it may desire to obtain in performing any of its functions under this Act.

(2) A person associated with the Board under sub-section (1) for any purpose shall have a right to take part in the discussions of the Board relevant to that purpose, but shall not have a right to vote at a meeting of the Board, and shall not be a member for any other purpose.

(3) A person associated with the Board under sub-section (1) for any purpose shall be paid such fees and allowances, for attending its meetings and for attending to any other work of the Board, as may be prescribed.

VACANCY IN BOARD NOT TO INVALIDATE ACTS AND PROCEEDINGS

No act or proceeding of a Board or any committee thereof shall be called in question on the ground merely of the existence of any vacancy in, or any defect in the constitution of, the Board or such committee, as the case may be.

[19][11A.Delegation of powers to Chairman

The chairman of a Board shall exercise such powers and perform such duties as may be prescribed or as may, from time to time, be delegated to him by the Board]

MEMBER-SECRETARY AND OFFICERS AND OTHER EMPLOYEES OF BOARD

(1) Terms and conditions of service of the member-secretary shall be such as may be prescribed.

(2) The member-secretary shall exercise such powers and perform such duties as may be prescribed or as may, from time to time, he delegated to him by the Board or its chairman.

(3) Subject to such rules as may be made by the Central Government or, as the case may be, the State Government in this behalf, a Board may appoint such officers and employees as it considers necessary for the efficient performance of its functions

(3A) The method of recruitment and the terms and conditions of service (including the scales or pay) of the officers (other than the member-secretary) and other employees of the Central Board or a State Board shall be such as may be determined by regulations made by the Central Board or, as the case may be, by the State Board:

Provided that no regulation made under this sub-section shall take effect unless —

(a) in the case of a regulation made by the Central Board, it is approved by the Central Government; and

(b) in the case of a regulation made by a State Board, it is approved by the State Government

(3B) The Board may, by general or special order, and subject to such conditions and limitations, if any, as may be specified in the order, delegate to any officer of the Board such of its powers and functions under this Act as it may deem necessary

(4) Subject to such conditions as may be prescribed, a Board may from time to time appoint any qualified person to be a consulting engineer to the Board and pay him such salaries and allowances and subject him to such other terms and conditions of service as it thinks fit.

JOINT BOARDS

Constitution of Joint Board

(1) Notwithstanding anything contained in this Act, an agreement may be entered into—

(a) by two or more Governments of contiguous States, or

(b) by the Central Government (in respect of one or more Union territories) and one or more Government of State Government contiguous to such Union territory or Union territories, to be in force for such period and to be subject to renewal for such further period if any, as may be specified in the agreement to provide for the constitution of a Joint Board—

(i) in a case referred to in clause (a), for all the participating States, and

(ii) in a case referred to in clause (b), for the participating Union territory or Union territories and the State or States.

(2) An agreement under this section may —

(a) provide, in a case referred to in clause (a) of sub-section (1), for the apportionment between the participating States and in a case referred to in clause (b) of that sub-section, for the apportionments between the Central Government and the participating State Government or State Governments, of the expenditure in connection with the Joint Board;

(b) determine, in a case referred to in clause (a) of sub-section (1), which of the participating State Governments and in a case referred to in clause (b) of that sub-section, whether the Central Government or the participating State Government (if there are more than one participating State, also which of the participating State Governments) shall exercise and perform the several powers and functions of the State Government under this Act and the references in this Act to the State Government shall be construed accordingly;

(c) provide for consultation, in a case referred to in clause (a) of sub-section (1), between the participating State Governments and in a case referred to in clause (b) of that sub-section, between the Central Government and the participating State Government or State Governments either generally or with reference to particular matters arising under this Act;-

(d) make such incidental and ancillary provisions, not inconsistent with this Act, as may be deemed necessary or expedient for giving effect to the agreement.

(3) An agreement under this section shall be published, in a case referred to in clause (a) of sub-section (1), in the Official Gazette of the participating States and in a case referred to in clause (b) of that sub-section, in the Official Gazette of

participating Union territory or Union territories and participating State or States.

Composition of Joint Boards

(1) A Joint Board constituted in pursuance of an agreement entered into under clause (a) of sub-section (1) of section 13 shall consist of the following members, namely:—

(a) a full-time chairman, being a person having special knowledge or practical experience in respect of [matters relating to environmental protection] or a person having knowledge and experience in administering institutions dealing with the matters aforesaid, to be nominated by the Central Government;

(b) two officials from each of the participating States to be nominated by the concerned participating State Government to represent that Government;

(c) one person to be nominated by each of the participating State Governments from amongst the members of the local authorities functioning within the State concerned;

(d) one non-official to be nominated by each of the participating State Governments to represent the interests or agriculture, fishery or industry or trade in the State concerned or any other interest which, in the opinion of the participating State Government, is to be represented;

(e) two persons to be nominated by the Central Government to represent the companies or corporations owned, controlled or managed by the participating State Government;

(f) a full-time member-secretary, possessing qualifications, knowledge and experience of scientific, engineering or management aspects of pollution control, to be appointed by the Central Government.

(2) A Joint Board constituted in pursuance of an agreement entered into under clause (b) of sub-section (1) of section 13 shall consist of the following members, namely:-

(a) a full-time chairman, being a person having special knowledge or practical experience in respect of [matters relating to environmental protection] or a person having knowledge and experience in administering institutions dealing with the matters aforesaid, to be nominated by the Central Government;

(b) two officials to be nominated by the Central Government from the participating Union territory or each of the participating union territories, as the case may be, and two officials to be nominated, from the participating State or each of the participating States, as the case may be by the concerned participating State Government;

(c) one person to be nominated by the Central Government from amongst the members of the local authorities functioning within the participating Union territory or each of the participating Union territories, as the case may be and one person to be nominated, from amongst the members of the local authorities functioning within the participating State or each of the participating States, as the case may be, by the concerned participating State Government;

(d) one non-official to be nominated by the Central Government and one person to be nominated by the participating State Government or State Governments to represent the interests of agriculture, fishery or industry or trade in the Union territory or in each of the Union territories or the State or in each of the States, as the case may be, or any other interest which in the opinion in the Central Government or, as the case may be, of the State Government is to be represented.

(e) two persons to be nominated by the Central Government to represent the companies or corporations owned, controlled or managed by the Central Government and situate in the participating Union territory or territories and two persons to be nominated by Central Government to represent the companies or corporations owned, controlled or managed by the participating State Government;

(f) a full-time member-secretary, possessing qualifications, knowledge and experience of scientific, engineering or management aspects of pollution control, to be appointed by the Central Government.]

(3) When a Joint Board is constituted in pursuance of an agreement under clause (b) of sub-section (1) of section 13, the provisions of sub-section (4) of section 4 shall cease to apply in relation to the Union territory for which the Joint Board is constituted.

(4) Subject to the provisions of sub-section (3), the provisions of sub-section (3) of section 4 and sections 5 to 12 (inclusive) shall apply in relation tot he Joint Board and its member-secretary as they apply in relation to a State Board and its member-secretary.

(5) Any reference in this Act to the State Board shall, unless the context otherwise requires, be construed as including a Joint Board.

Special Provision Relating to Giving of Directions

Notwithstanding anything contained in this Act where any Joint Board is constituted under section 13 —

(a) the Government of the State for which the Joint Board is constituted shall be competent to give any direction under this Act only in cases where such direction relates to a matter within the exclusive territorial jurisdiction of the State;

(b) the Central Government alone shall be competent to give any direction under this Act where such direction relates to a matter within the territorial jurisdiction of two or more States or pertaining to a Union territory.

POWERS AND FUNCTIONS OF BOARDS

Functions of Central Board

(1) Subject to the provisions of this Act, the main function of the Central Board shall be to promote cleanliness of streams and wells in different areas of the States.

(2) In particular and without prejudice to the generality of the foregoing function, the Central Board may perform all or any of the following functions, namely:—

(a) advise the Central Government on any matter concerning the prevention and control of water pollution;

(b) co-ordinate the activities of the State Boards and resolve disputes among them;

(c) provide technical assistance and guidance to the State Boards, carry out and sponsor investigations and research relating to problems of water pollution and prevention, control or abatement of water pollution;

(d) plan and organise the training of persons engaged or to be engaged in programs for the prevention, control or abatement of water pollution on such terms and conditions as the Central Board may specify;

(e) organise through mass media a comprehensive programme regarding the prevention and control of water pollution;

(ee) perform such of the functions of any State Board as may be specified in an order made under sub-section (2) of section 18;

(f) collect, compile and publish technical and statistical data relating to water pollution and the measures devised for its effective prevention and control and prepare manuals, codes or guides relating to treatment and disposal of sewage and trade effluents and disseminate information connected therewith;

(g) lay down, modify or annul, in consultation with the State Government concerned, the standards for a stream or well: Provided that different standards may be laid down for the same stream or well or for different streams or wells, having regard to the quality of water, flow characteristics of the stream or well and the nature of the use of the water in such stream or well or streams or wells;

(h) plan and cause to be executed a nation-wide programme for the prevention, control or abatement of water pollution;

(i) perform such other functions as may be prescribed.

(3) The Board may establish or recognise a laboratory or laboratories to enable the Board to perform its functions under this section fficiently, including the analysis of samples of water from any stream or well or of samples of any sewage or trade effluents.

Functions of State Board

(1) Subject to the provisions of this Act, the functions of a State Board shall be —

(a) to plan a comprehensive programme for the prevention, control or abatement of pollution of streams and wells in the State and to secure the execution thereof;

(b) to advise the State Government on any matter concerning the prevention, control or abatement of water pollution;

(c) to collect and disseminate information relating to water pollution and the prevention, control or abatement thereof;

(d) to encourage, conduct and participate in investigations and research relating to problems of water pollution and prevention, control or abatement of water pollution;

(e) to collaborate with the Central Board in organising the training of persons engaged or to be engaged in programmes relating to prevention, control or abatement of water pollution and to organise mass education programmes relating thereto;

(f) to inspect sewage or trade effluents, works and plants for the treatment or sewage and trade effluents and to review plans, specifications or other data relating to plants set up for the treatment of water, works for the purification thereof and the system for the disposal of sewage or trade effluents or in connection with the grant of any consent as required by this Act;

(g) lay down, modify or annul effluent standards for the sewage and trade effluents and for the quality of receiving waters (not being water in an inter-State stream) resulting from the discharge of effluents and to classify waters of the State;

(h) to evolve economical and reliable methods of treatment of sewage and trade effluents, having regard to the peculiar conditions of soils, climate and water resources of different regions and more specially the prevailing flow characteristics of water in streams and wells which render it impossible to attain even the minimum degree of dilution;

(i) to evolve methods of utilisation of sewage and suitable trade effluents in agriculture;

(j) to evolve efficient methods of disposal of sewage and trade effluents on land, as are necessary on account of the predominant conditions of scant stream flows that do not provide for major part of the year the minimum degree of dilution;

(k) to lay down standards of treatment of sewage and trade effluents to be discharged into any particular stream taking into account the minimum fair weather dilution available in that stream and the tolerance limits of pollution permissible in the water of the stream, after the discharge of such effluents;

(l) to make, vary or revoke any order —

(i) for the prevention, control or abatement of discharge of waste into streams or wells;

(ii) requiring any person concerned to construct new systems for the disposal of sewage and trade effluents or to modify, alter or extend any such existing system or to adopt such remedial measures as are necessary to prevent control or abate water pollution;

(m) to lay down effluent standards to be complied with by persons while causing discharge of sewage or sullage or both and to lay down, modify or annul effluent standards for the sewage and trade effluents;

(n) to advice the State Government with respect to the location of any industry the carrying on of which is likely to pollute a stream or well;

(o) to perform such other functions as may be prescribed or as may, from time to time be entrusted to it by the Central Board or the State Government.

(2) The Board may establish or recognise a laboratory or laboratories to enable the Board to perform its functions under this section efficiently, including the analysis of samples of water from any stream or well or of samples of any sewage or trade effluents.

Powers to Give Directions

(1) In the performance of its functions under this Act —

(a) the Central Board shall be bound by such directions in writing the Central Government may give to it; and

(b) every State Board shall be bound by such directions in writing as the Central Government or the State Government may give to it:

Provided that where a direction given by the State Government is inconsistent with the direction given by the Central Board, the matter shall be referred to the Central Government for its decision.

(2) Where the Central Government is of the opinion that and State Board has defaulted in complying with any directions given by the Central Government under sub-section (1) and as a result of such default a grave emergency has arisen and it is necessary or expedient so to do in the public interest, it may, by order, direct the Central Board to perform any of the functions of the State Board in relation to such area for such period and for such purposes, as may be specified in the order.

(3) Where the Central Board performs any of the functions of the State Board in pursuance of a direction under sub-section (2), the expenses, if any, incurred by the Central Board with respect to performance of such functions may, if the State Board is empowered to recover such expenses, be recovered by the Central Board with interest (at such reasonable rate as the Central Government may, by order, fix) from the date when a demand for such expenses is made until it is paid from the person or persons concerned as arrears of land revenue or of public demand.

(4) For the removal of doubts, it is hereby declared that any directions to perform the functions of any State Board given under sub-section (2) in respect of any area would not preclude the State Board from performing such functions in any other area in the State or any of its other functions in that area.

PREVENTION AND CONTROL OF WATER POLLUTION

Power of State Government to Restrict the Application of the Act to Certain Areas

(1) Notwithstanding contained in this Act, if the State Government, after consultation with, or on the recommendation of, the State Board, is of opinion that the provisions of this Act need not apply to the entire State, it may, by notification in the Official Gazette, restrict the application of this Act to such area or areas as may be declared therein as water pollution, prevention and control area or areas and thereupon the provisions of this Act shall apply only to such area or areas.

(2) Each water pollution, prevention and control area may be declared either by reference to a map or by reference to the line of any watershed or the boundary of any district or partly by one method and partly by another.

(3) The State Government may, by notification in the Official Gazette-

(a) alter any water pollution prevention and control area whether by way of extension or reduction; or

(b) define a new water pollution, prevention and control area in which may be merged one or more water pollution, prevention and control areas, or any part or parts thereof.

Power to Obtain Information

(1) For the purpose of enabling a State Board to perform the function conferred on it by or under this Act, the State Board or any officer empowered by it in that behalf, may make surveys of any area and gauge and keep records of the flow or volume and other characteristics of an stream or well in such area, and may take steps for the measurement and recording of the rainfall in such area or any part thereof and for the installation and maintenance for those purposes of gauges or other apparatus and works connected therewith, and carry out stream surveys and may take such other steps as may be necessary in order to obtain any information required for the purposes aforesaid.

(2) A State Board may give directions requiring any person who in its opinion is abstracting water from any such stream or well in the area in quantities which are substantial in relation to the flow or volume of that stream or well or is discharging sewage or trade effluent into any such stream or well, to give such information as to the abstraction or the discharge at such times and in such form as may be specified in the directions.

(3) Without prejudice to the provisions of sub-section (2), a State Board may, with a view to preventing or controlling pollution of water, give directions requiring any person in charge of any establishment where any [1][industry, operation or process, or treatment and disposal system is carried on, to furnish to it information regarding the construction, installation or operation of such establishment or of any disposal system or of any extension or addition thereto in such establishment and such other particulars as may be prescribed.

Power to Take Samples of Effluents and Procedure to be Followed in Connection Therewith

(1) A State Board or any officer empowered by it in this behalf shall have power to take for the purpose of analysis

samples of water from any stream or well or samples of any sewage of trade effluent which is passing from any plant or vessel or from or over any place into any such stream or well.

(2) The result of any analysis of a sample of any sewage or trade effluent taken under sub-section (1) shall not be admissible in evidence in an legal proceeding unless the provisions of sub-sections (3), (4) and (5) are complied with.

(3) Subject to the provisions of sub-sections (4) and (5), when a sample (composite or otherwise as may be warranted by the process used) of any sewage or trade effluent is taken for analysis under sub-section (1), the person taking the sample shall —

(a) serve on the person in charge of, or having control over, the plant or vessel or in occupation of the place (which person is hereinafter referred to as the occupier) or any agent of such occupier, a notice, then and there in such form as may be prescribed of his intention to have it so analysed;

(b) in the presence of the occupier or his agent, divided the sample into two parts;

(c) cause each part to be placed in a container which shall be marked and sealed and shall also be signed both by the person taking the sample and the occupier or his agent;

(d) send one container forthwith,—

(i) in a case where such sample is taken from any area situated in a Union territory, to the laboratory established or recognised by the Central Board under section; and

(ii) in any other case, to the laboratory established or recognised by the State Board under section 17;

(e) on the request of the occupier or his agent, send the second container —

(i) in a case where such sample is taken from any area situated in a Union territory, to the laboratory established or specified under sub-section (1) of section 51; and

(ii) in an other case, to the laboratory established or specified under sub-section (1) of section 52.

(4) When a sample of any sewage of trade effluent is taken for analysis under sub-section (1) and the person taking the sample serves on the occupier or his agent, a notice under clause (a) of sub-section (3) and the occupier or his agent wilfully absents himself, then —

(a) the sample so taken shall be placed in a container which shall be marked and sealed and shall also be signed by the person taking the sample and the same shall be sent forthwith by such person for analysis to the laboratory referred to in sub-clause (i) or sub-clause (ii), as the case may be, of clause (e) of sub-section (3) and such person shall inform the Government analyst appointed under sub-section (1) or sub-section (2), as the case may be, of section 53, in writing about the wilful absence of the occupier or his agent; and

(b) the cost incurred in getting such sample analysed shall be payable by the occupier or his agent and in case of default of such payment, the same shall be recoverable from the occupier or his agent, as the case may be, as an arrear of land revenue or of public demand:

Provided that no such recovery shall be made unless the occupier or, as the case may be, his agent has been given a reasonable opportunity of being heard in the matter.

(5) When a sample of any sewage or trade effluent is taken for analysis under sub-section (1) and the person taking the sample serves on the occupier or his agent a notice under clause (a) of sub-section (3) and the occupier or his agent who is present at the time of taking the sample does not make a request for dividing the sample into two parts as provided in clause (b) of sub-section (3), then, the sample so taken shall be placed in a container which shall be marked and sealed and shall also be signed by the person taking the sample and the same shall be sent forthwith by such person for analysis to the

laboratory referred to in sub-clause (i) or sub-clause (ii), as the case may be, of clause (d) of sub-section (3).

Reports of Results of Analysis on Samples Taken Under Section 21

(1) Where a sample of any sewage or trade effluent has been sent for analysis to the laboratory established or recognised by the Central Board or, as the case may be, the State Board, the concerned Board analyst appointed under sub-section (3) of section 53 shall analyse the sample and submit a report in the prescribed form of the result of such analysis in triplicate to the Central Board or the State Board, as the case may be.

(2) On receipt of the report under sub-section (1), one copy of the report shall be sent by the Central Board or the State Board, as the case may be, to the occupier or his agent referred to in section 21, another copy shall be preserved for production before the court in case any legal proceedings are taken against him and the other copy shall be kept by the concerned Board.

(3) Where a sample has been sent for analysis under clause (e) of sub-section (3) or sub-section (4) of section 21 to any laboratory mentioned therein, the Government analyst referred to in that sub-section shall analyse the sample and submit a report in the prescribed form of the result of the analysis in triplicate to the Central Board or, as the case may be, the State Board which shall comply with the provisions of sub-section (2).

(4) If there is any inconsistency or discrepancy between, or variation in the results of, the analysis carried out by the laboratory established or recognised by the Central Board or the State Board, as the case may be, and that of the laboratory established or specified under section 51 or section 52, as the case may be, the report of the latter shall prevail.

(5) Any cost incurred in getting any sample analysed at the request of the occupier or his agent shall be payable by

such occupier or his agent and in case of default the same shall be recoverable from him as arrears of land revenue or of public demand.

POWER OF ENTRY AND INSPECTION

(1) Subject to the provisions of this section, any person empowered by a State Board in this behalf shall have a right at any time to enter, with such assistance as he considers necessary, any place—

(a) for the purpose of performing any of the functions of the Board entrusted to him;

(b) for the purpose of determining whether and if so in what manner, any such functions are to be performed or whether any provisions of this Act or the rules made thereunder of an notice, order, direction or authorisation served, made, given, or granted under this Act is being or has been complied with;

(c) for the purpose of examining any plant, record, register, document or any other material object or for conducting a search of any place in which he has reason to believe that an offence under this Act or the rules made thereunder has been or is being or is about to be committed and for seizing any such plant, record, register, document or other material object, if he has reason to believe that it may furnish evidence of the commission of an offence punishable under this Act or the rules made thereunder:

Provided that the right to enter under this sub-section for the inspection of a well shall be exercised only at reasonable hours in a case where such well is situated in any premises used for residential purposes and the water thereof is used exclusively for domestic purposes.

(2) The provisions of [3][the Code of Criminal Procedure, 1973, or, in relation to the State of Jammu and Kashmir, the provisions of any corresponding law in force in that State, shall, so far as may be, apply to an search or seizure under this section as they apply to any search or seizure made under the

authority of a warrant issued under [4][section 94] of the said Code, or, as the case may be, under the corresponding provisions of the said law.

Explanation — For the purposes of this section, "place" includes vessel.

PROHIBITION ON USE OF STREAM OR WELL FOR DISPOSAL OF POLLUTING MATTER, ETC.

(1) Subject to the provisions of this section —

(a) no person shall knowingly cause or permit any poisonous, noxious or polluting matter determined in accordance with such standards as may be laid down by the State Board to enter (whether directly or indirectly) into any [5][stream or well or sewer or on land]; or

(b) no person shall knowingly cause or permit to enter into any stream any other matter which may tend, either directly or in combination with similar matters, to impede the proper flow of the water of the stream in a manner leading or likely to lead to a substantial aggravation of pollution due to other causes or of its consequences.

(2) A person shall not be guilty of an offence under sub-section (1), by reason only of having done any of the following acts, namely;—

(a) constructing, improving a maintaining in or across or on the bank or bed of any stream any building, bridge, weir, dam, sluice, dock, pier, drain or sewer or other permanent works which he has a right to construct, improve or maintain;

(b) depositing any materials on the bank or in the bed of any stream for the purpose of reclaiming land or for supporting, repairing or protecting the bank or bed of such stream provided such materials are not capable of polluting such stream;

(c) putting into an stream any sand or gravel or other natural deposit which has flowed from or been deposited by the current of such stream;

(d) causing or permitting, with the consent of the State Board, the deposit accumulated in a well, pond or reservoir to enter into any stream.

(3) The State Government may, after consultation with, or on the recommendation of, the State Board, exempt, by notification in the Official Gazette, any person from the operation of sub-section (1) subject to such conditions, if any, as may be specified in the notification and any conditions so specified may by a like notification and be altered, varied or amended.

RESTRICTIONS ON NEW OUTLETS AND NEW DISCHARGES

(1) Subject to the provisions of this section, no person shall, without the previous consent of the State Board,—

(a) establish or take any steps to establish any industry, operation or process, or any treatment and disposal system or an extension or addition thereto, which is likely to discharge sewage or trade effluent into a stream or well or sewer or on land (such discharge being hereafter in this section referred to as discharge of sewage); or

(b) bring into use any new or altered outlets for the discharge of sewage; or

(c) begin to make any new discharge of sewage; Provided that a person in the process of taking any steps to establish any industry, operation or process immediately before the commencement of the Water (Prevention and Control of Pollution) Amendment Act, 1988, for which no consent was necessary prior to such commencement or, if he has made an application for such consent, within the said period of three months, till the disposal of such application.

(2) An application for consent of the State Board under sub-section (1) shall be made in such form, contain such particulars and shall be accompanied by such fees as may be prescribed.

(3) The State Board may make such inquiry as it may deem fit in respect of the application for consent referred to in sub-

section (1) and in making any such inquiry shall follow such procedure as may be prescribed.

(4) The State Board may —

(a) grant its consent referred to in sub-section (1), subject to such conditions as it may impose, being—

(i) in cases referred to in clauses (a) and (b) of sub-section (1) of section 25, conditions as to the point of discharge of sewage or as to the use of that outlet or any other outlet for discharge of sewage;

(ii) in the case of a new discharge, conditions as to the nature and composition, temperature, volume or rate of discharge of the effluent from the land or premises from which the discharge or new discharge is to be made; and

(iii) that the consent will be valid only for such period as may be specified in the order, and any such conditions imposed shall be binding on any person establishing or taking any steps to establish any industry, operation or process, or treatment and disposal system or extension or addition thereto, or using the new or altered outlet, or discharging the effluent from the land or premises aforesaid; or

(b) refuse such consent for reasons to be recorded in writing.

(5) Where, without the consent of the State Board, any industry operation or process, or any treatment and disposal system or any extension or addition thereto, is established, or any steps for such establishment have been taken or a new or altered outlet is brought into use for the discharge of sewage or a new discharge of sewage is made, the State Board may serve on the person who has established or taken steps to establish any industry, operation or process, or any treatment and disposal system or any extension or addition thereto, or using the outlet, or making the discharge, as the case may be, a notice imposing any such conditions as it might have imposed on an application for its consent in respect of such establishment, such outlet or discharge.

(6) Every State Board shall maintain a register containing particulars or conditions imposed under this section and so much of the register as relates to any outlet, or to any effluent, from any land or premises shall be open to inspection at all reasonable hours by any person interested in, or affected by such outlet, land or premises, as the case may be, or by any person authorised by him in this behalf and the conditions so contained in such register shall be conclusive proof that the consent was granted subject such conditions]

(7) The consent referred to in sub-section (1) shall, unless given or refused earlier, be deemed to have been given unconditionally on the expiry of a period of four months of the making of an application in this behalf complete in all respects to the State Board.

(8) For the purposes of this section and sections 27 and 30 —

(a) the expression "new or altered outlet" means any outlet which is wholly or partly constructed on or after the commencement of this Act or which (whether so constructed or not) is substantially altered after such commencement;

(b) the expression "new discharge" means a discharge which is not, as respects the nature and composition, temperature, volume, and rate of discharge of the effluent substantially a continuation of a discharge made within the preceding twelve months (whether by the same or different outlet), so however that a discharge which is in other respects a continuation of previous discharge made as aforesaid shall not be deemed to be a new discharge by reason of any reduction of the temperature or volume or rate of discharge of the effluent as compared with the previous discharge.

PROVISION REGARDING EXISTING DISCHARGE OF SEWAGE OR TRADE EFFLUENT

Where immediately before the commencement of this Act any person was discharging any sewage or trade effluent into a stream or well or sewer or on land], the provisions of section 25 shall, so far as may be, apply in relation to such person as they apply in relation to the person referred to in that section subject to the modification that the application for consent to be made under sub-section (2) of that section shall be made on or before such date as may be specified by the State Government by notification in this behalf in the Official Gazette.

REFUSAL OR WITHDRAWAL OF CONSENT BY STATE BOARD

(1) A State Board shall not grant its consent under sub-section (4) of section 25 for the establishment of any industry, operation or process, or treatment and disposal system or extension or addition thereto, or to the bringing into use of a new or altered outlet unless the industry, operation or process, or treatment and disposal system or extension or addition thereto, or the outlet is so established as to comply with an conditions imposed by the Board to enable it to exercise its right to take samples of the effluent.

(2) A State Board may from time to time review —

(a) any condition imposed under section 25 or section 26 and may serve on the person to whom a consent under section 25 or section 26 is granted a notice making any reasonable variation of or revoking any such condition.

(b) the refusal of any consent referred to in sub-section (1) of section 25 or section 26 or the grant of such consent without any condition, and may make such orders as it deemed fit.

(3) Any conditions imposed under section 25 or section 26 shall be subject to any variation made under sub-section (2) and shall continue in force until revoked under that sub-section.

APPEALS

(1) Any person aggrieved by an order made by the State Board under Section 25, section 26 or section 27 may within thirty days from the date on which the order is communicated to him, prefer an appeal to such authority (hereinafter referred

to as the appellate authority) as the State Government may think fit to constitute: Provided that the appellate authority may entertain the appeal after the expiry of the said period of thirty days if such authority is satisfied that the appellant was prevented by sufficient cause from filing the appeal in time.

(2) An appellate authority shall consist of a single person or three persons as the State Government may think fit, to be appointed by that Government.

(3) The form and manner in which an appeal may be preferred under sub-section (1), the fees payable for such appeal and the procedure to be followed by the appellate authority shall be such as may be prescribed.

(4) On receipt of an appeal preferred under sub-section (1), the appellate authority shall, after giving the appellant and the State Board an opportunity of being heard, dispose of the appeal as expeditiously as possible.

(5) If the appellate authority determines that any condition imposed, or the variation of any condition, as the case may be, was unreasonable, then,—

(a) where the appeal is in respect of the unreasonableness of any condition imposed, such authority may direct either that the condition shall be treated as annulled or that there shall be substituted for it such condition as appears to it to be reasonable;

(b) where the appeal is in respect of the unreasonableness of any variation of a condition, such authority may direct either that the condition shall be treated as continuing in force unvaried or that it shall be varied in such manner as appears to it to be reasonable.

REVISION

(1) The State Government may at any time either of its own motion or on an application made to it in this behalf, call for the records of any case where an order has been made by the State Board under section 25, section 26 or section 27 for the purpose of satisfying itself as to the legality or propriety of any

such order and may pass such order in relation thereto as it may think fit: Provided that the State Government shall not pass any order under this sub-section without affording the State Board and the person who may be affected by such order a reasonable opportunity of being heard in the matter.

(2) The State Government shall not revise any order made under section 25, section 26 or section 27 where an appeal against that order lies to the appellate authority, but has not been preferred or where an appeal has been preferred such appeal is pending before the appellate authority.

POWER OF STATE BOARD TO CARRY OUT CERTAIN WORKS

(1) Where under this Act, any conditions have been imposed on any person while granting consent under section 25 or section 26 and such conditions require such person to execute any work in connection therewith and such work has not been executed within such time as may be specified in this behalf, the State Board may serve on the person concerned a notice requiring him within such time (not being less than thirty days) as may be specified in the notice to execute the work specified therein]

(2) If the person concerned fails to execute the work as required in the notice referred to in sub-section (1), then, after the expiration of the time specified in the said notice, the State Board may itself execute or cause to be executed such work.

(3) All expenses incurred by the State Board for the execution of the aforesaid work, together with interest, at such rate as the State Government may, by order, fix, from the date when a demand for the expenses is made until it is paid, may be recovered by that Board from the person concerned, as arrears of land revenue, or of public demand.

FURNISHING OF INFORMATION TO STATE BOARD AND OTHER AGENCIES IN CERTAIN CASES

(1) If at any place where any industry, operation or process, or any treatment and disposal system or any extension or

addition thereto is being carried on, due to accident or other unforeseen act or event, any poisonous, noxious or polluting matter is being discharged, or is likely to be discharged into a stream or well or sewer or on land and, as a result of such discharge, the water in any stream or well is being polluted, or is likely to be polluted, then the person incharge of such place shall forthwith intimate the occurrence of such accident, act or event to the State Board and such other authorities or agencies as may be prescribed]

(2) Where any local authority operates any sewerage system or sewage works the provisions of sub-section (1) shall apply to such local authority as they apply in relation to the person in charge of the place where an industry or trade is being carried on.

EMERGENCY MEASURES IN CASE OF POLLUTION OF STREAM OR WELL

(1) Where it appears to the State Board that any poisonous, noxious or polluting matter is present in [16][any stream or well or on land by reason of the discharge of such matter in such stream or well or on such land or has entered into that stream or well due to any accident or other unforeseen act or event, and if the Board is of opinion that it is necessary or expedient to take immediate action, it may for reasons to be recorded in writing, carry out such operations as it may consider necessary for all or any of the following purposes, that is to say —

(a) removing that matter from the stream or well or on land and disposing it of in such manner as the Board considers appropriate;

(b) remedying or mitigating any pollution caused by its presence in the stream or well;

(c) issuing orders immediately restraining or prohibiting the persons concerned from discharging any poisonous, noxious or polluting matter [18][into the steam or well or on land] or from making insanitary use of the stream or well.

(2) The power conferred by sub-section (I) does not include the power to construct any works other than works of a temporary character which are removed on or before the completion of the operations.

POWER OF BOARD TO MAKE APPLICATION TO COURTS FOR RESTRAINING APPREHENDED POLLUTION OF WATER IN STREAMS OF WELLS

(1) Where it is apprehended by a Board that the water in any stream or well is likely to be polluted by reason of the disposal or likely disposal of any matter in such stream or well or in any sewer, or on any land, or otherwise, the Board may make an application to a court, not inferior to that of a Metropolitan Magistrate or a Judicial Magistrate of the first class, for restraining the person who is likely to cause such pollution from so causing.]

(2) On receipt of an application under sub-section (I) the court make such order as it deems fit.

(3) Where under sub-section (2) the court makes an order restraining any person from polluting the water in any stream or well, it may in that order-

(i) direct the person who is likely to cause or has caused the pollution of the water in the stream or well, to desist from taking such action as is likely to cause pollution or, as the case may be, to remove such stream or well, such matter, and

(ii) authorise the Board, if the direction under clause (i) (being a direction for the removal of any matter from such stream or well) is not complied with by the person to whom such direction is issued, to undertake the removal and disposal of the matter in such manner as may be specified by the court.

(4) All expenses incurred by the Board in removing any matter in pursuance of the authorisation under clause (ii) of sub-section (3) or in the disposal of any such matter may be defrayed out of any money obtained by the Board from such disposal and any balance outstanding shall be recoverable from

the person concerned as arrears of land revenue or of public demand.

POWER TO GIVE DIRECTIONS

Notwithstanding anything contained in any other law, but subject to the provisions of this Act, and to any directions that the Central Government may give in this behalf, a Board may, in the exercise of its powers and performance of its functions under this Act, issue any directions in writing to any person, officer or authority, and such person, officer or authority shall be bound to comply with such directions.

Explanation.-For the avoidance of doubts, it is hereby declared that the power to issue directions under this section includes the power to direct-

(a) the closure, prohibition or regulation of any industry, operation or process; or

(b) the stoppage or regulation of supply of electricity, water or any other service.

FUNDS, ACCOUNTS AND AUDIT

Contributions by Central Government

The Central Government may, after due appropriation made by Parliament by law in this behalf, make in each financial year such contribution to the Central Board as it may think necessary to enable the Board to perform its functions under this Act.

CONTRIBUTIONS BY STATE GOVERNMENT

The State Government may, after due appropriation made by the Legislature of the State by law in this behalf, make in each financial year such contributions to the State Board as it may think necessary to enable that Board to perform its functions under this Act.

FUND OF CENTRAL BOARD

(1) The Central Board shall have its own fund, and all sums which may, from time to time, be paid to it by the Central

Government and all other receipts (by way of gifts, grants, donations, benefactions fees or (otherwise) of that Board shall be carried to the fund of the Board and all payments by the Board shall be made therefrom.

(2) The Central Board may expend such sums as it thinks fit for performing its functions under this Act, and, where any law for the time being in force relating to the prevention, control of abatement or air pollution provides for the performance of any function under such law by the Central Board, also for performing its functions under such [law] and such sums shall be treated as expenditure payable out of the funds of that Board.

FUND OF STATE BOARD

(1) The State Board shall have its own fund, and the sums which may, from time to time, be paid to it by the State Government and all other receipts (by way of gifts, grants, donations, benefactions [fees] or (otherwise) of that Board shall be carried to the fund of the Board and all payments by the Board shall be made therefrom.

(2) The State Board may expend such sums as it thinks fit for performing its functions under this Act, [and, where any law for the time being in force relating to the prevention, control or abatement of air pollution provides for the performance of any function under such law by the State Board, also for performing its functions under such law] and such sums shall be treated as expenditure payable out of the fund of that Board.

Borrowing Powers of Board

A Board may, with the consent of, or in accordance with, the terms of any general or special authority given to it by the Central Government or, as the case may be, the State Government, borrow money from any source by way of loans or issue of bonds, debentures or such other instruments, as it may deem fit, for the performance of all or any of its functions under this Act].

BUDGET

The Central Board or, as the case may be, the State Board shall, during each financial year, prepare, in such form and at such time as may be prescribed, a budget in respect of the financial year next ensuing showing the estimated receipt and expenditure, and copies thereof shall be forwarded to the Central Government, or as the case may be, the State Government.

ANNUAL REPORT

(1) The Central Board shall, during each financial year, prepare, in such form as may be prescribed, an annual report giving full account of its activities under this Act during the previous financial year and copies thereof shall be forwarded to the Central Government within four months from the last date of the previous financial year and that Government shall cause every such report to be laid before both Houses of Parliament within nine months from the last date of the previous financial year.

(2) Every State Board shall, during each financial year, prepare, in such form as may be prescribed, an annual report giving full account of its activities under this Act during the previous financial ear and copies thereof shall be forwarded to the State Government within four months from the last date of the previous financial year and that Government shall cause every such report to be laid before the State legislature within a period of nine months from the last date of the previous financial year]

ACCOUNT AND AUDIT

(1) Every Board shall maintain proper accounts and other relevant records and prepare an annual statement of accounts in such form as may be prescribed by the Central Government or, as the case may be, the State Government.

(2) 1 of 1956.

The accounts of the Board shall be audited by an auditor duly qualified to act as an auditor of companies under section 226 of the Companies Act, 1956.

(3) The said auditor shall be appointed by the Central Government or, as the case may be, the State Government on the advice of the Comptroller and Auditor-General of India.

(4) Every auditor appointed to audit the accounts of the Board under this Act shall have the right to demand the production of books, accounts, connected vouchers and other documents and papers and to inspect any of the offices of the Board.

(5) Every such auditor shall send a copy of his report together with an audited copy of the accounts to the Central Government or, as the case may be, the State Government.

(6) The Central Government shall, as soon as may be after the receipt of the audit report under sub-section (5), cause the same to be laid before both Houses of Parliament.

(7) The State Government shall, as soon as may be after the receipt of the audit report under sub-section (5), cause the same to be laid before the State Legislature.

PENALTIES AND PROCEDURE

"41. Failure to comply with directions under sub-section (2) or sub-section (3) of section of 20, or orders issued under clause (c) of sub-section (1) of 32 or directions issued under sub-section (2) of section 33 or section 33A.

(1) Whoever fails to comply with any direction given under sub-section (2) or sub-section (3) of section 20 within such time as may be specified in the direction shall, or conviction, be punishable with imprisonment for a term which may extend to three months or with fine which may extend to ten thousand rupees or with both and in case the failure continues, with an additional fine which may extend to five thousand rupees for every day during which such failure continues after the conviction for the first such failure.

(2) Whoever fails to comply with any order issued under clause (c) of sub-section (1) of section 32 or any direction issued by a court under sub-section (2) of section 33 or any direction issued under section 33A shall, in respect of each such failure

and on conviction, be punishable with imprisonment for a term which shall not be less than one year and six months but which may extend to six years and with fine, and case the failure continues, with an additional fine which may extend to five thousand rupees for every day during which such failure continues after the conviction for the first such failure.

(3) If the failure referred to in sub-section (2) continues beyond a period of one year after the date of conviction, the offender shall, on conviction, be punishable with imprisonment for a term which shall not be less than two years but which may extend to seven years and with fine]

PENALTY FOR CERTAIN ACTS

(1) Whoever —

(a) destroys, pulls down, removes, injures or defaces any pillar, post or stake fixed in the ground or any notice or other matter put up, inscribed or placed, by or under the authority of the Board, or

(b) obstructs any person acting under the orders or directions of the Board from exercising his powers and performing his functions under this Act, or

(c) damages any works or property belonging to the Board, or

(d) fails to furnish to any officer or other employees of the Board any information required by him for the purpose of this Act, or

(e) fails to intimate the occurrence of an accident or other unforeseen act or even under section 31 to the Board and other authorities or agencies as required by that section, or

(f) in giving any information which he is required to give under this Act, knowingly or wilfully makes a statement which is false in any material particular, or

(g) for the purpose of obtaining any consent under section 25 or section 26, knowingly or willfully makes a statement which is false in any material particular shall be punishable with imprisonment for a term which may extend to three months or with fine which may extend to [2][ten thousand rupees or with both.

(2) Where for the grant of a consent in pursuance of the provisions of section 25 or section 26 the use of a meter or gauge or other measure or monitoring device is required and such device is used for the purposes of those provision, any person who knowingly or willfully alters or interferes with that device so as to prevent it from monitoring or measuring correctly shall be punishable with imprisonment for a term which may extend to three months or with fine which may extend to [2][ten thousand rupees] or with both.

PENALTY FOR CONTRAVENTION OF PROVISIONS OF SECTION 24

Whoever contravenes the provisions of section 24 shall be punishable with imprisonment for a term which shall not be less than [one year and six months] but which may extend to six years and with fine.

PENALTY FOR CONTRAVENTION OF SECTION 25 OR SECTION 26

Whoever contravenes the provision of section 25 or section 26 shall be punishable with imprisonment for a term which shall not be less than [4][two years] but which may extend to six years and with fine.

ENHANCED PENALTY AFTER PREVIOUS CONVICTION

If any person who has been convicted of any offence under section 24 or 25 or section 26 is again found guilty of an offence involving a contravention of the same provision, he shall, on the second and on every subsequent conviction, be punishable with imprisonment for a term which shall not be less than [4][one and half years] but which may extend to seven years and with fine: Provided that for the purpose of this section no cognizance shall be taken of any conviction made more than two years before the commission of the offence which is being punished.

PENALTY FOR CONTRAVENTION OF CERTAIN PROVISIONS OF THE ACT

[5][Whoever contravenes any of the provisions of this Act or fails to comply with any order or direction given under this Act, for which no penalty has been elsewhere provided in this Act, shall be punishable with imprisonment which may extend to three months or with fine which may extend to ten thousand rupees or with both and in the case of a continuing contravention or failure, with an additional fine which may extend to five thousand rupees for every day during which such contravention or failure continues after conviction for the first such contravention or failure.

PUBLICATION OF NAMES OF OFFENDERS

If any person convicted of an offence under this Act commits a like offence afterwards it shall be lawful for the court before which the second or subsequent conviction takes place to cause the offender's name and place of residence, the offence and the penalty imposed to be published at the offender's expense in such newspapers or in such other manner as the court may direct and the expenses of such publication shall be deemed to be part of the cost attending the conviction and shall be recoverable in the same manner as a fine.

OFFENCES BY COMPANIES

(1) Where an offence under this Act has been committed by a company, every person who at the time the offence was committed was in charge of, and was responsible to the company for the conduct of, the business of the company, as well as the company, shall be deemed to the guilty of the offence and shall be liable to be proceeded against and punished accordingly: Provided that nothing contained in this sub-section shall render any such person liable to any punishment provided in this Act if he proves that the offence was committed without his knowledge for that he exercised all due diligence to prevent the commission of such offence.

(2) Notwithstanding anything contained in sub-section (1), where an offence under this Act has been committed by a

company and it is proved that the offence has been committed with the consent or connivance of, or is attributable to any neglect on the part of, any director, manager, secretary or other officer of the company, such director, manager, secretary or other officer shall also be deemed to be guilty of that offence and shall be liable to be proceeded against and punished accordingly.

Explanation—For the purpose of this section,—

(a) "company" means any body corporate, and includes a firm or other association of individuals; and

(b) "director" in relation to a firm means a partner in the firm.

OFFENCES BY GOVERNMENT DEPARTMENTS

Where an offence under this Act has been committed by any Department of Government, the Head of the Department shall be deemed to be guilty of the offence and shall be liable to be proceeded against and punished accordingly:

Provided that nothing contained in this section shall render such Head of the Department liable to any punishment if he proves that the offence was committed without his knowledge or that he exercised all due diligence to prevent the commission of such offence.

COGNIZANCE OF OFFENCES

(1) No court shall take cognizance of any offence under this Act except on a complaint made by—

(a) a Board or any officer authorised in this behalf by it; or

(b) any person who has given notice of not less than sixty days, in the manner prescribed, of the alleged offence and of his intention to make a complaint, to the Board or officer authorised as aforesaid, and no court inferior to that of a Metropolitan Magistrate or a Judicial Magistrate of the first class shall try any offence punishable under this Act.

(2) Where a complaint has been made under clause (b) of sub-section (1), the Board shall, on demand by such person, make available the relevant reports in its possession to that person:

Provided that the Board may refuse to make any such report available to such person if the same is, in its opinion, against the public interest.

Notwithstanding anything contained in section 29 of the Code of Criminal Procedure, 1973"], it shall be lawful for any Judicial Magistrate of the first class or for any Metropolitan Magistrate" to pass a sentence of imprisonment for a term exceeding two years or of fine exceeding two thousand rupees on any person convicted of an offence punishable under this Act.

MEMBERS, OFFICERS AND SERVANTS OF BOARD TO BE PUBLIC SERVANTS

All members, officers and servants of a Board when acting or purporting to act in pursuance of any of the provisions of this Act (45 of 1860) and the rules made thereunder shall be deemed to be public servants within the meaning of section 21 of the Indian Penal Code.

MISCELLANEOUS

Central Water Laboratory

(1) The Central Government may, by notification in the Official Gazette —

(a) establish a Central Water Laboratory; or

(b) specify any laboratory or institute as a Central Water Laboratory, to carry out the functions entrusted to the Central Water Laboratory under this Act.

(2) The Central Government may, after consultation with the Central Board, make rules prescribing—

(a) the functions of the Central Water Laboratory;

(b) the procedure for the submission to the said laboratory of samples of water or of sewage or trade effluent for analysis or tests, the form of the laboratory's report thereunder and the fees payable in respect of such report;

(c) such other matters as may be necessary or expedient to enable that laboratory to carry out its functions.

STATE WATER LABORATORY

(1) The State Government may, by notification in the Official Gazette —

(a) establish a State Water Laboratory; or

(b) specify any State laboratory or institute as a State Water Laboratory, to carry out the functions entrusted to the State Water Laboratory under this Act.

(2) The State Government may, after consultation with the State Board, make rules prescribing —

(a) the functions of the State Water Laboratory;

(b) the procedure for the submission to the said laboratory of samples of water or of sewage or trade effluent for analysis or rests, the form of the laboratory's report thereon and the fees payable in respect of such report;

(c) such other matters as may be necessary or expedient to enable that laboratory to carry out its functions.

ANALYSTS

(1) The Central Government may, by notification in the Official Gazette appoint such persons as it thinks fit and having the prescribed qualifications to be Government analysts for the purpose of analysis of samples of water or of sewage or trade effluent sent for analysis to any laboratory established or specified under sub-section (1) of section 51.

(2) The State Government may, by notification in the Official Gazette, appoint such persons as it thinks fit and having the prescribed qualifications to be Government analysts for the purpose of analysis of water or of sewage or trade effluent sent for analysis to any laboratory established or specified under sub-section (1) of section 52.

(3) Without prejudice to the provisions of sub-section (3) of section 12, the Central Board or, as the case may be, the State Board may, by notification in the Official Gazette, and with the approval of the Central Government or the State Government, as the case may be, appoint such persons as it thinks fit and having the prescribed qualifications to be Board analysts for the purpose of analysis of samples of water or of sewage or trade effluent sent for analysis to any laboratory established or recognised under section 16, as the case may be, under section 17.

REPORTS OF ANALYSTS

Any document purporting to be report signed by a Government analyst or, as the case may be, a Board analyst may be used as evidence of the facts stated therein in any proceeding under this Act.

LOCAL AUTHORITIES TO ASSIST

All local authorities shall render such help and assistance and furnish such information to the Board as it may require for the discharge of its functions, and shall make available to the Board for inspection and examination such records, maps, plans and other documents as may be necessary for the discharge of its functions.

COMPULSORY ACQUISITION OF LAND FOR THE STATE BOARD

Any land required by a State Board for the efficient performance of its function under this Act shall be deemed to be needed for a public purpose and such land shall be acquired for the State Board under the provisions of the Land Acquisition Act, 1894 (1 of 1984), or under any other corresponding law for the time being in force.

RETURNS AND REPORTS

The Central Board shall furnish to the Central Government, and a State Board shall furnish to the State Government and to the Central Board such reports, returns, statistics, accounts and other information with respect to its fund or activities as that government, or, as the case may be, the Central Board may, from time to time, require.

BAR OF JURISDICTION

No civil court shall have jurisdiction to entertain any suit or proceeding in respect of any matter which an appellate authority constituted under this Act is empowered by or under this Act to determine, and no injunction shall be granted by any court or other authority in respect of any action taken or to be taken in pursuance of any power conferred by or under this Act.

PROTECTION OF ACTION TAKEN IN GOOD FAITH

No suit or other legal proceedings shall lie against the Government or any officer of Government or any member or officer of a Board in respect of anything which is in good faith done or intended to be done in pursuance of this Act or the rules made thereunder.

OVERRIDING EFFECT

The provisions of this Act shall have effect notwithstanding anything inconsistent therewith contained in any enactment other than this Act.

POWER OF CENTRAL GOVERNMENT TO SUPERSEDE THE CENTRAL BOARD AND JOINT BOARDS

(1) If at any time the Central Government is of opinion —

(a) that the Central Board or any Joint Board has persistently made default in the performance of the functions imposed on it by or under this Act; or

(b) that circumstances exist which render it necessary in the public interest so to do, the Central Government may, by notification in the Official Gazette, supersede the Central Board or such Joint Board, as the case may be, for such period not exceeding one year, as may be specified in the notification: Provided that before issuing a notification under this sub-section for the reasons mentioned in clause (a), the Central Government shall give a reasonable opportunity to the Central Board or such Joint Board, as the case may be, to show cause why it should not be superseded and shall consider the explanations and objections if any, of the Central Board or such Joint Board, as the case may be.

(2) Upon the publication of notification under sub-section (1) superseding the Central Board or any Joint Board,

(a) all the members shall, as from the date of supersession vacate their offices as such;

(b) all the powers, functions and duties which may, by or under this Act, be exercised, performed or discharged by the Central Board or such Joint Board, shall, until the Central Board or the Joint Board, as the case may be, is reconstituted under sub-section (3) be exercised, performed or discharged by such person or persons as the Central Government may direct;

(c) all property owned or controlled by the Central Board or such Joint Board shall, until the Central Board or the Joint Board, as the case may be, is reconstituted under sub-section (3) vest in the Central Government.

(3) On the expiration of the period of supersession specified in the notification issued under sub-section (1), the Central Government may —

(a) extend the period of supersession for such further term, not exceeding six months, as it may consider necessary; or

(b) reconstitute the Central Board or the Joint Board, as the case may be, by fresh nomination or appointment, as the case may be, and in such case any person who vacated his office under clause (a) of sub-section (2) shall not be deemed disqualified for nomination or appointment: Provided that the Central Government may at any time before the expiration of the period of supersession, whether originally specified under sub-section (1) or as extended under this sub-section, take action under clause (b) of this sub-section.

POWER OF STATE GOVERNMENT TO SUPERSEDE STATE BOARD

(1) If at any time the State Government is of opinion —

(a) that the State Board has persistently made default in the performance of the functions imposed on it by or under this Act; or

(b) that circumstances exist which render it necessary in the public interest so to do, the State Government may, by notification in the Official Gazette, supersede the State Board for such period, not exceeding one year, as may be specified in the notification: Provided that before issuing a notification under this sub-section for the reasons mentioned in clause (a), the State Government shall give a reasonable opportunity to the State Board to show cause why it should not be superseded and shall consider the explanations and objections, if any, of the State Board.

(2) Upon the publication of a notification under sub-section (1) superseding the State Board, the provisions of sub-sections (2) and (3) of section 61 shall apply in relation to the supersession of the State Board as they apply in relation to the supersession of the Central Board or a Joint Board by the Central Government.

POWER OF CENTRAL GOVERNMENT TO MAKE RULES

(1) The Central Government may, simultaneously with the constitution of the Central Board, make rules in respect of the matters specified in sub-section (2) : Provided that when the Central Board has been constituted, no such rule shall be made, varied, amended or repealed without consulting the Board.

(2) In particular, and without prejudice to the generality of the foregoing power, such rules may provide for all or any of the following matters namely :-

(a) the terms and conditions of service of the members (other than the chairman and member-secretary) of the Central Board under sub-section (8) of section 5;

(b) the intervals and the time and place at which meetings of the Central Board or of any committee thereof constituted under this Act, shall be held and the procedure to be followed at such meetings, including the quorum necessary for the transaction of business under section 8, and under sub-section (2) of section 9;

(c) the fees and allowances to be paid to such members of a committee of the Central Board as are not members of the Board under sub-section (3) of section 9;

(d) the manner in which and the purposes for which persons may be associated with the Central Board under sub-section (1) of section 10 and the fees and allowances payable to such persons;

(e) the terms and conditions of service of the chairman and the member-secretary of the Central Board under sub-section (9) of section 5 and under sub-section (1) of section 12;

(f) conditions subject to which a person may be appointed as a consulting engineer to the Central Board under sub-section (4) of section 12;

(g) the powers and duties to be exercised and performed by the chairman and member-secretary of the Central Board;

(j) the form of the report of the Central Board analyst under sub-section (1) of section 22;

(k) the form of the report of the Government analyst under sub-section (1) of section 22;

(l) the form in which the time within which the budget of the Central Board may be prepared and forwarded to the Central Government under section 38;

(ll) the form in which the annual report of the Central Board may be prepared under section 39;

(m) the form in which the accounts of the Central Board may be maintained under section 40;

(mm) the manner relating to the Central Board, including the powers and functions of that Board in relation to Union territories;

(o) any other matter which has to be, or may be, prescribed.

(3) Every rule made by the Central Government under this Act shall be laid, as soon as may be after it is made, before each House of Parliament while it is in session for a total period of thirty days which may be comprised in one session or in two or more successive sessions, and if, before the expiry of the session immediately following the session or the successive sessions aforesaid, both Houses agree in making any modification in the rule of both Houses agree that the rule should not be made, the rule shall thereafter have effect only in such modified form or be of no effect, as the case may be; so, however, that any such modification or annulment shall be without prejudice to the validity of anything previously done under that rule.

POWER OF STATE GOVERNMENT TO MAKE RULES

(1) The State Government may, simultaneously with the constitution of the State Board, make rules to carry out the purposes of this Act in respect of matters not falling within the purview of section 63; Provided that when the State Board has been constituted, no such rule shall be made, varied, amended or repealed without consulting that Board.

(2) In particular, and without prejudice to the generality of the foregoing power, such rules may provide for all or any of the following matters, namely:—

(a) the terms and conditions of service of the members (other than the chairman and the member-secretary) of the State Board under sub-section (8) of section 5;

(b) the time and place of meetings of the State Board or of any committee of that Board constituted under this Act and the procedure to be followed at such meeting, including in quorum necessary for the transaction of business under section 8 and under sub-section (2) of section 9;

(c) the fees and allowances to be paid to such members of a committee of the State Board as are not members of the Board under sub-section (3) of section 9;

(d) the manner in which and the purpose for which persons may be associated with the State Board under sub-section (1) of section 10 [6][and the fees and allowances payable to such persons;

(e) the terms and conditions of service of the chairman and the member secretary of the State Board under sub-section (9) of section 5 and under sub-section (1) of section 12;

(f) the conditions subject to which a person may be appointed as a consulting engineer to the State Board under sub-section (4) of section 12;

(g) the powers and duties to be exercised and discharged by the chairman and the member-secretary of the State Board;

(h) the form of the notice referred to in section 21;

(i) the form of the report of the State Board analyst under sub-section (3) of section 22.

(j) the form of the report of the Government analyst under sub- section (3) of section 22;

(k) the form of application for the consent of the State Board under sub-section (2) of section 25 and the particular it may contain;

(l) the manner in which inquiry under sub-section (3) of section 25 may be made in respect of an application for obtaining consent of the State Board and the matters to be taken in to account in granting or refusing such consent;

(m) the form and manner in which appeals may be filed, the fees payable in respect of such appeals and the procedure to be followed by the appellate authority in disposing of the appeals under sub-section (3) of section 28;

[7][(n) the form in which and the time within which the budget of the State Board may be prepared and forwarded to the State Government under section 38;

(nn) the form in which the annual report of the State Board may be prepared under section 39;

(o) the form in which the accounts of the State Board may be maintained under sub-section (1) of section 40;

(oo) the manner in which notice of intention to make a complaint shall be given to the State Board or officer authorised by it under section 49;

(p) any other matter which has to be, or may be, prescribed.

4

National Environment Appellate Authority Act

An Act to provide for the establishment of a National Environment Appellate Authority to hear appeals with respect to restriction of areas in which any industries, operations or processes or class of industries, operations or processes shall not be carried out or shall be carried out subject to certain safeguards under the Environment (Protection) Act, 1986 and for matters connected therewith or incidental thereto. Be it enacted by Parliament in the Forty-eighth Year of the Republic of India as follows:-

PRELIMINARY

1. (1) This Act may be called the National Environment Appellate Authority Act, 1997. (2) It shall be deemed to have come into force on the 30th day of January, 1997.

2. In this Act, unless the context otherwise requires,- (a) "Act" means the Environment (Protection) Act, 1986; (b) "Authority" means the National Environment Appellate Authority established under sub-section (1) of section 3; (c) "Chairperson" means the Chairperson of the Authority; (d) "Member" means a Member of the Authority; (e) "prescribed" means prescribed by rules made under this Act; (f) "Vice-Chairperson" means the Vice-Chairperson of the Authority.

ESTABLISHMENT OF AUTHORITY

3. (1) The Central Government shall, by notification in the Official Gazette, establish a body to be known as the National

Environment Appellate Authority to exercise the powers conferred upon, and to perform the functions assigned to, it under this Act. (2) The head office of the Authority shall be at Delhi.

4. The Authority shall consist of a Chairperson, a Vice-Chairperson and such other Members not exceeding three, as the Central Government may deem fit.

5. (1) A person shall not be qualified for appointment as a Chairperson unless he has been- (a) a Judge of the Supreme Court; or (b) the Chief Justice of a High Court. (2) A person shall not be qualified for appointment as a Vice-Chairperson unless he has- (a) for at least two years held the post of a Secretary to the Government of India or any other post under the Central or State Government carrying a scale of pay which is not less than that of a Secretary to the Government of India; and (b) expertise or experience in administrative, legal, managerial or technical aspects of problems relating to environment. (3) A person shall not be qualified for appointment as a Member unless he has professional knowledge or practical experience in the areas pertaining to conservation, environmental management, law or planning and development. (4) The Chairperson, the Vice-Chairperson and the Members shall be appointed by the President.

6. (1) In the event of the occurrence of any vacancy in the office of the Chairperson by reason of his death, resignation or otherwise, the Vice-Chairperson shall act as the Chairperson until the date on which a new Chairperson appointed in accordance with the provisions of this Act to fill such vacancy enters upon his office. (2) When the Chairperson is unable to discharge his functions owing to absence, illness or any other cause, the Vice-Chairperson or, as the case may be, such one of the Member as the Central Government may, by notification, authorise in this behalf, shall discharge the functions of the Chairperson until the date on which the Chairperson resumes his duties.

7. The Chairperson, the Vice-Chairperson or a Member shall hold office as such for a term of three years from the date

on which he enters upon his office, but shall be eligible for re-appointment for another term of three years: Provided that no Chairperson, Vice-Chairperson or Member shall hold office as such after he has attained,- (a) in the case of the Chairperson, the age of seventy years; and (b) in the case of the Vice-Chairperson or a Member, the age of sixty-five years.

8. (1) The Chairperson, the Vice-Chairperson or a Member may, by notice in writing under his hand addressed to the President, resign his office: Provided that the Chairperson, the Vice-Chairperson or a Member shall, unless he is permitted by the President to relinquish his office sooner, continue to hold office until the expiry of three months from the date of receipt of such notice or until a person duly appointed as his successor enters upon his office or until the expiry of his term of office, whichever is the earliest. (2) The Chairperson, the Vice-Chairperson or a Member shall not be removed from his office except by an order made by the President on the ground of proved misbehaviour or incapacity after an inquiry made by a Judge of the Supreme Court in which such Chairperson, the Vice-Chairperson or a Member had been informed of the charges against him and given a reasonable opportunity of being heard in respect of those charges. (3) The President may suspend from office the Chairperson, the Vice-Chairperson or a Member in respect of whom a reference has been made to the Supreme Court under sub-section (2) until the President has passed orders on receipt of the report of the Supreme Court on such reference. (4) The Central Government may, by rules, regulate the procedure for the investigation of misbehaviour or incapacity of the Chairperson, the Vice-Chairperson or a Member referred to in sub-section (2).

9. The salaries and allowances payable to, and the other terms and conditions of service (including ponsion, gratuity and other retirement benefits) of, the Chairperson, the Vice-Chairperson and the Members shall be such as may be prescribed by the Central Government.

10. No act or proceedings of the Authority shall be questioned or shall be invalid merely on the ground of existence of any vacancy or defect in the establishment of the Authority.

JURISDICTION AND POWERS OF AUTHORITY

11. (1) Any person aggrieved by an order granting environmental clearance in the areas in which any industries, operations or processes or class of industries, operations and processes shall not be carried out or shall be carried out subject to certain safeguards may, within thirty days from the date of such order, prefer an appeal to the Authority in such form as may be prescribed: Provided that the Authority may entertain any appeal after the expiry of the said period of thirty days but not after ninety days from the date aforesaid if it is satisfied that the appellant was prevented by sufficient cause from filing the appeal in time.

(2) For the purposes of sub-section (1), "person" means- (a) any person who is likely to be affected by the grant of environmental clearance; (b) any person who owns or has control over the project with respect to which an application has been submitted for environmental clearance; (c) any association of persons (whether incorporated or not) likely to be affected by such order and functioning in the field of environment; (d) the Central Government, where the environmental clearance is granted by the State Government and the State Government, where the environmental clearance is granted by the Central Government; or (e) any local authority, any part of whose local limits is within the neighbourhood of the area wherein the project is proposed to be located.

(3) On receipt of an appeal preferred under sub-section (1), the Authority shall, after giving the appellant an opportunity of being heard, pass such orders, as it thinks fit.

(4) The Authority shall dispose of the appeal within ninety days from the date of filing the appeal: Provided that the Authority may for reasons to be recorded in writing, dispose of the appeal within a further period of thirty days.

12. (1) The Authority shall not be bound by the procedure laid down in the Code of Civil Procedure, 1908, but shall be guided by the principles of natural justice and subject to the other provisions of this Act and of any rules made by the Central Government, the Authority shall have power to regulate

its own procedure including the fixing of places and times of its inquiry and deciding whether to sit in public or in private.

(2) The Authority shall have, for the purposes of discharging its functions under this Act, the same powers as are vested in a civil court under the Code of Civil Procedure, 1908, while trying a suit, in respect of the following matters, namely:- (a) summoning and enforcing the attendance of any person and examining him on oath; (b) requiring the discovery and production of documents; (c) receiving evidence on affidavits; (d) subject to the provisions of sections 123 and 124 of the Indian Evidence Act, 1872 requisitioning any public record or document or copy of such record or document from any office; (e) issuing commissions for the examination of witnesses or documents; (f) reviewing its decisions; (g) dismissing a representation for default or deciding it, *ex parte*; (h) setting aside any order of dismissal of any representation for default or any order passed by it *ex parte*; and (i) any other matter which is required to be, or may be, prescribed by the Central Government.

13. The Chairperson shall exercise such financial and administrative powers as may be vested in him under the rules: Provided that the Chairperson shall have authority to delegate such of his financial and administrative powers as he may think fit to the Vice-Chairperson or any other officer subject to the condition that the Vice-Chairperson or such other officer shall, while exercising such delegated powers, continue to act under the direction, control and supervision of the Chairperson.

14. (1) The Central Government shall determine the nature and categories of the officers and other employees required to assist the Authority in the discharge of its functions and provide the Authority with such officers and other employees as it may think fit. (2) The officers and other employees of the Authority shall discharge their functions under the general superintendence of the Chairperson. (3) The salaries and allowances and conditions of service of the officers and other employees shall be such as may be prescribed.

MISCELLANEOUS

15. With effect from the date of establishment of the Authority, no civil court or other authority shall have jurisdiction to entertain any appeal in respect of any matter with which the Authority is so empowered by or under this Act.

16. All proceedings before the Authority shall be deemed to be judicial proceedings within the meaning of sections 193, 219 and 228 of the Indian Penal Code.

17. The Chairperson, the Vice-Chairperson and the Members and the officers and other employees of the Authority shall be deemed to be public servants within the meaning of section 21 of the Indian Penal Code.

18. No suit, prosecution or other legal proceeding shall lie against the Central Government or against the Chairperson, the Vice-Chairperson or a Member of the Authority or any other person authorised by the Chairperson, the Vice-Chairperson or a Member for anything which is in good faith done or intended to be done in pursuance of this Act or any rule or order made thereunder.

19. Whoever fails to comply with any order made by the Authority, he shall be punishable with imprisonment for a tenn which may extend to seven years, or with fine which may extend to one lakh rupees, or with both.

20. (1) Where any offence under this Act has been committed by a company, every person who, at the time the offence was committed, was directly in charge of, and was responsible to, the company for the conduct of the business of the company, as well as the company, shall be deemed to be guilty of the offence and shall be liable to be proceeded against and punished accordingly: Provided that nothing contained in this sub-section shall render any such person liable to any punishment provided in this Act, if he proves that the offence was committed without his knowledge or that he has exercised all due diligence to prevent the commission of such offence. (2) Notwithstanding anything contained in sub-section (1), where an offence under this Act has been committed by a company and it is proved that

the offence has been committed with the consent or connivance of, or is attributable to any neglect on the part of, any director, manager, secretary or other officer of the company, such director, manager, secretary or other officer shall also be deemed to be guilty of that offence and shall be liable to be proceeded against and punished accordingly.

Explanation. For the purposes of this section,- (a) "company" means any body corporate and includes a firm or other association of individuals; and (b) "director", in relation to a firm, means a partner in the firm.

21. (1) If any difficulty arises in giving effect to the Provisions of this Act, the Central Government may, by order published in the Official Gazette, make such provisions, not inconsistent with the provisions of this Act, as appear to it to be necessary or expedient for removing the difficulty: Provided that no such order shall be made after the expiry of the period of three years from the date on which this Act receives the assent of the President. (2) Every order made under this section shall, as soon as may be after it is made, be laid before each House of Parliament.

22. (1) The Central Government may, by notification, make rules for carrying out the provisions of this Act. (2) In particular, and without prejudice to the generality of the foregoing power, such rules may provide for all or any of the following matters, namely:- (a) the procedure under sub-section (4) of section 8 for the investigation of misbehaviour or incapacity of the Chairperson, the Vice-Chairperson or a Member; (b) the salaries and allowances payable to and the other terms and conditions of service of the Chairperson, the Vice-Chairperson and the Members under section 9; (c) the form which an appeal shall contain under sub-section (1) of section 11; (d) financial and administrative powers of the Chairperson under section 13; (e) the salaries and allowances and conditions of service of the officers and other employees of the Authority; (f) any other matter which is required to be, or may be, prescribed.

(3) Every rule made under this Act shall be laid, as soon as may be after it is made, before each House of Parliament, while it is in session, for a total period of thirty days which may

be comprised in one session or in two or more successive sessions, and if, before the expiry of the session immediately following the session or the successive sessions aforesaid, both Houses agree in making any modification in the rule or both Houses agree that the rule should not be made, the rule shall thereafter have effect only in such modified form or be of no effect, as the case may be; so, however, that any such modification or annulment shall be without prejudice to the validity of anything previously done under that rule.

23. (1) The National Environment Appellate Authority Ordinance, 1997 is hereby repealed. (2) Notwithstanding such repeal, anything done or any action taken under the said Ordinance, shall be deemed to have been done or taken under the corresponding provisions of this Act.

NATIONAL ENVIRONMENT TRIBUNAL ACT

An Act to provide for strict liability for damages arising out of any accident occurring while handling any hazardous substance and for the establishment of a National Environment Tribunal for effective and expeditious disposal of cases arising from such accident, with a view to giving relief and compensation for damages to persons, property and the environment and for matters connected therewith or incidental thereto.

WHEREAS decisions were taken at the United Nations Conference on Environment and Development held at Rio de Janeiro in June, 1992, in which India participated, calling upon the States to develop national laws regarding liability and compensation for the victims of pollution and other environmental damages;

AND WHEREAS it is considered expedient to implement the decisions of the aforesaid Conference so far as they relate to the protection of environment and payment of compensation for damage to persons, property and the environment while handling hazardous substances;

BE it enacted by Parliament in the Forty-sixth Year of the Republic of India as follows:-

PRELIMINARY

1. Short title and commencement. (1) This Act may be called the National Environment Tribunal Act, 1995. (2) It shall come into force on such date or dates as the Central Government may, by notification, appoint, and different dates may be appointed for different States and any reference in any provision of this Act to the commencement of this Act shall be construed in relation to any State or part thereof as a reference to the coming into force of that provision in that State or part thereof.

2. Definitions. In this Act, unless the context otherwise requires;— (a) "accident" means an accident involving a fortuitous or sudden or unintended occurrence while handling any hazardous substance resulting in continuous or intermittent or repeated exposure to death of, or injury to, any person or damage to any property or environment but does not include an accident by reason only of war or radio-activity; (b) "Bench" means a Bench of the Tribunal; (c) "Chairperson" means the Chairperson of the Tribunal; (d) "environment" includes water, air and land and the interrelationship which exists among and between water, air and land, and human beings, other living creatures, plants, microorganism and property; (e) "handling", in relation to any hazardous !substance, means the manufacture, processing; treatment; package; storage; transportation by vehicle, use, collection, destruction, conversion, offering for sale, transfer or the like of such hazardous substance; (f) "hazardous substance" means any substance or preparation which is defined as hazardous substance in the Environment (Protection) Act, 1986, (29 of 1986.) and exceeding such quantity as specified by the Central Government under the Public Liability Insurance Act, 1991; (6 of 1991.) (g) "Judicial Momber" means a Member of the Tribunal appointed as such under this Act, and includes,the Chairperson or a Vice-Chairperson who possesses any of the qualifications specified in sub-section (3) of section 10; (h) "Member" means a Member (whether Judicial or Technical) of the Tribunal and includes the Chairperson and a Vice-Chairperson; (i) "notification" means a notification published in the official Gazette; (j) "prescribed' means prescribed by ruler. made under this Act; (k) "rules" means the rules made under this Act; (l) "Technical Member" means a Member of the Tribunal who is not a Judicial Member within the meaning of clause (g); (m) "Tribunal" means the National Environment Tribunal established under section 8; (n) "Vice-Chairperson" means the Vice-Chairperson of the Tribunal.

Explanation.-In the case of the Tribunal having two or more Vice-Chairpersons, references to the Vice-Chairperson in this Act shall be construed as a reference to each of those Vice-Chairpersons; (o) "owner" means a person who owns, or has control over handling, any hazardous substance at the time of accident and includes,- (i) in the case of a firm, any of its partners; (ii) in the case of an association, any of its members; and (iii) in the case of a company, any of its directors, managers, secretaries or other officers who is directly in charge of, and is responsible to, the company for the conduct of the business of the company.

COMPENSATION FOR DEATH OF, OR INJURY TO, A PERSON AND DAMAGE TO PROPERTY AND ENVIRONMENT

3. Liability to pay compensation in certain cases on principle of o fault. (1) Where death of, or injury to, any person (other than a workman) or damage to any property or environment has resulted 'from an accident, the owner shall be liable to pay compensation for such death, injury or damage under all or any of the heads specified in the Schedule. (2) In any claim for compensation under sub-section (1), the claimant shall not be required to plead and establish that the death, injury or damage in respect of which the claim has been made was due to any wrongful act, neglect or default of any person.

Explanation-For the purposes of this section- (i) "workman" has the meaning assigned to it in the Workmen's Compensation Act, 1923; (8 of 1923.) (ii) "injury" includes permanent total or permanent partial disability or sickness resulting out of an accident. (3) If the death, injury or damage caused by an accident cannot be attributed to any individual activity but is the combined or resultant effect of several such activities, operation and processes, the Tribunal may apportion the liability for compensation amongst those responsible for such activities, operations and processes on an equitable basis.

4. Application for claim for compensation.

(1) An application for claim for compensation may be made- (a) by the person who has sustained the injury; (b) by the owner of the property to which the damage has been caused; (c) where death has resulted from the accident, by all or any of the legal representatives of the deceased; (d) by any agent duly authorised by such person or owner of such property or all or any of the legal representatives of the deceased, as the case may be; (e) by any representative body or Organisation, functioning in the field of environment and recognised in this behalf by the Central Government, under all or any of the heads specified in the Schedule; or (f) by the Central Government or a State Government or a local authority under all or any of the heads specified in the Schedule: Provided that where all the legal representatives of the deceased have not joined in any such application for compensation, the application shall be made on behalf of or for the benefit of all the legal representatives of the deceased and the legal representatives who have not so joined shall be impleaded as respondents to the application.

(2) The Tribunal may, if it thinks fit, take up the cases for claims for compensation *suo motu*.

(3) Any claimant making an application under sub-section (1) may also make an application before the Tribunal for such relief as is provided in the Public Liability Insurance Act, 1991: (6 of 1991.) Provided that no such application shall be made if the relief has been received by the claimant earlier or an application made by the claimant to the Collector under the said Act is pending and has not been withdrawn.

(4) The Tribunal shall have, and exercise, the same jurisdiction, powers and authority in respect of the matters specified in the Public Liability Insurance Act, 1991 (6 of 1991.) as the Collector has and may exercise and, for this purpose;

the provisions of that Act shalt have effect subject to the modification that the references therein to the Collector shall be construed as including a reference to the Tribunal.

(5) Every application under sub-section (1) shall be made to the Tribunal and shall contain such particulars and shall be accompanied by such documents and such fee, not exceeding one thousand rupees, as may be prescribed: Provided that no fee shall be payable by a person whose annual income is below the prescribed limit or by a representative body or Organisation referred to in clause (e) of sub-section (1) or by the Central Government, a State Government or a local authority.

(6) No application for compensation shall be entertained unless it is made within five years of the occurrence of the accident

5. Procedure and powers of Tribunal.

(1) On receipt of an application under sub-section (1) of section 4, the Tribunal may, after such inquiry as it may deem fit, reject the application summarily.

(2) Where the Tribunal does not reject the application under sub-section (1), the Tribunal may, after giving notice of the application to the owner and after giving the parties an opportunity of being heard, hold an inquiry into the claim or each of the claims and may make art award determining the amount of compensation which appears to be just and specifying the person or persons to whom such amount of compensation shall be paid.

(3) The Tribunal shall not be bound by the procedure laid down by the Code of Civil Procedure, 1908, (5 of 1908.) but shall be guided by the principles of natural justice and, subject to the other provisions of this Act and of any rules, the Tribunal shall have power o regulate its own procedure including the fixing of places and times of its inquiry.

(4) The Tribunal shall have, for the purpose of discharging its functions under this Act, the same powers as are vested in a civil court under the Code of Civil Procedure, 1908, (5 of 1908.) while trying a suit, in respect of the following matters.

namely:- (a) summoning and enforcing the attendance of any person and examining him on oath; (b) requiring the discovery and production of documents; (c) receiving evidence on affidavits; (d) subject to the provisions of sections 123 and 124 of the Indian Evidence Act, 1872, (1 of 1872.) requisitioning any public record or document or copy of such record or document from any office; (e) issuing commissions for the examination of witnesses or documents; (f) reviewing its decisions; (g) dismissing an application or deault or deciding it *ex parte*; (h) setting aside any order of dismissal of any application for default or any order passed by it *ex parte*; and (i) any other matter which is to be, or may be, prescribed.

6. Conditions as to making of interim orders.

Notwithstanding anything contained in any other provision of this Act or in any other law for the time being in force, no interim order (whether by way of injunction or stay or in any other manner) shall be made on, or in any proceedings relating to, an application unless- (a) copies of such application and of all documents in support of the plea for such interim order are furnished to the party against whom such application is made or proposed to be made; and (b) opportunity is given to such party to be heard in the matter: provided that the Tribunal may dispense with the requirements of clauses (a) and (b) and make an interim order as an exceptional measure if it is satisfied, for reasons to be recorded in writing, that it is necessary so to do for preventing any loss or damage being caused to the applicant which cannot be adequately compensated in Money but any such interim order shall, if it is not Sooner vacated, cease to have effect on the expiry of a period of fourteen clays from the date on which it is made unless the said requirement have been complied with before the expiry of that period and the Tribunal has continued the operation of the interim order.

7. Reduction of amount of relief paid under any other law.

Where in respect of death of, or injury to, any person or damage to any property, the owner, liable to pay compensation under this Act, is also liable to pay any amount as relief under the Public Liability Insurance Act, 1991 (6 of 1991.) or any other compensation under any other law, the amount of compensation payable under this Act shall be reduced by the amount of relief and other compensation paid under any other law.

ESTABLISHMENT OF NATIONAL ENVIRONMENT TRIBUNAL AND BENCHES THEREOF

8. Establishment of National Environment Tribunal. The Central Government shall, by notification, establish a Tribunal, to be known as the National Environment Tribunal, to exercise the jurisdiction, powers and authority Conferred on it by or under this Act.

9. Composition of Tribunal and Benches thereof.

(1) The Tribunal shall consist of a Chairperson and such number of Vice-Chairpersons, Judicial Members and Technical Members as the Central Government may deem fit and, subject to the other provisions if this Act, the jurisdiction, powers and authority of the Tribunal may be exercised by Benches thereof.

(2) Subject to the other provisions of this Act, a Bench shall consist of one Judicial Member and one Technical Member.

(3) Notwithstanding anything contained in sub-section (1), the Chairperson- (a) may, in addition to discharging the functions of the Judicial Member of the Technical Member of the Bench to which he is appointed, discharge the functions of the Judicial Member or, as the case may be, the Technical Member, of any other Bench; (b) may transfer the Vice-Chairperson or other Member from one Bench to another Bench; (c) may authorise the Vice-Chairperson or the Judicial Member or the Technical Member appointed to one Bench to discharge also the functions of the Vice-Chairperson or, as the case may be, the Judicial Member or the Technical Member of another Bench; and (d) may, for the purpose of securing that any case or cases which, having regard to the nature of the questions involved, requires or require, hi his opinion or under the rules made by the Central Government in this behalf, to be decided by a Bench composed of more than two Members issue such general or special orders, as he may deem fit: Provided that every Bench constituted in pursuance of this clause shall include at least one Judicial Member and one Technical Member.

(4) Notwithstanding anything contained in the foregoing provisions of this section, it shall be competent for the Chairperson or any other Member authorised by the Chairperson in this behalf to function as a Bench consisting of a single Member and exercise the jurisdiction, powers and authority of the Tribunal in respect of such classes of cases or such matters pertaining to such classes, of cases as the Chairperson may, by general or special order, specify: Provided that if at any stage of the hearing of any such case or matter, it appears to the Chairperson or such Member that the case or matter is of such a nature that, it ought to be, heard by a Bench consisting of two Members, the case or matter may be transferred by the Chairperson or, as the, case pay be referred to him for transfer to such Bench as the Chairperson may deem fit.

(5) Subject to the other provisions of this Act, the Benches of the Tribunal shall ordinarily sit at New Delhi (which shall be known as the principal Bench) and at such other places as the Central Government may, by notification, specify.

10. Qualifications for appointment as Chairperson, Vice-Chairperson or other Member.

(1) A person shall not be qualified for appointment as the Chairperson unless he.- (a) is, or has been, a Judge of the Supreme Court or a High Court; or (b) has, for at last two year", held the office of Vice-Chairperson.

(2) A person shell not be qualified for appointment as the Vice-Chairperson unless he- (a) is, or has been, a Judge of a High Court; or (b) has, for at least two years, held the post of a Secretary to the Government of India or any other post under the Central or a State Government carrying a scale of pay which is not less then that of a Secretary to the Government of India; or (c) (i) has, for at least five years, held the post of an Additional Secretary to the Government of India or any other post under the Central or a State Government carrying a scale of pay which is not less than that of an Additional Secretary to the Government of India; and (ii) has adequate, knowledge of, or experience in, legal, administrative, scientific or technical aspects of the problems relating to environment;

or (d) has for at least three years, held office as a Judicial Member or a Technical Member,

(3) A person shall not be qualified for appointment as a Judicial Member unless he— (a) is, or has been, or is qualified to be, a Judge of a High Court; or (b) has been a member of the Indian Legal Service and has held a post in grade I of that Service for at least three years.

(4) A person shall not be qualified for appointment as a Technical Member unless he has adequate knowledge of, or experience in, or capacity to deal with, administrative, scientific or technical aspects of the problems relating to environment.

(5) Subject to the provisions of subsections (6) and (7), the Chairperson, Vice-Chairperson and every other Member of the Tribunal shall be appointed by the President.

(6) No appointment of a person possessing the qualifications specified in this section as the Chairperson or the Vice-Chairperson shall be made except after consultation with the Chief Justice of India.

(7) No appointment of a person as a Judicial Member or a Technical Member shall be made except on the recommendation of a Selection Committee appointed by the Central Government consisting of the following, namely:-

(a)	Chairperson of the Tribunal.	Chairperson of the Committee, ex officio;
(b)	Secretary to the Government of India in the Ministry of Environment and Forests	member, ex Officio;
(c)	Secretary to the Government of India in the Ministry of Law, justice and company Affairs (Department of Legal Affairs)	member, ex Officio;
(d)	Director-General, Council of Scientific and Industrial Research.	member, ex officio;
(e)	an Environmentalist to be nominated by the central Government	member.

11. Vice-Chairperson to act as Chairperson or to discharge his functions in certain circumstances. (1) In the event of the occurrence of any vacancy in the office of the Chairperson by reason of his death, resignation or otherwise, the Vice-Chairperson or, as the case may be, such one of the' Vice-Chairpersons' as the Central Government may, by notification, authorise in this behalf, shall act as the Chairperson until the date on which a new Chairperson, appointed in accordance with the provisions of this Act to fill such vacancy, enters upon his office. (2) When the Chairperson is unable to discharge his functions owing to absence, illness of any other cause, the Vice-Chairperson or, as the case may be, such one of the Vice-Chairpersons, as the Central Government may, by notification, authorise in this behalf, shall discharge the functions of the Chairperson until the date on which the Chairperson resumes his duties.

12. Term of office. The Chairperson, Vice-Chairperson and other Member shall hold office as such for a term of five years from the date on which he enters upon his office, but shall be eligible for re-appointment for another term of five years: Provided that no Chairperson, Vice-Chairperson or other Member shall hold office as such after he has attained,- (a) in the case of the Chairperson, the age of seventy years; (b) in the case of the Vice-Chairperson, the age of sixty-five years; and (c) in the case of any other Member, the age of sixty-two years.

13. Resignation and removal.

(1) The Chairperson, Vice-Chairperson or other Member may, by notice in writing under his hand addressed to the President, resign his office: Provided that the Chairperson, Vice-Chairperson or other Member shall unless he is permitted by the President to relinquish his office sooner, continue to hold office until the expiry of three months from the date of receipt of such notice or until a person duly appointed as his successor enters upon his office or until the expiry of his term of office, whichever is the earliest.

(2) The Chairperson, Vice-Chairperson or any other Member shall not be removed from his office except, by an order made

by the President on, the ground of proved misbehaviour or incapacity after an inquiry made by a Judge of the Supreme Court in which such Chairperson, Vice-Chairperson or other Member had been informed of the charges against him and given a reasonable opportunity of being heard in respect of those charges.

(3) The Central Government may, by rules, regulate the procedure for the investigation of misbehaviour or incapacity of the Chairperson, Vice-Chairperson or other Member referred to in sub-section (2).

14. Salaries and allowances and other terms and conditions of service of Chairperson, Vice-Chairperson and other Member. The salaries and allowances payable to, and the other terms and conditions of service (including pension, gratuity and other retirement benefits) of, the Chairperson, Vice-Chairperson and other Member shall be such as may be prescribed: Provided that neither the salary and allowances nor the, other terms and conditions of service of the Chairperson, Vice-Chairperson or other Member shall be varied to his disadvantage after his appointment.

15. Provision as to the holding of Offices, by Chairperson, etc, on ceasing to be such Chairperson, etc. On ceasing to hold office,- (a) the Chairperson of the Tribunal shall be ineligible for further employment either under the Government of India or under the Government of a State; (b) the Vice-Chairperson of the Tribunal shall, subject to theother provisions of this Act, be eligible for appointment as the Chairperson of the Tribunal, but not for any other employment either under the Government of India or under the government of a State; (c) a Member (other than the Chairperson or Vice-Chairperson) of the Tribunal shall, subject to the other provisions of this Act, be eligible for appointment as the Chairperson or Vice-Chairperson of the Tribunal or as the Chairperson, Vice-Chairperson or Member of any other Tribunal, but not for any other employment either under the Government of India or under the Government of a State; (d) the Chairperson, Vice-Chairperson or other Member shall not appear, act or plead before the Tribunal.

Explanation.— For the purposes of this section, employment under the Government of India or under the Government of a State includes employment under any local or other authority within the territory of India or under the control of the Government of India or under any corporation or society owned or controlled by the Government.

16. Financial and administrative powers of Chairperson.

The Chairperson shall exercise such financial and administrative powers over Benches as may be vested in him under the rules: Provided that the Chairperson shall have authority to delegate such of his financial and administrative powers as he may think fit to the Vice-Chairperson or any other officer of the Tribunal subject to the condition that the Vice-Chairperson or such officer shall, which exercising such delegated powers, continue to act under the direction, control and supervision of the Chairperson.

17. Staff of the Tribunal.

(1) The Central Government shall determine the nature and categories of the officers and other employees required to assist the Tribunal in the discharge of its functions and provide the Tribunal with such officers and other employees as it may think fit. (2) The officers and other employees of the Tribunal shall discharge: their functions under the general superintendence of the Chairperson. (3) The salaries and allowances and conditions of service of the officers and other employee of the Tribunal shall be such as may be prescribed.

18. Distribution of business amongst the Benches.

(1) Where any Benches of the Tribunal are constituted, the Central Government may, from time to time by notification, make provisions as to the distribution of the business of the Tribunal amongst the Benches and specify, the matters which may be dealt with by each Bench.

(2) If any question arises as to whether any matter falls within the purview of the business allocated to a t3ench, the decision of the Chairperson shall be final.

Explanation. For the removal of doubts, it is hereby declared that the expression "matter" includes applications for interim relief.

JURISDICTION AND PROCEEDINGS OF THE TRIBUNAL

19. Bar of jurisdiction.

On and from the commencement of this Act, no court or Other authority except the Tribunal shall have, or the entitled to exercise, any jurisdiction, powers or authority to entertain any application or action for any claim for compensation which may entertained or dealt with by the Tribunal.

20. Power of Chairperson to transfer cases from one Bench to another.

On the application of any of the parties and after notice to the parties, and after hearing such of them as he may desire to be heard, or on his own motion without such notice, the Chairperson may transfer any case pending before one Bench, for disposal, to any other Bench.

21. Decision to be taken by majority.

If the Members of a Bench differ in opinion on any point, the point shall be (decided according to the opinion of the majority, if there is a majority, but if the Members are equally divided they shall state the point or points on which they differ, and make a reference to the Chairperson who shall either hear the point or points himself or refer the case for hearing on such point or points by one or more of the other Members and such point or points shall be decided according to the opinion of the majority of the Members who have heard the case including those who first heard it.

22. Deposit of amount payable for damage to environment.

(1) Where any amount of compensation is ordered to he paid under any award by the Tribunal on the ground of any damage to environment, that amount shall be remitted to the authority specified under sub-section (3) of section 7A of the Public Liability insurance Act, 1991 for being credited to the Environmental

Relief Fund established under that section. (2) The amount of compensation credited to the Environmental Relief Fund under sub-section (1) may be utilised by such person or authority, in such manner and for such purposes of environment as may be prescribed.

23. Extension of award or order of Tribunal.

(1) An award made by the Tribunal under this Act shall be executable by the Tribunal as a decree of civil court, and for this purpose, the Tribunal shall have all the powers of a civil court. (2) Notwithstanding anything contained in sub-section (1), the Tribunal may transmit to the Collector having jurisdiction over the area in which the accident has occurred the copy of the order made by it for payment of relief as provided in the Public Liability Insurance Act, 1991 and the Collector shall execute the order in the same manner as if it were an order made by him under that Act. (3) Where the owner against whom the award or order is made by the Tribunal fails to make the payment or deposit the amount as directed by the Tribunal within the period specified in the award or order, such amount shall be recoverable from the owner as arrears of land revenue or of public demand.

24. Appeals.

(1) Save as provided in sub—section (2) and notwithstanding anything contained in the Code of Civil Procedure, 1908 or in any other law, an appeal shall lie against any award or other order, not being an interlocutory order, of the Tribunal to the Supreme Court on one or more of the grounds specified in section 100 of that Code. (2) No appeal shall lie against an award or other order made by the Tribunal with the consent of the parties. (3) Every appeal under this section shall be preferred within a period of ninety days from the date of the award or other order appealed against: Provided that no appeal by the person who is required to pay any amount in terms of such award shall be entertained by the Supreme Court unless he has deposited with it the amount so awarded in the manner directed by the Supreme Court: Provided further that the Supreme Court may entertain the appeal after the expiry of

the said period of ninety days, if it is satisfied that the appellant was prevented by sufficient cause from preferring the appeal in time.

MISCELLANEOUS

25. Penalty for failure to comply with orders of Tribunal.

Whoever fails to comply with any order made by the Tribunal, he shall be punishable with imprisonment for a term which may extend to three years, or with fine which may extend to ten lakh rupees, or with both.

26. Offences by companies

(1) Where any offence under this Act has been committed by a company, every person who, at the time the offence was committed, was directly in charge of, and was responsible to, the company for the conduct of the business of the company, as well as the company, shall be deemed to be guilty of the offence and shall be liable to be proceeded against and punished accordingly: Provided that nothing contained in this sub-section shall render any such person liable to any punishment provided in this Act, if he proves that the offence was committed without his knowledge or that he had exercised all due diligence to prevent the commission of such offence. (2) Notwithstanding anything contained in sub-section (1), where an offence under this Act has been committed by a company and it is proved that; the offence has been committed with the consent or connivance of, or is attributable to any neglect on the part of, any director, manager, secretary or other officer of the company, such director, manager, secretary or other officer shall also be deemed to be guilty of that offence and shall be liable to be proceeded against and punished accordingly.

Explanation.-For the purposes of this section,-

(a) "company" means any body corporate and includes a firm or other association of individuals; and (b) "director", in relation to a firm, means a partner in the firm.

27. Proceedings before the Tribunal to be judicial proceedings.

All proceedings before the Tribunal shall be deemed to be Judicial proceedings within the meaning of sections 193, 219 and 228 of the Indian Penal Code.

28. Members and staff of Tribunal to be public servants.

The Chairperson, Vice-Chairperson and other Members and the officers and other employees of the Tribunal shall be deemed to be public servants within the meaning of section 21 of the Indian Penal Code.

29. Protection of action taken in good faith

No suit, prosecution or other legal proceeding shall lie against the Central Government or against the Chairperson, Vice-Chairperson or other Member of the Tribunal or any other person authorised by the Chairperson, Vice-Chairperson or other Member for anything which is in good faith done or intended to be done in pursuance of this Act or any rule or order made thereunder.

30. Act to have overriding effect

Save as provided in the Public Liability Insurance Act, 1991, the provisions of this Act shall have effect notwithstanding anything inconsistent therewith contained in any other law for the time being in force or in any instrument having effect by virtue of any law other than this Act.

31. Power to make rules

(1) The Central Government may, by notification, make rules for carrying out the purposes of this Act.

(2) In particular, and without prejudice to the generality of the foregoing power, such rules may provide for all or any of the following matters, namely:- (a) the particulars which an application shall contain, the documents and the fee which shall be accompanied with it and the limit of annual income of a person so as to enable him to make application without paying any fee, under sub-section (5) of section 4; (b) any such matter in respect on which the Tribunal shall have powers of a civil court, under clause (i) of sub-section (4) of section 5; (c) the case or cases which, having regard to the nature of the questions involved, requires or require! to be decided by a

Bench of more than two members, under clause (d) of suNsection (3) of section 9; (d) procedure for the investigation of misbehaviour or incapacity of the Chairperson, Vice-Chairperson or other Member of the Tribunal under sub-section (3) of section 13; (e) the salaries and allowances payable to, and the other terms and conditions of service of, the Chairperson, Vice-Chairperson and other Members under section 14; (f) financial and administrative powers of the Chairperson over the Benches under section 16; (g) the salaries and allowances and conditions of service of the officers and other employees of the Tribunal under sub-section (3) of section 17; (h) the person or the authority by whom, the manner in which and the purposes of environment for which the amount of compensation credited to the Environmental Relief Fund shall be utilised under sub-section (2) of section 22; and (i) any other matter which is required to be, or may be, prescribed.

(3) Every rule made under this Act shall be laid, as soon as may be after it is made, before each House of Parliament, while it is in session, for a total period of thirty days which may be comprised in one session or in two or more successive sessions, and if, before the expiry of the session immediately following the session of the successive sessions aforesaid, both Houses agree in making any modification in the rule or both Houses agree that the rule Should not be made, the rule shall thereafter have effect only in such modified from or no effect, as the case may be; so, however, that any such modification or annulment shall be without prejudice to the validity of anything previously done under that rules.

THE SCHEDULE

Heads Under Which Compensation for Damages may be Claimed

(a) Death;

(b) Permanent, temporary, total or partial disability or other injury or sickness;

(c) Loss of wages due to total or partial disability or permanent or temporary disability;

(d) Medical expenses incurred for treatment of injuries or sickness;

(e) Damages to private property;

(f) Expenses incurred by the Government or any local authority in providing relief aid and rehabilitation to the affected persons;

(g) Expenses incurred by Government for any administrative or legal action or to cope with any harm or damage, including compensation for environmental degradation and restoration of the quality of environment;

(h) Loss to Government or local authority arising out of, or connected with, the activity causing any damage;

(i) Claims on account of any harm, damage or destruction to the fauna including milch and draught animals and aquatic fauna;

(j) Claims on account of any harm, damage or destruction to flora including aquatic flora, crops, vegetables, trees and orchards;

(k) Claims including cost of restoration on account- of any harm or damage to environment including pollution of soil, air, water, land and eco-systems;

(l) Loss and destruction of any property other than private property;

(m) Loss of business or employment or both;

(n) any other claim arising out of, or connected with, any activity of handling of hazardous substance.

5

THE PREVENTION OF CRUELTY TO ANIMALS ACT

PRELIMINARY

1. Short title, extent and commencement :

(1) This Act may be called the Prevention of Cruelty to Animals Act, 1960.

(2) It extends to the whole of India except the State of Jammu and Kashmir.

(3) It shall come into force on such date as the Central Government may, by notification in the official Gazette, appoint, and different dates may be appointed for different States and for the different provisions comained in this Act.

2. Definitions : In this Act, unless the context otherwise. requires,

(a) "animal" means any living creature other than a human being,

(b) "Board" means the Board established under Section 4. and as reconstituted from time to time under Section 5A]

(c) "captive animal" means any animal (not being a domestic animal) which is in capacity or confinement, whether permanent or temporary, or which is subjected to any appliance of contrivance for the purpose of hindering or preventing its escape from captivity or confinement or which is pinioned or which is or appears to be. maimed;

a. "domestic animal" means any animal which is tamed or which has been or is being sufficiently tamed to serve some purpose for the use of man or which, although it neither has been nor is intended to be so tamed, is or has become in fact wholly or partly tamed-,

(e) "local authority" means a municipal committee, district board or other authority for the time being invested by law with the control and administration of any matters within a specified local area;

(f) "owner", used with reference to an animal, includes not only the owner but also any other person for the time being in possession or custody of the animal, whether with or without the consent of the owner.

(g) "phooka" or "doom dev" includes any process of introducing air or any substance into the female organ of a milch animal with the object of drawing off from the animal any secretion of milk;

(h) "prescribed" means prescribed by Rules made under this Act;

(i) "street" includes any way, road, lane, square, court, alley, passage or open space, whether a thoroughfare or not to which the public have access.

3. Duties of persons having charge of animals : It shall be the duty of every person having the care or charge of any animal to take all reasonable measures to ensure the well-being of such animal and to prevent the infliction upon such animal of unnecessary pain or suffering.

ANIMAL WELFARE BOARD OF INDIA

4. Establishment of Animal Welfare Board of India :

(1) For the promotion of animal welfare generally and for the purpose of protecting animals from being subjected to unnecessary pain or suffering, in particular, there shall be established by the Central Government, as soon as may be after the commencement of this Act, a Board to be called the (Animal Board of India.)

(2) The Board, shall be a body corporate having perpetual succession and a common seal with power, subject to the provisions of this Act, to acquire, hold and dispose of property and may by its name sue and be sued.

5. Constitution of the Board :

(1) The Board shall consist of the following persons, namely:

(a) the Inspector General of Forests, Government of India, ex-officio,

(b) the Animal Husbandry Commissioner to the Government of India, ex-officio;

(ba) two persons to represent respectively the Ministries of the Central Government dealing with Home Aff airs and Education, to be appointed by the Central Government;

(bb) one person to represent the Indian Board for Wild Life, to be appointed by the Central Government;

(bc) three persons who, in the opinion of the Central Government, are or have been actively engaged in animal welfare work and are well-known humanitarians, to be nominated by the Central Government;)

(c) one person to represent such association of veterinary practitioners as in the opinion of the Central Government ought to be represented on the Board, to be elected by that association in the prescribed manner;

(d) two persons to represent practitioners of modern and indigenous systems of medicine, to be nominated by the Central Government;

(e) one person to represent each of such two municipal corporations as in the opinion of the Central Government ought to be represented on the Board, to be elected by each of the said corporations in the prescribed manner

(f) one person to represent each of such three organisations actively interested in animal welfare as in the opinion of the Central Government ought to be represented on the Board, to be chosen by each of the said organisations in the prescribed manner;

(g) one person to represent each of such three societies dealing with prevention of cruelty to animal as in the opinion of the Central Government ought to be represented on the Board, to be chosen, in the prescribed manner;

(h) three persons to be nominated by the Central Government,

(i) six Members of Parliament, four to be elected by the House of the People (Lok Sabha) and two by the Council of States (Rajya Sabha).

(2) Any of the persons referred to in clause 9a) or [6][clause (b) or clause (ba) or clause (bb) of sub-section (1) may depute any other person to attend any of the meetings of the Board.

(3) The Central Government shall nominate one of the members of the Board to be its Chairman and another member of the Board to be its Vice-Chairman.

5A. Reconstitution of the Board :

5.A (1) In order that the Chairman and other members of the Board hold off ice till the same date and that their terms of off ice come to an end on the same date, the Central Government may, by notification in the Official Gazette, reconstitute, as soon as may be after the Prevention of Cruelty to Animals (Amendment) Act, 1982 comes into force, the Board.

(2) The Board as reconstituted under sub-section (1) shall be reconstituted from time to time on the expiration of every third year, from the date of its reconstitution under sub-section (1).

(3) There shall be included amongst the members of the Board reconstituted under sub-section (1), all persons who immediately before the date on which such reconstitution is to take effect, are Members of the Board but such persons shall hold office only for the unexpired portion of the term for which they would have held office if such reconstitution had not been made and the vacancies arising as a result of their ceasing to be Members of the Board shall be filled up as casual vacancies for the remaining period of the term of the Board as so reconstituted: Provided that nothing in this sub-section shall

apply in relation to any person who ceases to be member of the Board by virute of the amendment made in sub-section (1) of section 5 by sub-clause (ii) of clause (a) of section 5 of the Prevention of Cruelty to Animals (Amendement) Act, 1982).

6. Term of off ice and conditions of service of Members of the Board : (1) The term for which the Board may be reconstituted under section 5A shall be three years from the date of the reconstitution and the Chairman and other Members of the Board as so reconstituted shall hold office till the expiry of the term for which the Board has been so reconstituted.

(2) Notwithstanding anything contained in sub-section (1):

a. the term of office of an ex-officio Member shall continue so long as he holds the off ice by virtue of which he is such a Member;

(b) the term of off ice of a Member elected or chosen under clause (c), clause (e), clause (g), clause (h) or clause (i) of section 5 to represent anybody of persons shall come to an end as soon as he ceases to be a Member of the body which elected him or in respect of which he was chosen;

(c) the term of office of a Member appointed, nominated, elected or chosen to fill a casual vacancy shall continue for the remainder of the term of office of the Member in whose place he is appointed, nominated, elected or chosen;

(d) the Central Government may, at any time, remove for reasons to be recorded in writing a member from office after giving him a reasonable opportunity of showing cause against the proposed removal and any vacancy caused by such removal shall be treated as casual vacancy for the purpose of clause (c).

(3) 'The members of the Board shall receive such allowance, if any, as the Board may, subject to the previous approval of the Central Government, provided by regulations made in this behalf,

(4) No act done or proceeding taken by the Board shall be questioned on the ground merely of the existence of any vacancy in, or defect in the constitution of the Board and in particular, and without prejudice to the generality of the foregoing, during

the period intervening between the expiry of the term for which the Board has been reconstituted under section 5A and its further reconstitution under that section, the ex-officio members of the Board shall discharge all the powers and function of the Board.)

7. Secretary and other employees of the Board :

(1) The Central Government shall appoint [10]xxxxx the Secretary of the Board.

(2) Subject to such rules as may be made by the Central Government in this behalf, the Board may appoint such number of other officers and employees as may be necessary for the exercise of its powers and the discharge of its functions and may determine the terms and conditions of service of such officers and other employees by regulations made by it with the previous approval of the Central Government.

8. Funds of the Board :

The funds of the Board shall consist of grants made to it from time to Board time by the Government and of contributions, subscriptions, bequests, gifts and the like made to it by any local authority or by any other person.

9. Functions of the Board :

The functions of the Board shall be Board :

(a) to keep the law in force in, India for the prevention of cruelty to animals under constant study and advise the Government on the amendments to be undertaken in any such law from time to time;

(b) to advise the Central Government on the making of rules under this Act with a view to preventing unnecessary pain or suffering to animals generally, and more particularly when they are being transported from one place to another or when they are used as performing animals or when they are kept in captivity or confinement;

(c) to advise the Government or any local authority or other person on improvements in the design of vehicles so as to lessen the burden on draught animals;

(d) to take all such steps as the Board may think fit for [11](amelioration of animals) by encouraging or providing for, the construction of sheds, water-troughs and the like and by providing for veterinary assistance to animals:

(e) to advise the Government or any local authority or other person in the design of slaughter-houses or the maintenance of slaughter houses or in connection with slaughter of animals so that unnecessary pain or suffering, whether physical or mental, is eliminated in the pre-slaughter stages as far as possible, and animals are killed; wherever necessary, in as humane a manner as possible;

(f) to take all such steps as the Board may think fit to ensure that unwanted animals are destroyed by local authorities, whenever it is necessary to do so, either instantaneously or after being rendered insensible to pain or suffering.

(g) to encourage by the grant of financial assistance or otherwise, [12](the formation or establishment of pinjrapoles, rescue homes, animal shelters, sanctuaries and the like) where animals and birds may find a shelter when they have become old and useless or when they need protection:

(h) to co-operate with, and co-ordinate the work of, associations or bodies established for the purpose of preventing unnecessary pain or suffering to animals or for the protection of animals and birds;

(i) to give financial and other assistance to animal welfare organisations functioning in any local area or to encourage the formation of animal welfare organisations in any local area which shall work under the general supervision and guidance of the Board;

(j) to advise the Government on matters relating to the medical care and attention which may be provided in animal hospital, and to give financial and other assistance to animal hospitals whenever the Board thinks it necessary to do so;

(k) to impart education in relation to the humane treatment of animals and to encourage the formation of public opinion against the infliction of unnecessary pain or suffering to animals and for the promotion of animal welfare by means of lectures, books, posters, cinematographic exhibitions and the like;

(l) to advise the Government on any matter connected with animal welfare or the prevention of infliction of unnecessary pain or suffering on animals.

10. Power of Board to make regulations : The Board may, subject to the previous approval of the Central Government, make such regulations as it may think fit for the administration of its affairs and for carrying out its functions.

CRUELTY TO ANIMALS GENERALLY

11. Treating animals cruelly :

(1) If any person

(a) beats, kicks, over-rides, over-drives, over-loads, tortures or otherwise treats any animal so as to subject it to unnecessary pain or suffering or causes, or being the owner permits, any animal to be so treated; or

(b) [13](employs in any work or labour or for any purpose any animal which, by reason of its age or any disease) infirmity; wound, sore or other cause, is unfit to be so employed or, being the owner, permits any such unfit animal to be employed; or

(c) wilfully and unreasonably administers any injurious drug or injurious substance to [14](any animal) or wilfully and unreasonably causes or attempts to cause any such drug or substance to be taken by [15](any animal;) or

(d) conveys or carries, whether in or upon any vehicle or not, any animal in such a manner or position as to subject it to unnecessary pain or suffering; or

(e) keeps or confines any animal in any cage or other receptacle which does not measure sufficiently in height, length and breadth to permit the animal a reasonable opportunity for movement; or

(f) keeps for an unreasonable time any animal chained or tethered upon an unreasonably short or unreasonably heavy chain or cord; or

(g) being the owner, neglects to exercise or cause to be exercised reasonably any dog habitually chained up or kept in close confinement; or

(h) being the owner of (any animal) fails to provide such animal with sufficient food, drink or shelter; or

(i) without reasonable cause, abandons any animal in circumstances which tender it likely that it will suffer pain by reason of starvation thirst; or

(j) wilfully permits any animal, of which he is the owner, to go at large in any street, while the animal is affected with contagious or infectious disease or, without reasonable excuse permits any diseased or disabled animal, of which he is the owner, to die in any street; or

(k) offers for sale or without reasonable cause, has in his possession any animal which is suffering pain by reason of mutilation, starvation, thirst, overcrowding or other illtreatment; or

[16]{(1) mutilates any animal or kills any animal (including stray dogs) by using the method of strychnine injections, in the heart or in any other unnecessarily cruel manner or;)

[17]{(m) solely with a view to providing entertainment

(i) confines or causes to be confined any animal (including tying of an animal as a bait in a tiger or other sanctuary) so as to make it an object or prey for any other animal; or

(n) [18][xxxx] organises, keeps uses or acts in the management or, any place for animal fighting or for the purpose of baiting any animal or permits or offers any place to be so used or receives money for the admission of any other person to any place kept or used for any such purposes; or

(o) promotes or takes part in any shooting match or competition wherein animals are released from captivity for the purpose of such shooting: he shall be punishable [19](in the case of a first offence, with fine which shall not be less than ten rup6es but which may extend to fifty rupees and in the case of a second or subsequent offence committed within three years of the previous offence, with fine which shall not be less than twenty-five rupees but which may extend, to one hundred rupees or with imprisonment for a term which may extend, to three months, or with both.]

(2) For the purposes of section (1) an owner shall be deemed to have committed an offence if he has failed to exercise reasonable care and supervision with a view to the prevention of such offence;

Provided that where an owner is convicted permitting cruelty by reason only of having failed to exercise such care and supervision, he shall not be liable to imprisonment without the option of a fine.

(3) Nothing in this section shall apply to -

(a) the dehorning of cattle, or the castration or branding or noseroping of any animal in the prescribed manner, or

(b) the destruction of stray dogs in lethal chambers [20][by such other methods as may be prescribed] or

(c) the extermination or destruction of any animal under the authority of any law for the time being in force; or

(d) any matter dealt with in Chapter IV; or

(e) the commission or omission of any act in the course of the destruction or the preparation for destruction of any animal as food for mankind unless such destruction or preparation was accompanied by the infliction of unnecessary pain or suffering.

12. Penalty for practising phooka or doom dev :

If any persons upon any cow or other milch animal the operation called practising phooka or doom dev or any other operation (including injection of any or doom dev. substance) to improve lactation which is injurious to the health of the animal] or permits such operation being performed upon any such animal in his possession or under his control, he shall be punishable with fine which may extend to one thousand rupees, or with imprisonment for a term which may extend to two years, or with both, and the animal on which the operation was performed shall be forfeited to the Government.

13. 'Destruction of suffering animals' :

(1) Where the owner of an animal is convicted of an offence under section 11, it shall be lawful for the court, if the court is satisfied that it would be cruel to keep the animal alive, to direct that the animal be destroyed and to assign the animals to any suitable person for that purpose, and the person to whom such animal is so assigned shall as soon as possible, destroy such animal or cause such animal to be destroyed in his presence without unnecessary suffering: and any reasonable expense incurred in destroying the animal may be ordered by the court, if the court is satisfied that it would be cruel to keep the animal alive, to direct that the animal be destroyed and to assign the animal to any reasonable expense incurred in destroying the animal mal be ordered by the court to be recovered from the owner as if it were a fine:

Provided that unless the owner assents thereto, no order shall be made under this section except upon the evidence of a veterinary officer in charge of the area.

(2) When any magistrate, commissioner of police or district superintendent of police has reason to believe that an offence under section 11 has been committed in respect of any animal, he may direct the immediate destruction of the animal, if in his opinion, it would be cruel to keep the animal alive.

(3) Any police officer above the rank of a constable or any person authorised by the State Government in this behalf who finds any animal so diseased or so severely injured or in such a physical condition that in his opinion it cannot be removed without cruelty, may, if the owner is absent or refuses his consent to the destruction of the animal, forth with summon the veterinary officer in charge of the area in which the animal is found, and if the veterinary officer certifies that the animal is mortally injured or so severely injured or in such a physical condition that it would be cruel to keep it alive, the police officer or the person authorised, as the case may be, may, after obtaining orders from a magistrate, destroy the animal injured or cause it to be destroyed; in such manner as may be prescribed.

(4) No appeal shall lie from any order of a magistrate for the destruction of an animal.

EXPERIMENTATION OF ANIMALS

14. Experiments on animals :

Nothing contained in this Act shall render unlawful the performance of experiments (including) experiments involving operations) on animals for the purpose of advancement by new discovery of physiological knowledge or of knowledge which will be useful for saving or for prolonging life or alleviating suffering or for combating any disease, whether of human beings, animals or plants.

15. Committee for control and supervision of experiments on animals :

(1) If at any time, on the advice of the Board, the Central Government is of opinion that it is necessary so to do for the purpose of controlling "and supervising experiments on animals it may be notification in the Official Gazette Constitute a Committee consisting of such number of officials and non-officials, as it may think fit to appoint thereto.

(2) The Central Government shall nominate one of the Members of the Committee to be its Chairman.

(3) The Committee shall have power to regulate its own Procedure in relation to the performance of its duties.

(4) The funds of the Committee shall consist of grants made to it from time to time by the Government and of contributions, donations, subscriptions, bequests, gifts and the like made to it by any person.

15A. Sub-Committee :

(1) The Committee may constitute as many sub-committees as it thinks fit for exercising any power or discharging any duty of the Committee or for inquiring into or reporting and advising on any matter which the Committee may refer.

(2) A sub-committee shall consist exclusively of the Members of the Committee.)

16. Staff of the Committee : Subject to the control of the Central Government, the Committee may committee appoint such number of officers and other employees as may be necessary to enable it to exercise ills powers and perform its duties and may determine the remuneration and other terms and conditions of service of such officers and other employees.

17. Duties of the Committee and power of the Committee to make rules relating to experiments on animals :

(1) It shall be the duty of the Committee to take all such measures as may be necessary to ensure that animals are not subjected to unnecessary pain or suffering before, during or after the performance of experiments on them, and for the purpose it may, by notification in the Gazette of India and subject to the condition of previous publication, make such rules as it may think fit in animals relation to the conduct of such experiments.

(1A)In particular, and without prejudice to the generality to the foregoing power, such rules may provide for the following matters namely:

(a) the registration of persons or institutions carrying on experiments on animals;

(b) the reports and other information which shall be forwarded to the Committee by persons and institutions carrying on experiments or, animals.

(2) In particular, and without prejudice to the generality of the foregoing power, rules made by the Committee shall be designed to secure the following objects, namely:

(a) that in cases where experiments are performed in any institution, the responsibility therefore is placed on the person in charge of the institution and that, in cases where experiments are performed outside an institution by individuals, the individuals, are performed outside an institution by individuals, the individuals, are qualified in that behalf and the experiments are performed on their full responsibility;

(b) that experiments are performed with due care and humanity and that as far as possible experiments involving operations are performed under the influence of some anaesthetic of sufficient power to prevent the animals feeling pain;

(c) that animals which, in the course of experiments under the influence of anaesthetics, are so injured that their recovery would involve serious suffering, are ordinarily destroyed while still insensible;

(d) that experiments on animals are avoided wherever it is possible to do so; as for example; in medical schools, hospitals, colleges and the like, if other teaching devices such as books, models, films and the. like, may equally suffice;

(e) that experiments on larger animals are avoided when it is possible to achieve the same results by experiments upon small laboratory animals like guinea-'pigs, rabbits, frogs and rats;

(f) that, as far as possible, experiments are not performed merely for the purpose of acquiring manual skill;

(g) that animals intended for the performance of experiments are properly looked after both before and after experiments;

(h) that suitable records are maintained with respect to experiments performed on animals

(3) In making any rules under this section, the Committee shall be guided by such directions as the Central Government (consistently with the objects for which the Committee is set up) may give to it, and the Central Government is hereby authorised to give such direction.

(4) All rules made by the Committee shall be binding on all individuals performing experiments outside institutions and on persons incharge of institutions in which experiments are performed.

18. Power of entry and inspection : For the purpose of ensuring that the rules made by it are being complied and with the Committee may authorise any of its officers or any other person in writing to inspect any institution or place where experiments are being carried on and report to it as a

result of such inspection, and any officer or person so authorised may-

(a) enter at any time considered reasonable by him and inspect any institution or place in which experiments on animals are being carried on; and

(b) require any person to produce any record kept by him with respect to experiments on animals.

19. Power to prohibit experiments on animals : If the Committee is satisfied, on the report of any officer or other person made to it as a result of any inspection under section 18 or otherwise that the rules made by it under section 17 are not being animals the Committee may, after giving an opportunity to the person or institution carrying on experiments on animals; the Committee may, after giving an opportunity to the person or institution of being heard in the matter, by order, prohibit the person or institution from carrying on any such experiments either for a specified period or indefinitely, or may allow the person or institution to carry on such experiments subject to such special conditions as the Committee may think fit to impose.

20. Penalties : If any person-

(a) contravenes any order made by the Committee under section 19; or

(b) commits a breach of any condition imposed by the Committee under that section: he shall be punishable with fine which may extend to two hundred rupees, and, when the contravention or breach of condition has taken place in any institution the person incharge of the institution shall be deemed to be guilty of the offence and shall be punishable accordingly.

PERFORMING ANIMALS

21. "Exhibit" and "train" defined : In this Chapter, " exhibit" means exhibit or any entertainment to which the public are admitted through sale of tickets, and "train" means train for the purpose of any such exhibition, and the expressions "exhibitor" and "trainer" have respectively the corresponding meanings.

22. Restriction on exhibition and training of performing animals: No person shall exhibit or train

(i) any performing animal unless he is registered in accordance with the provisions of this Chapter;

(ii) as a performing animal, any animal which the Central Government may, by notification in the official gazette, specify as an animal which shall not be exhibited or trained as a performing animal.

23. Procedure for registration :

(1) Every person desirous of exhibiting or training any performing animal shall, on making an application in the prescribed form to the prescribed authority and on payment of the prescribed fee, be registered under this Act unless he is a person who, by reason of an order made by the court under this Chapter, is not entitled to be so registered.

(2) An application for registration under this Chapter shall contain such particulars as to the animals and as to the general nature of the performances in which the animals are to be exhibited or for which they are to be trained as may be prescribed, and the particulars so given shall be entered in the register maintained by the prescribed authority.

(3) The prescribed authority shall give to every person whose name appears on the register kept by them, a certificate of registration in the prescribed form containing the particulars entered in the register.

(4) Every register kept under this Chapter shall at all reasonable times be open for inspection on payment of the prescribed fee, and any person shall, on payment of the prescribed fee, be entitled to obtain copies thereof or make extracts therefrom.

(5) Any person whose name is entered in the register shall, subject to the provisions of any order made under this Act by any court, be entitled, on making an application for the purpose, to have the particulars entered in the register with respect to him varied, and where any such particulars are so varied, the

existing certificate shall be cancelled and a new certificate issued.

24. Power of court to prohibit or restrict exhibition and training of performing animals :

(1) Where it is proved to the satisfaction of any magistrate on a complaint made by a police officer or an officer authorised in writing by the prescribed authority referred to in section 23, that the training or exhibition of any performing animals has been accompanied by unnecessary pain or suffering and should be prohibited or allowed only subject to conditions, the court may make an order against the person in respect of whom the complaint is made, prohibiting the training or exhibition or imposing such conditions in relation thereto, as may be specified by the order.

(2) Any court by which an order is made under this section, shall cause a copy of the order to be sent, as soon as may be after the order is made, to the prescribed authority by which the person against whom the order is made is registered, and shall cause the particulars of the order to be endorsed upon the certificate field by the person, and that person shall produce his certificate on being so required by the court for the purposes of endorsement, and the prescribed authority to which a copy of an order is sent under "his section shall enter the particulars of the order in that register;

25. Power to enter premises :

(1) Any person authorised in writing by the prescribed authority referred to in section 23 and any police officer not below the rank of a sub-inspector may

(a) enter at all reasonable times and inspect any premises in which any performing animals are being trained or exhibited or kept for training or exhibition, and any such animals found therein; and

(b) require any person who, he has reason to believe is a trainer or exhibitor of performing animals to produce his certificate of registration,

(2) No person or police officer referred to in sub section (1) shall be entitled under this section to go on or behind the stage during a public performance of performing animals.

26. Offences : If any person -

(a) not being registered under this chapter, exhibits or trains any performing animal; or

(b) being registered under the Act, exhibits or trains any performing animal with respect to which or in a manner with respect to which, he is not registered; or

(c) exhibits or trains as a performing animal, any animal which is not to be used for the purpose by reason of a notification issued under clause (ii) of section 22; or

(d) obstructs or wilfully delays any person or police officer referred to in section 25 in the exercise of powers under this Act as to entry and inspection; or

(e) conceals any animal with a view to avoiding such inspection: or

(f) being a person registered under 'the Act, on being duly required in pursuance of this Act to produce his certificate under this Act, fails without reasonable excuse so to do; or

(g) applies to be registered under this Act when not entitled to be so registered,

He shall be punishable on conviction with fine which may extend to five hundred rupees or with imprisonment which may extend to three months, or with both.

27. Exemptions : Nothing contained in this Chapter shall apply to -

(a) the training of animals for bonafide military or police purpose or the exhibition of any animals so trained; or

(b) any animals kept in any zoological garden or by any society or association which has for its principal object the exhibition of animals for educational or scientific purposes.

MISCELLANEOUS

28. Saving as respects manner of killing prescribed by religion : Nothing contained in this Act shall render it an offence to kill any animal in a manner required by the religion of any community.

29. Power of court to deprive person convicted of ownership of animal :

(1) If the owner of any animal is found guilty of any offence under this Act. the court upon his conviction thereof, may, if it thinks fit, in addition to any other punishment make an order that the animal with respect to which the offence was committed shall be forfeited to Government and may, further, make such order as to the disposal of the animal as it thinks fit under the circumstances.

(2) No order under sub section (1) shall be made unless it is shown by evidence as to a -previous conviction under this Act or as to the character of the owner or otherwise as to the treatment of the animal that the animal if left with the owner, is likely to be exposed to further cruelty.

(3) without prejudice to the provision contained in sub-section (1), the court may also order that a person convicted of an offence under this Act shall, either permanently or during such period as is fixed by the order, be prohibited from having the custody of any animal of any kind whatsoever, or as the court thinks fit of any animal of any kind or species specified in the order.

(4) No order under sub-section (3) shall be made unless

(a) it is shown by evidence as to a previous conviction or as to the character of the said person or otherwise as to the treatment of the animal in relation to which he has been convicted that an animal in the custody of the said person is likely to be exposed to cruelty;

(b) it is stated in the complaint upon which the conviction was made that it is the intention of the complaint upon the conviction of the accused to request that an order be made as aforesaid and

(c) the offence for which the conviction was made was committed in an area in which under the law for the time being in force a licence is necessary for the keeping of any such animal as that in respect of which the conviction was made.

(5) Notwithstanding anything to the contrary contained in any law for the time being in force, any person in respect of whom an order is made under sub-section (3) shall have no right to the custody of any animal contrary to the provisions of the order, and if he contravenes the provisions oil any order, he shall be punishable with fine which may extend to one hundred rupees, or. with imprisonment for a term which may extend to three months, or with both.

(6) Any court which has made an order under sub-section (3) may at any time, either on its own motion or on application made to it in this behalf, rescind or modify such order.

30. Presumptions as to guilt in certain cases :

If any person is charged with the offences of killing a goat, cow or its to guilt in progeny contrary to the provisions of clause (1) of sub section (1) or section 11, and it is proved that such person had in his possession, at the time the offence is alleged to have been committed, the skin of any such animal as is referred to in this section with any the skin of any such animal as is referred to in this section with any part of the skin of the head attached thereto, it shall be presumed until the contrary is proved that such animal was killed in a cruel manner.

31. Cognizability of offences :

Notwithstanding anything contained in the Code or Criminal procedure, 1898, (5 of 1898) an offence punishablo undcr clause (1) or clauso (n) or clause, (o) of sub-section (1) of section 11 or under section 12 shall be a cognizable offence within the meaning of that code.

32. Powers of search and seizure :

(1) If a police officer not below the rank of sub inspector, or any person authorised by the State Government in this behalf has reason to believe that an offence under clause (1) of sub-section (1) of section 11 in respect of any such animal

as is referred to in section 30 is being, or that any person has in his possession the skin of any such animal with any part of the skin of the head attached thereto, he, may enter and search such place or any place in which he has reason to believe any such skin to be, and may seize such skin or any article or thing used or intended to be used in the commission of such offence.

(2) If a police officer not below the rank of sub-inspector, or any person authorised by the State Government in this behalf, has reason to believe that phooka or [25](doom dev or any other operation of the nature referred to in section 12) has just been or is being, performed on any animal within the limits of his jurisdiction, he may enter any place in which he has reason to believe such animal to be, and may seize the animal and produce it for examination by the veterinary officer incharge of the area in which the animal is seized.

33. Search warrants :

(1) If a magistrate of the first or second class or a presidency magistrate or a commissioner of police or district superintendent of police, upon information in writing; and after such inquiry as he thinks necessary, has reason to believe that an offence under this Act is being, or is about to be, or has been committed in any place, he may either himself enter and search or by his warrant authorise any police officer not below the rank of sub-inspector to enter and search the place.

(2) The provisions of the Code of Criminal Procedure, 1898, relating to searches shall so far as those provision can be made applicable, apply to searches under this Act.

34. General Power of seizure for examination :

Any police officer above the rank of a constable or any person authorised seizure for by the State Government in this behalf, who has reason to believe that examination an offence against this Act has been or is being, committed in respect of any animal, may, if in his opinion the circumstances so require, seize the animal and produce the same for examination by the nearest magistrate or by such veterinary officer as may be prescribed; and such police officer or authorised person may, when seizing the animal, require the person in charge thereof to accompany it to the place of examination.

35. Treatment and care of animals :

(1) The State Government, may by general or special order appoint infirmaries for the treatment and care of animals in respect of which offences against this Act have been committed, and may authorise the detention therein of any animal pending its production before a magistrate.

(2) The magistrate before whom a prosecution for an offence against this Act has been instituted may direct that the animals concerned shall be treated and cared for in an infirmary, until it is fit to perform its usual work or is otherwise fit for discharge, or that it shall be sent to a pinjrapole, or if the veterinary officer in charge of the area in which the animal is found or such a veterinary officer as may be authorised in this behalf by rules made under this Act certifies that it is incurable or cannot be removed without cruelty, that it shall be destroyed.

(3) An animal sent for care and treatment to an infirmary shall not, unless the magistrate directs that it shall be sent to a pinjrapole or that it shall be destroyed, be released from such place except upon a certificate of its fitness for discharge issued by the veterinary officer in charge of the area in which the infirmary is situated or such other veterinary officer as may be authorised in this behalf by rules made under this Act.

(4) The cost of transporting the animal to an infirmary or pinjrapole and of its maintenance and treatment in an infirmary, shall be payable by the district magistrate, or, in presidency-towns, by the commissioner of police; Provided that when the magistrate so orders on account of the poverty of the owner of the animal, no charge shall be payable for the treatment of the animal.

(5) Any amount payable by an owner of an animal under sub-section (4) may be recovered in the same manner as an arrear of land revenue,

(6) If the owner refuses or neglects to remove the animal within such time as a magistrate may specify, the magistrate

may direct that the animal be sold and that the proceeds of the same be applied to the payment of such cost.

(7) The surplus, if any, of the proceeds of such sale shall, on application made by the owner within two months from the date of the sale be paid to him.

36. Limitation of prosecutions : A prosecution for an offence against this Act shall not be instituted after prosecutions the expiration of three months from the date of the commission of the offence.

37. Delegation of powers : The Central Government may, by notification in the official Gazette, direct that all or any of the powers exercisable by it under this Act, may, subject to such conditions as it may think fit to impose, be also exercisable by any State Government.

38. Power to make rules :

(1) The Central Government may, by notification in the Official Gazette and subject to the condition of previous publication, make rules to carry out the purposes of this Act.

(2) In particular, and without prejudice to the generality of the foregoing power, the Central Government may make rules providing for all or any of the following matters, namely:

(a) the (xxxx) conditions of service of members of the Board, the allowances payable to them and the manner in which they may exercise their powers and discharge their functions.

(aa) the manner in which the persons to represent municipal corporation are to be elected under clause (e) of sub-section (1) of section

(b) the maximum load (including any load occasioned by the weight of passengers) to be carried or drawn by any animal;

(c) the conditions to be observed for preventing the overcrowding of animals; the period during which, and the hours between which, any class of animals shall not be used for draught purposes:

(d) prohibiting the use of any bit or harness involving cruelty to animals;

(ea)the other methods of destruction of stray dogs referred to in clause (b) of sub-section (3) of section 11;

(eb) the methods by which any animal which cannot be removed without cruelty may be destroyed under sub-section (3) of section 13,

(f) requiring persons carrying on the business of a farrier to be licensed and registered by such authority as may be prescribed and levying a fee for the purpose;

(g) the precautions to be taken in the capture of animals for purposes of sale, export or for any other purpose, and the different appliances or devices that may alone be used for the purpose; and the licensing of such capture and the levying of fees for such licences;

(h) the precautions to be taken in the transport of animals whether by rail, road, inland waterway, sea or air and the manner in which and the cages or other receptacles in which they may be so transported;

(i) requiring person owning or in charge of premises in which animals are kept or milked to register such permises, to comply with such conditions as may be laid down in relation to the boundary walls or surroundings of such premises, to permit their inspection for the purpose of ascertaining whether any offence under this Act is being, or has been committed therein, and to expose in such premises copies of section 12 in a language or languages commonly understood in the locality;

(j) the form in which applications for registration under Chapter V may be made, the particulars to be contained therein the fees payable for such registration and the authorities to whom such applications may be made;

(ja) the fees which may be charged by the Committee constituted under section 15 for the registration of persons or institutions carrying on experiments on animals or for any other purpose;

(k) the purposes to which fines realised under the Act may be applied, including such purposes as the maintenance of infirmaries, pinjrapole and veterinary hospitals;

(l) any other matter which has to be, or may be prescribed.

(3) If any person contravenes, or abets the contravention of, any rules made under this section, he shall be punishable with fine which may extend to one hundred rupees, or with imprisonment for a term which may extend to three months, or with both.

38A. Rules and regulations to be laid before Parliament : Every rule made by the Central Government or by the Committee constituted under section 15 and every regulation made. by the Board shall be laid, as soon as may be after it is made, before each House of Parliament, while it is in session, for a total period of thirty days which may be comprised in one session or in two or more successive sessions, and if, before the expiry of the session immediately following the session or the successive sessions aforesaid, both Houses agree in making any modification in the rule or regulation, as the case may be, should not be made the rule or regulation shall there after have effect only in such modified form or be of no effect, as the case may be; so, however, that any such modification or annulment shall be without prejudice to the validity of anything previously done under that rule or regulation.

39. Persons authorised under section 34 to be public servants: Every person authorised by the State Government under section 34 shall be deemed to be a public servant within the meaning of section 21 of the Indian Penal code.

40. Indemnity : No suit, prosecution or other legal proceeding shall lie against any person who is, or who is deemed to be a public servant within the meaning of section 21 of the Indian Penal Code in respect of anything in good faith done or intended to be done under this Act.

41. Repeal of Act 11 of 1890 : Where in pursuance of a notification under subsection (3) of section 1 of 1890 any provision of this Act comes into force in any State, any provision of the Prevention of Cruelty to Animals Act, 1890, which corresponds to the provision so coming into force, shall thereupon stand repealed.

6

MINISTRY OF ENVIRONMENT AND FORESTS

S.O. 1818 (E). - Whereas certain draft rules to amend the Breeding of and Experiments on Animals (Control and Supervision) Rules, 1998 were published, as required by sub-sections(1), (1A) and (2) of section 17 of the Prevention of Cruelty to Animals Act, 1960 (59 of 1960), under the notification of the Government of India in the Ministry of Environment and Forests number S.O.42(E) dated 10th January, 2006 inviting suggestions from all the persons likely to be affected thereby, before the expiry of the period of thirty days from the date on which copies of the Gazette containing the said notification are made available to the public;

And whereas the said Gazette was made available to the public on 10th January, 2006;

And whereas the objections/suggestion received in respect of the said draft rules, have been duly considered;

Now, therefore, in exercise of the powers conferred by sub-section (1), (1A) and (2) of Section 17 of the Prevention of Cruelty to Animals Act, 1960 (59 of 1960), the Committee for the purpose of control and supervision of experiments on animals hereby makes the following rules to amend the Breeding of and Experiments on Animals (Control & Supervision) Rules, 1998, namely:-

1. (1) These rules may be called the Breeding of and Experiments on Animals (Control and Supervision) Amendment Rules, 2006.

(2) They shall come into force on the date of their final publication in the Official Gazette.

2. 2. In the Breeding of and Experiments on Animals (Control and Supervision) Rules, 1998 (hereinafter referred to as the said rules), in rule 2, for clause (e), the following clause shall be substituted, namely:-

'*(e)* "Experiment" means any programme or project involving use of animal(s) for the acquisition of knowledge of a biological, physiological, ethological, physical or chemical nature; and includes the use of animal(s) in the production of reagents and products such as antigens and antibodies, routine diagnostics, testing activity and establishment of transgenic stocks, for the purpose of saving or prolonging life or alleviating suffering or significant gains in well being for people of the country or for combating any disease whether of human beings or animals;'

3. In rule 9 of the said rules, -

(1) after clause (b), the following clause shall be inserted, namely:-

"(bb) animals lowest on the phylogenetic scale which may give scientifically valid results should be first considered for any experimental procedure and the experiment should be designed using minimum number of animals to give statistically valid results at 95% degree of confidence:

Provided that replacement alternatives not involving experiments on animals should be given due and full consideration and sound justification must be provided in case alternatives, though available, are not used;" ;

(2) after clause (c), the following clause shall be inserted, namely:

"(cc) (i) personnel using experimental animal(s) shall be responsible for the welfare of animal(s) during their use in experiments;

(ii) investigators shall be responsible for the aftercare and rehabilitation of animal(s) after experimentation, and shall not euthanise animal(s) except in situations as defined in clause (ff);

(iii) costs of aftercare and rehabilitation of animal(s) after experimentation shall be made part of research costs and shall be scaled in positive correlation with the level of costs involved in such aftercare and rehabilitation of the animal(s);

(iv) rehabilitation treatment of an animal after experimentation shall extend till the point the animal is able to resume a normal existence by providing a lump-sum amount as costs for rehabilitation and care of such animal to cover its entire statistical expected life span; and

(v) the establishment undertaking experiments or duly licensed and authorised animal welfare organization under the control of the Committee may, on payment of lump-sum amount, undertake rehabilitation of animals;";

(3) after clause (f), the following clause shall be inserted, namely:-

"(ff) the following parameters shall be adopted for application of euthanasia, namely:-

(i) when the animal is paralyzed and is not able to perform its natural functions or it becomes incapable of independent locomotion or it can no longer perceive the environment in an intelligible manner; or

(ii) if during the course of experimental procedure the animal has been left with a recurring pain wherein the animal exhibits obvious signs of pain and suffering; or

(iii) where the non-termination of the life of the experimental animal will be life threatening to human beings or other animals;".

4. In rule 10 of the said rules, -

(1) for clause (b), the following clause shall be substituted, namely:-

"(b) (i) an establishment shall acquire animal(s) for experiments from registered breeders only;

(ii) in case of non-availability of animal(s) from registered breeders, the animal(s) may be procured from alternate legal sources;

(iii) in case the animal is procured from the alternate legal sources, the same shall be procured after taking written permission from the authority competent under the law for the time being in force, to give such permission; and

(iv) the establishment procuring such animal shall maintain a record in this regard and shall produce the same before the Committee, whenever required;" ;

(2) for clause (e), the following clause shall be substituted, namely:-

"(e) In case an animal is not available from a registered breeder or from alternate legal sources within the country, genetically defined animals may be imported with permission of Directorate General of Foreign Trade:

Provided that the condition of non-availability within the country shall not apply for laboratory bred rats and mice of genetically defined strains;".

5. For rule 12 of the said rules, the following rule shall be substituted, namely:-

"12. Contract animal experiments.-Registered establishments may undertake contract research on behalf of any other agency in accordance with the Prevention of Cruelty to Animals Act, 1960 (59 of 1960) and the rules made thereunder.".

6. In rule 14 of the said rules, for clause (a), the following clause shall be substituted, namely:-

"(a) The Committee, if it is satisfied with the report of the Member-Secretary or the authorized officer of the Committee (made to it as a result of any inspection or information received or otherwise) that -

(i) the rules made by it are not being complied with by an establishment or breeder; or

(ii) a violation of the directions of the Committee has been committed by any establishment or breeder and the Committee's directions to rectify such violation have not been complied within the period so specified, the Committee may, by order in writing, suspend or revoke the registration of the establishment or breeder and/or direct closure of the animal house facility for such a period as may be specified in the order: Provided that no order under this clause shall be made without giving the establishment or breeder any opportunity of being heard in the matter: Provided further that no order for suspension or revocation of registration, or closure of animal house facility shall be issued in a case of minor violation.

Explanation: for the purposes of this clause, "minor violation" means an act of commission or omission which does not have direct bearing on the health of an animal which may not lead to adverse health effect or pain or suffering or death of an animal.".

S.O. 42(E). The following draft of the Breeding of and Experiments on Animals (Control and Supervision) Amendment Rules, 2005, which the Committee for the Purpose of Control and Supervision of Experiments on Animals proposes to make, in exercise of the powers conferred by sub-sections(1), (1A) and (2) of section 17 of the Prevention of Cruelty to Animals Act, 1960 (59 of 1960), are hereby published for information of all persons likely to be affected thereby, and notice is hereby given that the said draft rules shall be taken into consideration after the expiry of a period of thirty days from the date on which copies of the Gazette of India containing this notification are made available to the public;

Any person desirous of making any suggestion or objection in respect of the said draft rules may, within the period so specified, forward the same for consideration of the said Committee, addressed to the Member Secretary, Committee for the Purpose of Control and Supervision of Experiments on Animals, Animal Welfare Division, Ministry of Environment and Forests, 8th Floor, Jeevan Prakash Building, 25, Kasturba Gandhi Marg, New Delhi-110001.

DRAFT RULES

1. (1) These rules may be called the Breeding of and Experiments on Animals (Control and Supervision) Amendment Rules, 2005.

(2) They shall come into force on the date of their final publication in the Official Gazette.

3. 2. In the Breeding of and Experiments on Animals (Control and Supervision) Rules, 1998 (hereinafter referred to as the said rules), in rule 2, for clause (e), the following clause shall be substituted, namely:-

'*(e)* "Experiment" means any programme or project involving use of animal for the acquisition of knowledge of a biological, physiological, ethological, physical or chemical nature; and includes the use of animal in the production of reagents and products such as antigens and antibodies, routine diagnostics, testing activity and establishment of transgenic stocks, for the purpose of saving or prolonging life or alleviating suffering or significant gains in well being for people of the country or for combating any disease whether of human beings or animals ;'

3. In rule 9 of the said rules, -

(1) after clause (b), the following clause shall be inserted, namely:-

"(bb) animals lowest on the phylogenetic scale which may give scientifically valid results should be first considered for any experimental procedure and the experiment should be designed using minimum number of animals to give statistically valid results at 95% degree of confidence:

Provided that replacement alternatives not involving experiments on animals should be given due and full consideration and sound justification must be provided in case alternatives, though available, are not used;" ;

(2) after clause (c), the following clause shall be inserted, namely:

"(cc) (i) personnel using experimental animals shall be responsible for the welfare of animal during their use in experiments;

(ii) investigators shall be responsible for the aftercare and rehabilitation of animal after experimentation, and shall not euthanise animals except in situations as defined in clause (ff);

(iii) costs of aftercare and rehabilitation of animal after experimentation shall be made part of research costs and shall be scaled in positive correlation with the level of costs involved in such aftercare and rehabilitation of the animals;

(iv) rehabilitation treatment of animals after experimentation shall extend till the point the animal is able to resume a normal existence by providing a lump-sum amount as costs for rehabilitation and care of such animal to cover its entire statistical expected life span; and

(v) the establishment undertaking experiments or duly licensed and authorised animal welfare organization under the control of the Committee may, on payment of lump-sum amount, undertake rehabilitation of animals;";

(3) after clause (f), the following clause shall be inserted, namely:-

"(ff) the following parameters shall be adopted for application of euthanasia, namely:-

(i) when the animal is paralyzed and is not able to perform its natural functions or it becomes incapable of independent locomotion or it can no longer perceive the environment in an intelligible manner; or

(ii) if during the course of experimental procedure the animal has been left with a recurring pain wherein the animal exhibits obvious signs of pain and suffering; or

(iii) where the non-termination of the life of the experimental animal will be life threatening to human beings or other animals;".

4. In rule 10 of the said rules, -

(1) for clause (b), the following clause shall be substituted, namely:-

"(b) (i) an establishment shall acquire animal for experiments from registered breeders only;

(ii) in case of non-availability of animal from registered breeders, the animal may be procured from alternate legal sources;

(iii) in case the animal is procured from the alternate legal sources, the same shall be procured after taking written permission from the authority competent under the law for the time being in force, to give such permission; and

(iv) the establishment procuring such animal shall maintain a record in this regard and shall produce the same before the Committee, whenever required;" ;

(2) for clause (e), the following clause shall be substituted, namely:-

"(e) In case an animal is not available from a registered breeder or from alternate legal sources within the country, genetically defined animals may be imported with permission of Directorate General of Foreign Trade:

Provided that the condition of non-availability within the country shall not apply for laboratory bred rats and mice of genetically defined strains;".

5. For rule 12 of the said rules, the following rule shall be substituted, namely:-

"12. Contract animal experiments. - Registered establishments may undertake contract research on behalf of any other agency in accordance with the Prevention of Cruelty to Animals Act, 1960 (59 of 1960) and the rules made thereunder.".

6. In rule 14 of the said rules, for clause (a), the following clause shall be substituted, namely:-

"(a) The Committee, if it is satisfied with the report of the Member-Secretary or the authorized officer of the Committee (made to it as a result of any inspection or information received or otherwise) that -

(i) the rules made by it are not being complied with by an establishment or breeder; or

(ii) a violation of the directions of the Committee has been committed by any establishment or breeder and the Committee's directions to rectify such violation have not been complied within the period so specified, the Committee may, by order in writing, suspend or revoke the registration of the establishment or breeder and/or direct closure of the animal house facility for such a period as may be specified in the order:

Provided that no order under this clause shall be made without giving the establishment or breeder any opportunity of being heard in the matter:

Provided further that no order for suspension or revocation of registration, or closure or animal house facility shall be issued in a case of minor violation.

Explanation:- for the purposes of this clause, "minor violation" means an act of commission or omission which does not have direct bearing on the health of an animal which may not lead to adverse health effect or pain or suffering or death of an animal.".

NOTIFICATION

New Delhi, the 24th December, 2001

S.O. 1256 (E) - Whereas the draft Animal Birth Control (Dogs) Rules, 2001 were published, as required under the sub-section (1) of section 38 of the Prevention of Cruelty to Animals Act, 1960 (59 of 1960), vide Ministry of Culture notification number G.S.R.816(E) dated November 2, 2001 in the Gazette of India, Extraordinary, Part 11, Section 3, sub-section (i) dated November 2, 2001 and whereas objections and suggestions from all persons likely to be affected thereby were invited before the expiry of 30 days from the date on which copies of the gazette containing the said notification have been made available to the public;

And whereas copies of the said Gazette were made available to the public on November 2, 2001;

And whereas the objections/suggestions received from the public have been incorporated in the rules.

Now, therefore, in exercise of the powers conferred by the sub-sections (1) (2) of section 38 of the Prevention of Cruelty to Animals Act, 1960 (59 of 1960), the Central Government hereby makes the following rules, namely:

Short title and commencement :

(1) These rules may be called the Animal Birth Control (Dogs) Rules, 2001.

(2) They shall come into force on the date of their final publication in the Official Gazette.

Definition :

In these rules, unless the context otherwise requires, -

(a) "Act" means the Prevention of Cruelty to Animals Act, 1960.

(b) "Animal Welfare Organisation" means and includes the Society for Prevention of Cruelty to Animals and any other welfare organization for animals which is registered under the Societies Registration Act of 1860 (21 of 1860) or any other corresponding law for the time being in force and which is recognized by the Animal Welfare Board of India

(c) "Board" means the Animal Welfare Board of India, established under section 4 and as reconstituted under Section 5A of the Act;

(d) "Committee" means a committee appointed under these rules

(e) "local authority" means a municipal committee, district board or other authority for the time being invested by law with the control and administration of any matters within a specified local area;

(f) "owner" means the owner of an animal and includes any other person in possession or custody of such animal whether with or without the consent of the owner;

(g) "Veterinary doctor" means a person who holds a degree of a recognized veterinary college and is registered with the Indian Veterinary Council.

Classification of dogs and their Sterilization

(1) All dogs shall be classified in one of the following two categories (i) pet dogs, (ii) street dogs.

(2) The owner of pet dogs shall be responsible for the controlled breeding, immunization, sterlization and licensing in accordance with these rules and the law for the time being in force within a specified local area.

(3) The street dogs shall be sterilized and immunized by participation of animal welfare organizations, private individuals and the local authority.

Formation of Committtee

A monitoring committee consisting of the following persons shall be constituted by the local authority namely

(a) Commissioner/Chief of the local authority, who shall be the ex-officio Chairman of the Committee.

(b) A representative of the Public Health Department of the local authority.

(c) A representative of the Animal Welfare Department if any of the local authority.

(d) A veterinary doctor

(e) A representative of the district Society for Prevention of Cruelty to Animals (SPCA)

(f) At least two representatives from the Animal Welfare Organizations operating within the said local authority.

Functions of the Committee

The committee constituted under rule 4 shall be responsible for planning and management of dog control programme in accordance with these rules. The committee may:

(a) issue instructions for catching, transportation, sheltering, sterilisation, vaccination, treatment and release of sterilized vaccinated or treated dogs.

(b) authorize veterinary doctor to decide on case to case basis the need to put to sleep critically ill or fatally injured or rabid dogs in a painless method by using sodium pentathol. Any other method is strictly prohibited.

(c) create public awareness, solicit co-operation and funding.

(d) provide guidelines to pet dog owners and commercial breeders from time to time.

(e) get a survey done of the number of street dogs by an independent agency.

(f) take such steps for monitoring the dog bite cases to ascertain the reasons of dog bite, the area where it took place and whether it was from a stray or a pet dog.

(g) Keep a watch on the national and international development in the field of research pertaining to street dogs' control and management, development of vaccines and cost effective methods of sterilization, vaccination, etc.

Obligations of the Local Authority :

(1) The local authority shall provide for

(a) establishment of a sufficient number of dogs pounds including animal kennels/shelters which may be managed by animal welfare organizations;

(b) requisite number of dog vans with ramps for the capture and transportation of street dogs;

(c) one driver and two trained dog catchers to be provided for each dog van;

(d) an ambulance cum clinical van to be provided as mobile center for sterilisation and immunization;

(e) incinerators to be installed by the local authority for disposal of carcasses.

(f) periodic repair of shelter or pound.

(2) If the Municipal Corporation or the local authority thinks it expedient to control street dog population, it shall be incumbent upon them to sterilize and immunize street Dogs with the participation of animal welfare organizations, private individuals and the local authority.

(3) The animal welfare organizations shall be reimbursed the expenses of sterilization/immunization at a rate to be fixed by the Committee on fortnightly basis based on the number of sterilization/ immunization done.

Capturing/sterilization/immunization/release :

(1) Capturing of dogs shall be based on:

(a) Specific complaints (for which the local authority in consultation with the Monitoring Committee shall set up a dog control cell to receive complaints about dog nuisance, dog bites and information about rabid dogs) and

(b) General :

(i) On receipt of specific complaint about nuisance or dog bite the same shall be attended on priority basis, irrespective of the area from which the complaint comes. On receipt of such complaint the details such as name of the complainant, his complete address, date and time of complaint, nature of complaint etc. shall be recorded in a register to be maintained for permanent record.

(ii) Capturing for general purpose will be on such dates and time to be specified by the Committee.

The dog capturing squad shall consist of

(i) The driver of the dog van

(ii) Two or more trained employees of the local authority who are trained in capturing of dogs.

(iii) One representative of any of the animal welfare organization

Each member of the dog squad shall carry, a valid identity card issued by the local authority. The dog capturing squad will be accompanied by a representative of an Animal Welfare Organisation nominated for the purpose.

(3) On receipt of specific complaint or for capturing dogs in normal course the dog squad will visit the concerned area, capture the dogs identified by the complaint in case of complaint oriented capturing and other dogs in case of general capturing. All the dogs caught will be tagged for identification purposes and to ensure that the dogs are released in the same area after sterilization and vaccination. Only stipulated number of dogs, according to the Animal Birth Control Program target, shall

be caught by the van. A record of dogs captured shall be maintained in a register, mentioning therein the name of the area/locality, date and time of capture, names of persons in the dogs squad on that particular day and details about dogs captured such as number of male dogs, number of female dogs, number of puppies etc.

(4) The dogs shall be captured by using humane methods such as lassoing or soft-loop animal catchers such as those prescribed under the provisions of Prevention of Cruelty (Capture of Animals) Rules, 1979.

(5) While the dogs are being captured in any locality the representative of the local authority or of the animal welfare organization accompanying the dog squad will make announcements on a public address system that dogs are being captured from the area for the purpose of sterilization and immunization and will be released in the same area after sterilization and immunization. The announcement may also briefly educate the residents of the area about the dog control programme and solicit the support of all the residents reassuring them that the local authority is taking adequate steps for their safety.

(6) The captured dogs shall be brought to the dog kennels/ dog pounds managed by the Animal Welfare Organisations (AWOs). On reaching the dog pounds all the dogs shall be examined by the veterinarians and healthy and sick dogs should be segregated. Sick dogs should be given proper treatment in the hospitals run by Society for Prevention of Cruelty to Animals (SPCA)/other institutions and only after they are treated they should be sterilized and vaccinated. The dogs will be sterilized/ vacci noted under the supervision of the veterinarians of the hospital run by the Society for Prevention of Cruelty to Animals (SPCA), Animal Welfare Organization or other dog shelters. After necessary period of follow up, the dogs shall be released at the same place or locality from where they were captured and the date, time and place of their release shall be recorded. The representative of Animal Welfare Organisations (AWOs) shall accompany the dog squad at the time of release also.

(7) At a time only one lot of dogs shall be brought for sterilization, immunization at one dog kennel or dog pound and these dogs shall be from one locality. Two lots from different areas or localities shall not be mixed at the same dog pound or dog kennel.

(8) The dog kennel must have sufficient space for proper housing and free movement of dogs. The place should have proper ventilation and natural lighting and must be kept clean. Adults and puppies must be housed separately and amongst the adults the males and females also should be housed separately. Adequate arrangement for drinking water and food shall be made for dogs while in captivity.

(9) Female dogs found to be pregnant shall not undergo abortion (irrespective of stage of pregnancy) and sterilization and should be released till they have litter.

Identification and Recording

Sterilized dogs shall be vaccinated before release and the ears of these dogs should either be clipped and/ or tatooed for being identified as sterilized or immunised dogs. In addition, the dogs may be given token or nylon collars for identification and detailed records of such dogs shall be maintained. Branding of dogs would not be permitted.

Euthanasia of Street Dogs

Incurably ill and mortally wounded dogs as diagnosed by a qualified veterinarian appointed by the committee shall be euthanised during specified hours in a humane manner by administering sodium pentathol for adult dogs and Thiopental Introperitoneal for puppies by a qualified veterinarian or outhanised in any other humane manner approved by Animal Welfare Board of India. No dog shall be euthanised in the presence of another dog. The person responsible for euthanising shall make sure that the animal is dead, before disposal.

Furious or Dumb Rabid Dogs

(1) On the receipt of complaints from the public to the Dog Control Cell of the Local Authority or on its own, the dog squad

of the Local Authority would catch such dogs, suspected to be rabid.

(2) The caught dog would then be taken to the pound where it would be isolated in an isolation ward.

(3) The suspected rabid dog would then be subjected to inspection by a panel of two persons i.e.

(i) a veterinary surgeon appointed by the Local Authority and

(ii)a representative from an Animal Welfare Organisation

(4) If the dog is found to have a high probability of having rabies it would be isolated till it dies a natural death. Death normally occurs within 10 days of contracting rabies. Premature killings of suspected rabid dogs therefore prevents the true incidence of rabies from being known and appropriate action being taken.

(5) If the dog is found not to have rabies but some other disease it would be handed over to the AWOs who will take the necessary action to cure and rehabilitate the dog.

Disposal of Carcasses

The carcasses of such euthanised dogs shall be disposed of in an incinerator to be provided by the local authority.

Guidelines for Breeders

(i) A breeder must be registered with Animal Welfare Board of India.

(ii) Breeder must maintain full record of the number of pups born/died from individual bitches.

(iii) Breeder must maintain record of the person buying the pups. He should ensure that the buyer has the required knowledge for the upkeep of the pups.

Application of rules where local bye-laws etc., exist

If there is in force in any area to which these rules extend, any Act , rule, regulation or bye-low made under any law for the time being in force by the State or the Local Authority in respect of any of the matters for which provision is made in these rules, such rule, regulation or bye-law shall to the extent to which

(a) it contains provisions less irksome to the animal than those contained in these rules, shall prevail;

(b) it contains provisions more irksome to the animal than those contained in these rules, be of no effect.

S.O. 267 (E). - Whereas the draft Performing Animals (Registration) Rules, 2000 were published, as required by sub-section (1) of section 38 of the Prevention of Cruelty to Animals Act, 1960 (59 of 1960), under the notification of the Government of India in the Ministry of Social Justice and Empowerment number S.O. 1162 (E) dated the 26th December 2000 in the Gazette of India. Extraordinary, Part 11, Section 3, Sub Section (ii) dated the 27 th December, 2000 inviting objections and suggestions from all persons likely to be affected thereby, before the expiry of the period of sixty days from the date on which copies of the Gazette containing the said notification are made available to the public;

And, whereas, copies of the said Gazette were made available to the public on the 1st January, 2001;

And, whereas no objection or suggestion has been received from the public in respect of the said draft rules by the Central Government;

Now, therefore, in exercise of the powers conferred by sub-sections (1) and (2) of section 38 of the Prevention of Cruelty to Animals Act, 1960 (59 of 1960), the Central Government hereby makes the following rules, namely ;

1. Short Title and Commencement

(1) These rules may be called the Performing Animals (Registration) Rules, 2001.

(2) They shall come into force on the date of their publication in the Official Gazette.

2. Definitions : In these rules unless the context otherwise requires

(a) "Act" means the Prevention of Cruelty to Animals Act, 1960 (59 of 1960);

(b) "Board" means the Animal Welfare Board of India, established under section 4 and as reconstituted from time to time under section 5A of the Act;

(c) "film" means a cinematograph film as defined in the Cinematograph Act of 1952 (37 of 1952);

(d) "fitness certificate" means a certificate granted by a veterinary doctor to be nominated by the prescribed authority certifying the health and fitness of the animal;

(e) "owner' means the owner of an animal and includes any other person in possession or custody of such animal whether with or without the consent of the owner;

(f) ownership certificate" means a certificate granted under section 42 of the Wildlife (Protection) Act 1972 (53 of 1972);

(g) "prescribed authority" means the Board or such other authority or officer as may be authorised by the Board;

(h) "performing animal" means an animal which is used at or for the purpose of any entertainment including a film or an equine event to which the public are admitted;

(i) schedule" means a Schedule appended to these rules;

(j) "veterinary doctor' means a person registered with the Veterinary Council of India established under the Indian Veterinary Council Act, 1984 (52 of 1984).

3. Application of registration :

(1) Any person desirous of training or exhibiting a performing animal shall, within thirty days from the commencement of these rules, apply for registration to the prescribed authority and shall not exhibit or train any animal as a performing animal without being registered under these rules.

(2) Any person desirous of exhibiting or training any performing animal shall apply for registration in the form of application set out in the First Schedule.

(3) Every such application shall be made to the prescribed authority.

4. Fee and registration : Every application for registration shall be accompanied by a fee of Rupees five hundred which may be paid either in cash or in such other manner as may be specified by the Board for this purpose.

5. Power to call for additional information :

(1) The prescribed authority may call for such additional records and information as it may deem fit from the applicant in respect of the particulars furnished by it.

(2) If the prescribed authority is satisfied about the proposed performance and the method to be adopted for the training of such animals by the applicant it may grant registration,

(3) The prescribed authority while granting registration may impose such other conditions, as it may deem appropriate for the training and upkeep of such performing animals.

6. Form of certificate of registration

(1) The certificate of registration shall be issued by the prescribed authority in the form set out in the Second Schedule.

(2) Every registration shall be given a serial number in a order in which it is made, and it shall be indicated in the certificate of registration.

7. Prior information for use of performing animals in films:

(1) Every owner desirous of hiringout or lending a porforming animal in the making of a film shall give prior information in the format as specified by the prescribed authority for this purpose to specifying the kind of animal, age of animal, physical health of the animal, the nature of performance to be done by the animal, the duration for which the animal shall be used for such performance, the duration and method of training of the animal for such performance and justification

for the use of such animals in the film and such other information as may be required by that authority.

(2) Every such application shall be accompanied by a fitness certificate issued by a veterinary doctor certifying the health and fitness of the animal along with a ownership certificate in case of animals covered under the wildlife (Protection) Act, 1972 (53 of 1972).

8. General conditions for registration

(1) The prescribed authority while granting registration may impose such terms and conditions as it deems appropriate and shall impose the following conditions in granting registration, namely :

i. every owner who has ten or more such performing animals shall have a veterinarian as a regular employee for their care treatment and transport.

ii. the owner shall not transport such animals by road continuously for more than 8 hours and except in cages admeasuring as specified in the Fifth Schedule;

iii. the owner shall ensure proper watering and feeding halts during such transportation;

iv. the owner after transportation shall provide feeding and retiring enclosures in respect of the animal specified in the Sixth Schedule;

v. the owner shall ensure that any animal is no inflicted unnecessary pain or suffering before o during or after its training or exhibition;

vi. the owner shall not deprive the animal of feed c water in order to compel the said animal to train or perform any trick;

vii. the owner shall train an animal as a performing animal to perform an act in accordance with its basic natural instinct;

vii. the owner shall not make a performing animal perform if it is sick or injured or pregnant;

ix. the owner shall ensure that no sudden loud noise is deliberately created within the vicinity of any performing animal or bring an animal close to fire which may frighten the animal;

x. the owner in case the performing animal is to I exhibited under artificial light, the overall intensity of such light shall not be more than 500 LUX;

xi. the owner shall not subject the animals to a action which may either kill or injure or use the animal in scenes which may cause injury to the animals;

xii. the owner shall not use any tripping device wires or pitfalls for such animals;

xiii. the owner shall not expose any animal to either burning fire or to fire accidents;

xiv. the owner shall not keep any animal including horses in close proximity while shooting scenes involving explosives or other loud noises;

xv. the owner shall ensure that props such as spears nails splinters, barbed wires and other such pr shall not cause injury to the animals during performance;

xvi. the owner shall ensure that the equines are made to walk on hard surfaces without being shoed and shall further ensure that the animals are used in downhill slides or rodeo slide stops wit proper skid and hock boots;

xvii. the owner of any equine shall not use any other than an air cushioned shock absorbing which has been scientifically tested to provE it will not cause weals, bruising or other damage to the horse and subject to the conditions that (a) the whip shall not have raised binding, stitching seam or flap. (b) the whip shall be used by licenced jockeys only. (c) the owner shall also ensure the whip is not used other than either o quarters in either the forehand or the backhand position or down the shoulder in the backhand position or use the whip with the arm above shoulder height. (d) the whip shall not be used more than 3 times in a race;

xviii. the owner shall ensure that the animal is not used on floors that are very smooth without the use of non-skidding mats;

xix. the owner shall ensure that large gathering of animals is not allowed in such a way which may cause or result in stampede to the animals;

xx. the owner shall ensure that the animal is not made or incited to fight against other animals and shall further ensure that sedatives or tranquillisers or steroids or any other artificial enhancers are not administered to or inserted in any animal except the anaesthesia by a veterinary doctor for the purpose of treatment of an injured or sick animal;

xxi. the owner shall ensure that the animal shall not be transported or be kept or confined in cages and receptacles which do not measure in height, length or breadth as specified under the Transport of Animal Rules, 1978, the Recognition of Zoo Rules, 1992 or under any other Act, rule or order for this purpose;

xxii. the owner shall ensure that the animal is not 14. continuously used for excessive number of takes in shooting a film without providing adequate rest to the animal and in the event of a snake being used it shall not be made to ingest any substances or made to crawl across tarred or any other heatened surface and shall not be contorted to wrestle;

xxiii the owner shall ensure that while using an animal in shooting a film, the fight sequence shall not be shot in any livestock holding area including poultry area and shall further ensure that no birds are 15 shown in cages;

xxiv. the owner shall inform the prescribed authority at least four weeks in advance informing the place, date and time of the actual making of the film wherein the animal is to be used;

(2) The prescribed authority may also impose such other conditions for the grant of registration as may be deemed appropriate to it for the welfare of animals.

9. Register - Every person to whom a certificate of registration is issued under these rules shall have his name entered in a register which shall be kept in the form set out in the Third Schedule.

10. Inspection of register - The register kept for the purpose of these rules shall be open to inspection during office hours on any working day on payment of a fee of twenty rupees and

any person may take extract therefrom or may require the prescribed authority to issue to him a certified copy of any entry made therein on payment of a fee of fifty rupees.

11. Application for variation of entries in register - Every application for the variation of any particular entered in the register maintained for the purpose of these rules shall be in the form set out in the Fourth Schedule and when any particular is varied the existing certificate of registration shall be cancelled and a new certificate be issued.

12. Submission of report by veterinary doctor - Every person who has been granted registration under these rules shall ensure that a monthly report of all the performing animals in the form to be specified by the prescribed authority in respect of their health, deaths and births duly certified by a veterinary doctor is submitted to the prescribed authority on or before the 7th of every succeeding month.

13. Prohibition on exhibition and training of specified performing animals - Performing animals whose performance has been prohibited under sub section (2) of section 22 of the Act shall not be trained or exhibited as a performing animal.

14. Power to inspect -

(1) The prescribed authority may depute an officer or authorise any other person, to inspect the mode of transport, care and upkeep of the animals, or to be present at the time of training or exhibition of the performing animals or during making of a film to ensure that the conditions of registration are being complied with.

(2) The owner shall not obstruct the entry of such officer or authorised person and extend all possible assistance to enable him to discharge his duty.

15. Report of inspection - The officer deputed or person authorised under rule 14 shall after inspection submit a report to the prescribed authority about the compliance of the rules and the conditions as specified by the prescribed authority.

16. Cancellation of registration in respect of which registration has been granted :

1. Every animal in respect of which registration has been granted under rule 5 shall be exhibited and trained subject to the conditions of registration and these rules.

2. Every animal in respect of which registration has been granted under rule 5 shall be exhibited for a film subject to the conditions of registration and these rules.

3. The prescribed authority in the event of breach of any of the conditions of registration under rule 5 or any provision of the Act or the rules made thereunder may suspend the registration pending enquiry and after granting an opportunity of hearing revoke the registration so granted or issue such orders or directions as it may consider proper for the welfare of the animals.

17. Issue of duplicate copies of certificate - Any person who has been granted registration under these rule may, on proof by him that the original certificate registration has been lost or destroyed and on payment of a fee of one hundred rupees, be given a duplicate copy of the certificate of registration which for the purposes of these rules shall have the same effect the original certificate of registration.

FIFTH SCHEDULE

Suggestive Size of Cages for Transportation (See rule 8 (ii))

Species	Length (M)	Breadth (m)	Height (m)
Slender loris	0.40	0.25	0.35
Slow loris	0.60	0.25	0.45
Horse (domestic/wild)	3.00	1.00	1.75
Ass (domestic/wild)	2.25	80	1.28
Zebra	2.60	95	1.80
Elephant (Adult)	4.80	2.40	2.84
Hippopatamus (Common)	4.06	2.10	1.50
Pigmy Hippo	1.52	1.00	0.74
Civet	0.79	40	0.38
Mongoose	0.56	25	0.13
Duck	0.38 to 0.63	22-0.35	78
Dave	0.46	0.20	0.21

SIXTH SCHEDULE

Minimum prescribed size for feeding/retiring cubicle/ enclosures for Important mammalian species of captive animals

(see rule 8 (iv))

Name of the Species	Size of the cubicle/enclosures in meters		
	Length	Breadth	Height
Family – Felidae			
Leopard	2.00	1.50	2.00
Small cats	1.80	1.50	1.50
Family Elephantidae			
Elephant	8.0	6.0	5.5
Family – Rhinocerotidae			
One-horned Indian Rhinoceros	5.0	10	2.5
Family - Carvidae			
Brow antlered deer	3.0	2.0	2.5
Hangul	3.0	2.0	2.5
Swamp deer	3.0	2.0	2.5
Musk deer	2.5	1.5	2.0
Mouse deer	1.5	1.0	1.5
Family - Bovidae			
Nilgiri tahr	2.5	1.5	2.0
Chinkara	2.5	1.5	2.0
Four horned antelope	2.5	1.5	2.0
Wild Burrialo	3.0	1.5	2.0
Indian Bison	3.0	2.0	2.5
Yak	4.0	2.0	2.5
Bharal, goral, wild sheep and markhor	2.5	1.5	2.0
Family - Equidae			
Horses	6.0	4.0	3.0
Wild Ass	4.0	2.0	2.5

Family - Canidaê			
Jackal, wolf and wild dog	2.0	1.5	1.5
Family - Vivirridae			
Palm Civet	2.0	1.0	1.0
Large Indian civet & binturong	2.0	1.5	1.0
Family - Mustellidae			
Otter— all types	2.5	1.5	1.0
Rate/Hogbadger	2.5	1.5	1.0
Martens	2.0	1.5	1.0
Family - Procyonidae			
Red Panda	3.0	1.5	1.0
Family - Lorisidae			
Slow loris and slender Ions	1.0	1.0	1.5

S.O. 35(E).—Whereas the draft Performing Animals (Registration) amendment Rules, 2001, were published, as required by Sub-section (1) of Section 38 of the Prevention of Cruelty to Animals Act, 1960 (59 of 1960), vide Ministry of Culture Notification No. S.O. 1044(E), dated the 17th October, 2001 in the Gazette of India, Extraordinary, Part II, Section 3, Sub-section (ii), dated the 17th October, 2001 and whereas objection and suggestions from all persons likely to be affected thereby were invited before the expiry of the period of thirty days from the date on which copies of the Gazette containing the said notification have been made available to the public;

And, whereas, copies of the said Gazette were made available to the public on the 17th October, 2001;

And, whereas no objection for suggestion has been received from the public in respect of the said draft rules by the Central Government;

Now, therefore, in exercise of the powers conferred by sub-section (1) and (2) of section 38 of the Prevention of Cruelty to Animals Act, 1960 (59 of 1960), the Central Government hereby makes the following rules, namely:-

1. (1) These rules may be called the Performing Animals (Registration) Amendment Rules, 200 1.

(2) They shall come, into force on the date of their publication in the Official Gazette.

2. In the Performing Animals (Registration) Rules, 2001 (hereinafter referred to as the said rules), in rule 2, for clause (g), the following clause shall be substituted, namely:

'(g) "prescribed authority" means the Central Government, or such other authority including the Board or the State Government, as may be authorized by the Central Government;"

3. In the said rules, in rule 3, in sub-rule (1), the following proviso shall be added, namely:

"Provided that the race horses which have been registered by the owners with the Turf Authorities shall not, on intimation of such registration to the prescribed authority, require registration under this rule and the general conditions as specified in rule 8 shall apply to such registration subject to such other conditions as may be imposed by the prescribed authority".

4. In the said rules, in rule 8, in sub rule (1), -

(a) for the word "shall", the word "may" shall be substituted;

(b) in clause (xvii), -

(i) the words 'an air cushioned' shall be omitted;

(ii) for the figure and word "3 times", the words "eight times" shall be substituted,

(iii) after sub-clause (d), the following sub-clauses shall be inserted, namely:

"(e) each horse immediately after the race and again after a period of six hours but within eight hours of the race shall be subject to the veterinary inspection to check, for injuries.

(f) the horses shall be housed in stables admeasuring 12ft X 12ft with adequate 4cility for the horses to see each other with adequate provision for proper ventilation and protection against heat and an environmentally- friendly atmosphere as far as possible.";

(iv) the following proviso shall be added at the end, namely

"Provided that if the whip is used more than eight times in race, the prescribed authority in consultation with the Turf Authorities shall decide, if the use of such whip in excess of the number specified, was for any reason to save the horse or the jockey from any accident, for the purpose of initiating any action under the Act.";

(c) in clause xx, at the end, the following shall be added namely:

"and the use of steroids shall be avoided as far as possible provided the steroids may be used if no other option is available to be supported by a veterinary prescription and the 'purchase of such steroids shall be from a duly authorized source.";

(d) after clause xxiv, the following new clause shall be inserted, namely:

"xxv. 'persons desirous of transporting horses from one place to another shall adhere to the following minimum norms to enhance conditions of travel as also safety of the horses, namely:-

(a) no horse shall be tied up in such a way that his head and neck movements are unnaturally restricted while travelling.

(b) all horses must be watered at least every four hours and provided adequate ration of hay during the journey lasting more than eight hours.

(c) adequate ventilation and free flow of fresh air in the vehicle shall be ensured during transport:

(d) rubber mats shall preferably be used for flooring instead of straw bedding.

(e) horses shall not be transported within twenty four hours of having raced.

(f) no horse shall be raced, where the period of journey exceeds, six hours, unless twenty four hours have elapsed since completion of the travel."

S.O.271 (E) - Whereas the draft Prevention of Cruelty to Animals (Establishment and Regulation of Societies for

Prevention of Cruelty to Animals) Rules, 2000 were published as required by sub-section (1) of section 38 of the Prevention of Cruelty to Animals Act, 1960 (59 of 1960), under the notification of the Government of India in the Ministry of Social Justice and Empowerment number S.0 1166 (E) dated the 2611 December, 2000 in the Gazette of India, Extraordinary, Part 11, Section 3, Sub Section (ii) dated the 27th December, 2000 inviting objections and suggestions from all persons likely to be affected thereby, before the expiry of the period of sixty days from the date on which copies of the Gazette containing the said notification are made available to the public.

And, whereas, copies of the said Gazette were made available to the public on the 1 st January 2001.

And, whereas no objection or suggestion has been received from the public in respect of the said draft rules by the Central Government.

Now, therefore, in exercise of the powers conferred by sub-sections (1) and (2) of section 38 of the Prevention of Cruelty to Animals Act, 1960 (59 of 1960) the Central Government hereby makes the following rules, namely :

1. Short title and commencement - (1) These rules may be called the Prevention of Cruelty to Animals (Establishment and Regulation of Societies for Prevention of Cruelty to Animals) Rules, 2001

(2) They shall come into force on the date of their publication in the Official Gazette.

2. Definitions - In these rules, unless the context otherwise requires.

(a) "Act" means the Prevention of Cruelty to Animals Act, 1960 (59 of 1960)

(b) "Animal Welfare Organisation" means a Welfare Organisation for animals which is registered under the Societies Registration Act of 1860 (21 of 1860) or any other corresponding law for the time being in force and recognised by the Board or the Central Government.

(c) "Board" means the Animal Welfare Board of India established under the Act.

(d) "local authority, means a municipal board of municipal committee, a State Animal Welfare Board, district board or any local animal welfare organisation authorised by any law for the control and administration of any matter relating to animals within a specified local areas.

(e) "Society" means Society for Prevention of Cruelty to Animals (hereinafter referred to as SPCA) established in any district under the Societies Registration Act, 1860 (21 of 1860) or any other corresponding law applicable in a state and shall include the existing SPCA functioning in any district.

(f) "veterinary doctor" means a person registered with the Veterinary Council of India established under the Indian Veterinary Council Act, 1984 (52 of 1984).

3. Society for Prevention of Cruelty to animals in a district-(1) Every State Government shall by notification in the Official Gazette, establish, as soon as may be and in any event within six months from the date of commencement of these rules, a society for every district in the State to be the SPCA in that district.

Provided that any society for Prevention of Cruelty to Animals functioning in any district on the date of commencement of these rules shall continue to discharge its functions till establishment of the SPCA in that district under these rules.

(2) The Managing Committee of the Society shall be appointed by the State Government or the local authority of the district consisting of a Chairperson to be appointed by the State Government or the local authority of the district, as the case may be with the concurrence of the Board and shall consist of such number of other members as may be considered necessary by the State Government or the local authority of the district subject to the condition that

(i) at least two members shall be representatives of the Animal Welfare Organisations which are actively involved in the work of prevention of cruelty to animals and welfare of animals preferably from within the district; and

(ii) at least two members shall be the persons elected by the general body of members of the Society.

(3) The duties and powers of the Society shall be to aid the Government, the Board and local authority in enforcing the provisions of the Act and to make such bye-laws and guidelines as it may deem necessary for the efficient discharge of its duties.

(4) The Society, or any person authorized by it in this behalf, if it or he has reasonable grounds for believing that any person has committed an offence under the Act, it or such authorized person may require such person to produce forthwith any animal in his possession, control, custody or ownership, or any license, permit or any other document granted to such person or required to be kept by him under the provisions of the Act and may stop any vehicle or enter into any premises in order to conduct a search or inquiry and may seize an animal in respect of which it or such authorized person has reason to believe that an offence under the Act is being committed, and deal with it in accordance with law.

(5) In addition to the powers conferred by these rules, the State Government may, in consultation with the Board, confer such other powers upon any Society for exercising the powers and discharging the functions assigned to it under these rules.

4. Setting up of infirmaries and animal shelters - (1) Every State Government shall provide adequate land and other facilities to the Society for the purpose of constructing infirmaries and animal shelters.

(2) Every infirmary and animal shelter shall have -

(i) a full time veterinary doctor and other staff for the effective running and maintenance of such infirmary or animal shelter; and

(ii) an administrator who shall be appointed by the Society.

(3) Every Society shall, through its administrator or otherwise, supervise the overall functioning of the infirmaries and animal shelters under its control and jurisdiction.

(4) All cattle pounds and pinjrapoles owned and run by a local authority shall be managed by such authority jointly with the Society or Animal Welfare Organisations.

5. Regulation of SPCAs

(1) Every Society shall submit its annual report to the Board incorporating therein the activities undertaken by it for the welfare of animals and the steps or measures taken by it to implement various provisions of the Act and the rules made thereunder along with annual accounts duly audited by a chartered accountant or any other body authorised by law within a period of one month from the date of its accounts having been finalised by its managing committee.

(2) The Board shall examine such annual report and the annual accounts submitted by the Society and may give any directions to it for improvement of its functioning including the supercession of the managing committee of the Society with a view to give effect to the provisions of the Act and the rules made thereunder.

Provided that the Board shall give opportunity of personal hearing to the office bearers of the Society or any representative authorised by it before giving direction of its supercession and holding of fresh elections for electing a new managing committee as per bye-laws of the society.

(3) The Board shall give any direction to any Society in the interest of smooth and efficient functioning of the Society including the procedure for holding the election of the managing committee of the Society, utilisation of financial resources and management of assets of the Society with a view to give effect to the provisions of the Act and the rules made thereunder.

S.O.270(E) - Whereas the draft Prevention of Cruelty to Animals (Slaughter House) Rules, 2000 were published, as required by sub-section (1) of section 38 of the Prevention of Cruelty to Animals Act, 1960 (59 of 1960), under the notification of the Government of India in the Ministry of Social Justice and Empowerment number S.O. 1165 (E) dated the 26th December, 2000 in the Gazette of India, Extraordinary, Part II,

Section 3, Sub Section (ii) dated the 27th December, 2000 inviting objections and suggestions from all persons likely to be affected thereby, before the expiry of the period of sixty days from the date on which copies of the Gazette containing the said notification are made available to the public.

And, whereas copies of the said Gazette were made sufficient for livestock subject to veterinary inspection available to the public on the 1st January 2001.

And, whereas no objection or suggestion has been received from the public in respect of the said draft rules by the Central Government.

Now, therefore, in exercise of the powers conferred by sub-sections (1) and (2) of section 38 of the Prevention of Cruelty to Animals Act, 1960 (59 of 1960), the Central Government hereby makes the following rules, namely :

1. Short title and commencement: (1) These rules may be called the Prevention of Cruelty to Animals (Slaughter House) Rules, 2001 (2) They shall come into force on the date of their publication in the Official Gazette

2. Definitions - In these rules unless the context otherwise requires - a) "Act" means the Prevention of Cruelty to Animals Act, 1960 (59 of 1960); b) "Slaughter" means the killing or destruction of any animal for the purpose of food and includes all the processes and operations performed on all such animals in order to prepare it for being slaughtered. c) "Slaughter house" means a slaughter house wherein 10 or more than 10 animals are slaughtered per day and is duly licensed or recognised under a Central, State or Provincial Act or any rules or regulations made thereunder. d) "veterinary doctor' means a person registered with the Veterinary Council of India established under the Indian Veterinary Council Act, 1984 (52 of 1984).

3. Animals not to be slaughtered except in recognised or licensed houses - (1) No person shall slaughter any animal within a municipal area except in a slaughter house recognised or licensed by the concerned authority empowered under the law for the time being in force to do so. (2) No animal which- (i) is pregnant, or (ii) has an offspring less than three months old, or (iii) is under the age of three months or (iv) has not been certified by a veterinary doctor that it is in a fit condition to be slaughtered. (3) The municipal or other local authority specified by the Central Government for this purpose shall, having regard to the capacity of the slaughter house and the requirement of the local population of the area in which a slaughter house is situated, determine the maximum number of animals that may be slaughtered in a day.

4. Reception area or resting grounds -

(1) The slaughter house shall have a reception area of adequate size sufficient for livestock subject to veterinary inspection.

(2) The veterinary doctor shall examine thoroughly not more than 12 animals in an hour and not more than 96 animals in a day.

(3) The veterinary doctor after examining the animal shall issue a fitness certificate in the form specified by the Central Government for this purpose.

(4) The reception area of slaughter house shall have proper ramps for direct unloading of animals from vehicles or railway wagons and the said reception area shall have adequate facility sufficient for feeding and watering of animals.

(5) Separate isolation pens shall be provided in slaughter house with watering and feeding arrangements for animals suspected to be suffering from contagious and infectious diseases, and fractious animals, in order to segregate them from the remaining animals.

(6) Adequate holding area shall be provided in slaughter house according to the class of animals to be slaughtered and the said holding area shall have water and feeding facilities.

(7) The resting grounds in slaughter house shall have overhead protective shelters.

(8) Ante-mortem and pen area in slaughter house shall be paved with impervious material such as concrete non-slippery herring-bone type suitable to stand wear and tear by hooves, or brick, and pitched to suitable drainage facilities and the curbs of said impervious material 150 to 300 mm high shall be provided around the borders of livestock pen area, except at the entrances and such pen shall preferably be covered.

5. *Lairages* -

(1) Every animal after it has been subjected to veterinary inspection shall be passed on to a lairage for resting for 24 hours before slaughter.

(2) The lairage of the slaughter house shall be adequate in size sufficient for the number of animals to be [aired;

(3) The space provided in the pens of such lairage shall be not less than 2.8 sq.mt. per large animal and 1.6 sq.mt. per small animal;

(4) The animals shall be kept in such lairage separately depending upon their type and class and such lairage shall be so constructed as to protect the animals from heat, cold and rain;

(5) The lairage shall have adequate facilities for watering and post-mortem inspection.

6. *Slaughter* -

(1) No animal shall be slaughtered in a slaughter house in sight of other animals

(2) No animal shall be administered any chemical, drug or hormone before slaughter except drug for its treatment for any specific disease or ailment.

(3) The slaughter halls in a slaughter house shall provide separate sections of adequate dimensions sufficient for slaughter of individual animals to ensure that the animal to be slaughtered is not within the sight of other animals.

(4) Every slaughter house as soon as possible shall provide a separate space for stunning of animals prior to slaughter, bleeding and dressing of the carcasses

(5) Knocking section in slaughter house may be so planned as to suit the animal and particularly the ritual slaughter; if any and such knocking section and dry landing area associated with it shall be so built that escape from this section can be easily carried out by an operator without allowing the animal to pass the escape barrier.

(6) A curbed-in bleeding area of adequate size as specified by the Central Government shall be provided in a slaughter house and it shall be so located that the blood could not be splashed on other animals being slaughtered or on the carcass being skinned.

(7) The blood drain and collection in a slaughter house shall be immediate and proper

(8) A floor wash point shall be provided in a slaughter house for intermittent cleaning and a hand-wash basin and knife sterilizer shall also be provided for the sticker to sterilize knife and wash his hands periodically.

(9) Dressing of carcasses in a slaughter house shall not be done on floor and adequate means and tools for dehiding or belting of the animals shall be provided in a slaughter house with means for immediate disposal of hides or skins;

(10) Hides or skins shall be immediately transported from a slaughter house either in a closed wheelbarrow or by a chute provided with self-closing door and in no case such hides or skins shall be spread on slaughter floor for inspection

(11) Floor wash point and adequate number of hand wash basins with sterlizer shall be provided in a dressing area of a slaughter house with means for immediate disposal of legs, horns, hooves and other parts of animals through spring load floor chutes or sidewall doors or closed wheelbarrows and in case wheelbarrows or trucks are used in a slaughter house, care shall be taken that no point wheelbarrow or truck has to ply under the dressing rails and a clear passage is provided for movement of the trucks.

(12) Adequate space and suitable and properly located facilities shall be provided sufficient for inspection of the viscera

of the various types of animals slaughtered in a slaughter house and it shall have adequate facilities for hand washing, tool sterilisation and floor washing and contrivances for immediate separation and disposal of condemned material.

(13) Adequate arrangements shall be made in a slaughter house by its owner for identification, inspection and correlation of carcass, viscera and head.

(14) In a slaughter house, a curbed and separately drained area or an area of sufficient size, sloped 33 mm per metre to a floor drain, where the carcasses may be washed with a jet of water, shall be provided by the owner of such slaughter house.

7. *Slaughter house building* - The different construction of a slaughter house shall be built and maintained by its owner in the manner as specified below, namely :

a) Plant Building - (i) Materials used shall be impervious, easily cleansable, and resistant to wear and corrosion. (ii) Materials such as wood, plaster board, and porous acoustic-type boards, which are absorbent and difficult to keep clean shall not be used.

b) Floors - The floors shall be non-absorbent and nonslippery with rough finish and shall have suitable gradient for drainage.

c) Coves - Coves with radii sufficient to promote sanitation shall be installed at the juncture of floors and wall, in all rooms and which shall not be less than 100 mm

(d) Interior Walls - (i) interior walls shall be smooth and flat and constructed of impervious materials such a glazed brick, glazed tile, smooth surface Portland cement plaster, or other non toxic, non-absorber material applied to a suitable base. (ii) Walls shall b provided with suitable sanitary type bumpers to prevent damage by hand trucks, carcass shunks, and the like. (iii) The interior walls shall have washable surface up to the height of 2 meters from the floor so that the splashes may be washed and disinfected.

(e) Ceilings - (i) Ceilings shall be of the height of 5 mts or more in workrooms and so far as structure conditions permit,

ceilings shall be smooth and flat (ii) Ceilings shall be constructed of Portland cement plaster, large size cement asbestos boards with join sealed with a flexible sealing compound, or other acceptable impervious material and finished so as minimise condensation, mould development, flaking and accumulation of dirt. (iii) The walls above glazed type portion and ceiling shall be painted with water resistant paint to maintain them clean.

(f) Window Ledges - Window ledges shall be sloped 45 degrees to promote sanitation and to avoid damage to glass in windows from impact of hand trucks and similar equipment, the windowsills shall be 1200 mm above the floor level with proper ventilation through mechanical venting or through working vents shall be provided in the roof structure.

(g) Doorways and Doors - (i) Doorways through which product is transferred on rails or in hand trucks shall be at least 1500 mm high and shall be atleast 1500 mm wide. (ii) Doors shall either be of rust-resistant metal construction throughout, or if made with rust resistant metal having tight softwood, they shall be clad on both sides with soldered or welded seams. (iii) Doorjambs shall be clad with rust-resistant metal securely affixed so as to provide no crevices for dirt or vermin and the juncture at which the door joins the walls shall be effectively sealed with a flexible sealing compound.

(h) Screens and Insect control - All windows, doorways and other openings that may admit flies shall be equipped with effective insect and rodent screens and 'Fly chaser' fans and ducts or air curtains shall be provided over doorways in outside wall of food handing areas that are used for dispatch or receiving.

(i) Rodent-Proofing-Except in the case of solid masonry, walls constructed of glazed tile, glazed brick, and the like, expanded metal or wire mesh not exceeding 12.5 mm mesh, shall be embedded in walls and floor at their junction and such mesh shall extend vertically and horizontally to a sufficient distance to exclude the entrance of rats and other rodents.

(j) Vehicular areas for Trucks - (i) Concrete paved areas, properly drained and extending at least 6 metres from building, loading docks or livestock platforms shall be provided at places

where vehicles are loaded or unloaded. (ii) Pressure washing jets and disinfection facilities for trucks carrying animals shall also be provided at such places.

(k) Drainage - (i) All parts of floors where wet operations are conducted shall be well drained and as far as possible, one drainage inlet shall be provi.led for each 37 metre square of floor space (ii) A slope of about 20 mm per metre to drainage inlets shall be provided for usual conditions and it shall be ensured that the floor slopes uniformly to drains with no low spots, which collect liquid. (iii) Floor drains shall not be provided in freezer rooms or dry storage areas and when floor drains are installed in rooms where the water seal in traps is likely to evaporate without replenishment, they shall be provided with suitable removable metal screw plugs.

(l) Traps and vents on drainage lines - (i) Each floor drain, including blood drains, shall be equipped with a deep seal trap (P-, U-, or S-shape) (ii) Drainage lines shall be properly vented to the outside air and be equipped with effective rodent screens.

(m) Sanitary drainage lines - Drainage line from toilet pans and urinals shall not be connected with other drainage lines within the plant and s6l not discharge into a grease catch basin and such lines shall be installed so that if leakage develops, it shall not affect the product or the equipment.

(n) Lighting and ventilation - (i) Unrefrigerated work rooms shall be provided with adequate direct natural light and ventilation or ample artificial light and ventilation by mechanical means. (ii) Uncoloured glass having a high transmissibility of light shall be used in skylights and windows (iii) The glass area shall be approximately one fourth of the floor area of a workroom and such ratio shall be increased where there are obstructions, such as adjacent buildings, overhead catwalks, and hoists, which interfere with the admittance of direct natural light. (iv) Distributed artificial lighting of much quality and at such distances as may be specified by the Central Government shall be provided at all places where adequate natural light is not available or is insufficient.

(o) Every abattoir shall be provided with distributed artificial light of an overall intensity of not less than 200 lux at the distances as may be specified by the Central Government throughout the slaughter hall and workrooms and at places where meat inspection is carried out, the overall intensity of artificial light shall be not less than 500 lux.

(p) every abattoir shall be provided with suitable and sufficient means of ventilation to the outside air and the construction of the slaughter hall shall be so arranged that the dressed carcasses are not exposed to direct sunlight;

(q) a sufficient, safe, potable and constant supply of fresh water shall be available at adequate pressure through the premises.

(r) the pressure for the general purpose of floor washing may preferably be 200 to 330 kPa for through floor cleaning

(s) for thorough and efficient washing of carcasses, a higher pressure between 1000 kPa to 1 700 kPa shall be maintained.

(t) floor washing point shall be provided preferably for minimum 37 meter square on slaughter floor and working departments;

a. a constant supply of clean hot water shall be available in the slaughter hall and workrooms during working hours and the hotwater required for frequent sterilising of equipment shall not be less than 82 degree celsius;

b. where necessary for sanitary maintenance, equipment shall be constructed and installed so as to be completely self-draining.

c. the following materials shall not be used in an abattoir, namely –

(i) copper and its alloys in equipment used for edible products.

(ii) cadmium in any form in equipment handling edible products

(iii) equipment with painted surface in product zone

(iv) enamel containers or equipment is not desirable and

(v) lead;

(u) all permanently mounted equipment shall either be installed sufficiently away from walls (minimum 300 mm) to provide access for cleaning and inspection.

(v) all permanently mounted equipment shall either be installed sufficiently above the floor (minimum 300 mm) to provide access for cleaning and inspection or be completely sealed (watertight) to the floor area.

8. Engagement in slaughter house - (1) No owner or occupier of a slaughter house shall engage a person for slaughtering animals unless he possesses a valid license or authorisation issued by the municipal or other local authority. (2) No person who has not attained the age of 18 years shall be employed in any manner in a slaughter house. (3) No person who is suffering from any communicable or infectious disease shall be permitted to slaughter an animal.

9. Inspection of slaughter house -

(1) The Animal Welfare Board of India or any person or Animal Welfare Organisation authorised by it may inspect any slaughter house without notice to its owner or the person incharge of it at any time during the working hours to ensure that the provisions of these rules are being complied with.

(2) The person or the Animal Welfare Organisation authorised under sub rule (1) shall after inspection send its report to Animal Welfare Board of India as well as to the municipal or local authority for appropriate action including initiation of legal proceedings if any, in the event of violation of any provisions of these rules.

S.O.-268 (E) - Whereas the draft Prevention of Cruelty to Animals (Transport of Animals on Foot) Rules, 2000 were published as required by sub-section (1) of section 38 of the Prevention of Cruelty to Animals Act, 1960 (59 of 1960), under the notification of the Government of India in the Ministry of

Social Justice and Empowerment number S.O. I 163(E) dated the 26th December 2000 in the Gazette of India, Extraordinary, Part II, Section 3, Sub Section (ii) dated the 27th December, 2000 inviting objections and suggestions from all persons likely to be affected thereby, before the expiry of the period of sixty days from the date on which copies of the Gazette containing the said notification are made available to the public.

And, whereas copies of the said Gazette were made available to the public on the Ist January, 2001.

And, whereas no objection or suggestion has been received from the public in respect of the said rules by the Central Government.

Now, therefore, in exercise of the powers conferred by sub-sections (1) and (2) of section 38 of the Prevention of Cruelty to Animals Act, 1960 (59 of 1960), the Central Government hereby makes the following rules, namely:

1. Short title and commencement :

(1) These rules may be called the Prevention of Cruelty 5 to Animals (Transport of Animals on Foot) Rules, 2001

(2) They shall come into force on the date of their publication in the Official Gazette.

2. Definitions.- In these rules unless the context otherwise requires

a. "animal" means livestock and includes the following animals namely - (i) cattle including cow, bulls and bullocks, buffalo bulls and bullocks, cows, buffaloes, Mithuns, yaks and calves. (ii) equines includings horses, ponies, mules and donkeys. (iii) horse including entires (stallions), goldings, brood mares, colts and fillies. (iv) goat including adult goat, male or female of two years age and above. (v) ruck including male goat. (vi) kid young goat below one year of age. (vii) nanny female goat. (viii) sheep including adult sheep, male or female of two years age and above. (ix) ewe female sheep. (x) lamb young sheep below one year of age. (xi) ram male sheep. (xii) wether includes male lamb that has been castrated before reaching sexual maturity. (xiii) pig includes adult pig, male or female of one year of age or above. (xiv) piglet includes young pig below one year of age.

b. "veterinary doctor' means a person registered with the Veterinary Council of India established under the Indian Veterinary Council Act, 1984 (52 of 1984)

c. "Schedule" means a schedule appended to these rules.

3. *Application of the rules* - These rules shall apply to transport of animals on foot when the distance from the boundary of village or town or city of the origin of such transport to the last destination is 5 km or more than 5 km.

4. *Condition of health of animals transported on foot-*

(1) Every animal to be transported on foot shall be healthy and in good condition for such transport.

(2) A certificate of a veterinary doctor in respect of each animal to be transported to the effect that such animal is in a fit condition for such transportation and is not suffering from any infectious, contagious or parasitic diseases and that it has been vaccinated against any infectious, contagious or parasitic diseases shall accompany such animal

(3) The certificate under sub rule (1) shall be in the form as specified in the First Schedule.

5. *Certain animals not to transport on foot* - New born animals of which the navel has not completely healed, diseased, blind, emaciated, lame, fatigued, or having given birth during the preceding seventy two hours or likely to give birth during transport shall not be transported on foot.

6. *Transport in on-farm social group* - Animal shall be transported in their on farm social groups (established at least one week prior to journey)

7. *First aid equipment to accompany animals transported on foot* - The owner of the animals shall provide veterinary first aid equipment to be accompanied with such animals while transported on foot.

8. Certificate to be carried during transportation - In case the person transporting the animals on foot is not the owner of the animal then such person shall carry a certificate as specified in the Second Schedule during such transportation.

9. Watering arrangement during transportation of animals- The owner of the animals shall make watering arrangement in route during transport of such animals on foot.

10. Feed and fodder arrangements during transportation of animals-Sufficient feed and fodder with adequate reserve of such feed and fodder for the animals shall be made available by their owner during their transport on foot.

11. Prohibition of the use of whip, etc during transportation of animals on foot -

(1) No person shall use a whip or a stick in order to for the animal to walk or to hasten the pace of their w nor such person shall apply chillies or any oft substance to any part of the body of the animal for this purpose during their transportation on foot.

(2) If any animal needs to be tied during transport on foot, it shall be tied by a rope covered with suitable cushioning such as cloth around its leg and such animal shall not be tied by its nose, all legs or any other part of the body except by its neck.

(3) If more than one animal is to be tied adjacent to one another by a single rope during their transport on foot, the space between any two of such animals shall be minimum two feet and animals so tied shall be of similar physical condition and strength and no more than two such animals shall be tied adjacent to each other by a single rope.

12. Certain Prohibition on transport of animals on foot

(1) No person shall transport on foot an animal before sunrise or after sunset.

(2) No animal shall be transported on foot beyond the distance, time, rest interval and temperature specified for such animal in the Table below, namely:-

TABLE

Species (Animal)	Maximum distance covered/day/hour	Maximum no. of walking/day of hours (Travelling)	Period of rest (interval)	Temperature range Max. Min
Cattle (Cows)	30 km/day 4 km/hr	8 hours	At every 2hours for drinking and at every 4 hrs for feeding	12 deg. C to 30 deg.C
Buffaloes	25 km/day 3 km/hr	8 hours	At every 2 hours for drinking ano at every 4 hrs for feeding	12 deg. C to 30 deg. C
Cows and Buffaloes Calves	16 km/day 2.5 km/hr	6 hours	At every 1½ hrs for drinking and at every 3 hrs. for feeding	15 deg. C to 25 deg.C
Horses, Ponies, Mules, Donkeys	45 km/day 6 km/hr	8 hours	At every 3 hrs for drinking and at every 6 hrs. for feeding	12 deg. C to 30 deg. C
Young ones (Foal)	25 km/day 4 km/hr	6 hours	At every 2hrs. for drinking and at every 4 hrs. for feeding	15 deg. C to 25 deg. C
Goats and Sheep	30 km/day 4 km/hr	8 hours	At every 2 hrs. for drinking and at every 4 hrs. for feeding	12 deg. C to 30 deg. C
Kids and Lambs	16 km/day 2.5km/hr	6 hours	At every 1 1/2 hrs. for drinking and at every 3 hrs. for feeding	15 deg. C to 25 deg. C
Pigs	15 km/day 2 km/hr	8 hours	At every 1 Y2 hrs. for drinking and at every 3 hrs. for feeding	12 deg. C to 25deg. C
Piglets	10 krn/day 1.5 km/hr	6 hours	At every 1 Y2hrs. for drinking and at every 3 hrs. for feeding	15 deg. C to 25 deg. C

Note : After being provided with water every animal shall be given a break of 20 minutes before the commencement of the transport of the animal on foot and in case of feeding the break shall be given for one hour before the commencement of the transport of the animal on foot.

(3) No animal shall be made to walk under conditions of heavy rain, thunderstorms or extremely dry or sultry conditions during its transport on foot.

13. Transportation of animals in certain cases not permitted without shoes - Animals whose hooves are not provided with shoes (as in the case of pack or draught animals) shall not be transported on foot on hard cement, bitumen-coated or metalled roads, steep gradients or hilly and rocky terrain, irrespective of weather conditions (summer or winter)

14. Power of Police to require the owner to take animal to nearest Magistrate

(1) If any police officer above the rank of constable or any other person authorised in this behalf by the Central or state Government or by the Animal Welfare Board of India by the general or special order, has reason to believe that an offence has been or is being committed in respect of an animal in contravention of these rules, he may require the owner or other person in charges of such animal to take the animal to the nearest magistrate

(2) If the owner or the person in charge of the animals referred to in sub rule (1) refuses to comply with the demands of the police officer under that sub rule, it shall be lawful for such police officer or such other persons to take the animal to the nearest magistrate.

S.O. 134(E).—Whereas certain draft rules to amend the Breeding of and Experiments on Animals (Control and Supervision) Rules, 1998 were published, as required by sub-section (1) of section 17 of the Prevention of Cruelty to Animals Act, 1960 (59 of 1960) under the notification of the Government of India in the Ministry of Social Justice and Empowerment number S.O. 168(E) dated the 18th February, 2000 inviting objections and suggestions from all the persons likely to be affected thereby, before the expiry of the period of thirty days from the date on which copies the Gazette containing the said notification are made available to the public;

And whereas the said Gazette was made available to the public on 24th February, 2000;

And whereas the objections/suggestions received in respect of the said draft rules, have been duly considered by the

Committee for control, and supervision of experiments on animals; Now, therefore, in exercise of the powers conferred by sub-sections (1), (1A) and (2) of section 17 of the Prevention of Cruelty to Animals Act, 1960 (59 of 1960), the Committee for control am supervision of experiments on animals hereby makes the following rules to amend the Breeding of and Experiments on Animals (Control and Supervision) rules, 1998, namely:-

1. (1) These rules may be called the Breeding of and Experiments on animals (Control and Supervision) Amendment Rules, 2001. (2) They shall come Into force on the date of their publication in the Official Gazette.

2. In the Breeding of and Experiments on Animals (Control and Supervision) Rules, 1998 (hereinafter referred to as the sold rules), In rule 2, for the existing clause (e), the following clause shall be substituted, namely: (e) "experiment" means any programme/project Involving use of an animal/animals for the acquisition of knowledge of a biological, psychological, ethological, physical or chemical nature; and Includes ,the use of animal In the production of reagents and products such as ,antigens and antibodies, routine diagnostics, testing activity and establishment of transgenic stocks, for the purpose of, saving or prolonging life or alleviating suffering or for combating any disease whether on human beings or animals.

3. In the said rules, in rule 5, for sub-rule (c the following sub-rules shall be substituted, namely:-

"(c) A breeder or the establishment on registration for the purpose of performing experiments on animals shall comply with the conditions as may be specified at the time of registration by the Committee.

(d) The Committee or any other-officer authorized In this regard by the Committee shall take decision on the registration within three months of making the application.

(e) if any modification of facilities are required before registration, the details needed shall be communicated by the Committee."

(4) In the said rules, for rule 6, the following rule shall be substituted, namely:-

"6. Detail; of the experiments conducted:- (a) Every registered establishment shall- maintain a register of particulars about the animals used from: day to day for conducting experiments, with the number of animals, the species, the age, gender and other relevant particulars

"(b) "The Committee or any other officer authorized by the Committee may examine the register so maintained and if the Committee is not satisfied even after opportunities given for Improvement, It may take such action as may be appropriate under these rules"..

(5) In the said rules, in rule 7, after the existing condition (f), the following conditions shall be inserted, namely:-

"(g) - detailed specifications for housing, feeding and maintenance of various species to be used In animal experimentation as notified by the Committee, shall be adhered to by the registered establishment.

(h) In the Interim period fill such detailed specifications are notified, the breeders and establishments shall comply with the Indian National Science Academy Guidelines."

(6) In the said rules, in rule 9, - (i) for the existing condition (a), the following condition shall be substituted, namely:-

"(a) experiments shall be performed in every case by or under the supervision of a person duly qualified in that behalf, that is, Degree holders In Medicine or Veterinary Science, Post Graduate and above in life Sciences/Pharmaceutical Sciences or any other natural sciences, Degree or Diploma holders in Pharmacy, Diploma or Certificate In Laboratory Animal Techniques Sciences from a recognized Institution as Identified by Committee for the Purpose of Control and Supervision of Experiments on Animals for the purpose and under the responsibility of the person performing the experiment,";

(ii) for the -existing, condition (g), the following condition shall be substituted, namely:

(g) the experiments shall not be performed for the sole purpose of attaining or retaining manual skill except In schools, colleges and programmes duly scrutinized and permitted in registered establishments by the Committee;";

(iii) in the existing condition for the words, "the substance known as urari or curare or any such paralysan shall not be used", the words "no paralyzing agent, Including but not limited to curare, shall be used" shall be substituted.

7. In the said rules, in rule 10,-

(i) for sub-rule (b), the following sub-rules shall be substituted, namely:-

"(b) A breeder or establishment shall not acquire -any animal by sale or otherwise except from a registered breeder or establishment.

(bb) For the acquisition of laboratory bred experimental rats and mice species of genetically defined strains not available within the country, the registered breeders or establishments shall apply for permission to the Institutional Animal Ethics Committee recognized by the Committee for the Purpose of Control and Supervision of Experiments on Animals."

(ii) for sub-rule (e), the following-sub-rule shall be substituted, namely:-

"(e) No animal shall be Imported by a registered breeder or establishment, except genetically defined or laboratory bred experimental rats an! d mice of genetically defined strains, which is available in the country."

8. In the said rules, for rule 12, the following rule shall be substituted, namely:-

"12. Contract animal experiments. - No establishment shall contract or undertake to perform contract research or experiments on contract basis on behalf of any other establishment or research or educational Institution, except with prior permission of the committee:

Provided that no such restriction shall apply to collaborative research between academic Institutions."

S.O. 1074.—Whereas the draft Breeding of and Experiments on Animals (Control and Supervision) Rules, 1998 were published, as required by sub section (1) of Section 17 of, the Prevention of Cruelty to Animals Act, 1960 (59 of 1960) under the notification of the Government of India, Ministry of environment and Forests number S.O. 789(E) dated, the e September, 1998 in the Gazette of India, Extraordinary , Part II, section 31 Sub-section (ii) inviting objections and suggestion from all the persons likely to be affected thereby, before the expiry of the period of thirty days from the date on which copies of the Gazette, containing the said notification are made available to the public;

And, whereas the said Gazette was made available to the public on 8th September, 1998.

And whereas the objections/suggestions received in respect of the said draft rules, have been duly considered-by the Committee for control and supervision of experiments on animals;

Now, therefore, in exercise of the powers conferred by sub-section (1) (1A) and (2) of section 17 of the Prevention of Cruelty to Animals Act, 196 (59 of 1960), the Committee for control and supervision of experiments on animals hereby makes the following rules, namely:

1. *Short Title and commencement.* - (1) These rules may be called the Breeding of and Experiments on Animals (Control and Supervision) Rules, 1998. (2) They shall come into force on the date of their publication in the Official Gazette.

2. *Definitions.* - In these rules, unless the context otherwise requires -

(a) "Act" means the Prevention of Cruelty to Animals Act, 1960 (59 of 1960);

b. "breeder" means a person including an institution, which breeds animals for the purpose of transfer to other authorised institution for performing experiments;

c. "Committee" means the Committee under section 15 of the Act for control and supervision of experiments on animals;

(d) "establishment means any individual, company, firm, corporation, institution other than schools up to higher secondary level, which performs experiments on animals;

(e) "experiment" means any programme/project involving experiments on an animal /animals for the purpose of advancement by new discovery of physiological knowledge which will be useful for saving or prolonging life or alleviating suffering or for combating any disease whether on human beings or animals;

(f) "Institutional Animals Ethics Committee" means a body comprising of a group of persons recognised and registered by the Committee for the purpose of control and supervision of experiments on animal performed in an establishment which is constituted and operated in accordance with procedures specified for the purpose by the Committee;

(g) "contract Research" means any research undertaken by an individual, company, firm, corporation or institution on behalf of a foreign individual, company, firm, corporation or institution for any consideration;

(h) "collaborative research" means any research undertaken between two or more research institutions on an equal footing which does not involve any financial or monetary considerations and is undertaken solely for the purpose of advancement of scientific research and human welfare;

(i) "specified format" means the form specified for the purpose by the Committee from time to time.

3. Breading of animals - (a) No establishment shall carry on the business of breeding of animals or trade of animals for the purpose of experiments unless it is registered.

(b) Every breeder/establishment carrying on the business of breeding animals or trade of animals for the purpose of experiments, shall, apply for registration within sixty days from the date of commencement of these rules and, stop breeding of animals if registration is subsequently refused to it by the Committee.

4. *Registration of establishments.* - (a) No establishment shall perform any experiment on animals unless it is registered. (b) Every establishment performing experiments on animals, shall, apply for registration within sixty days from the date of commencement of these rules and, stop performing experiments on animals if registration is subsequently refused to it by the Committee.

5. *Application for registration.* - (a) The application for registration by a breeder under sub-rule (b) of rule 3 and an establishment under sub-rule (b) of rule 4 shall be made in the specified format to the Member- Secretary or any other officer authorised in this regard by the Committee. (b) The Member-Secretary or the authorised officer of the Committee, may for deciding the issue of registration, ask for information relating to premises where the experiments are to be conducted, animal housing facilities, details of breeding of animals and its trade, other infrastructure including availability of manpower trained in handling animals and for verification of facts mentioned in the application for registration, and if satisfied, shall register such establishment or the breeder. (c) A breeder or the establishment on registration for the purpose of performing experiments on animals shall comply with the conditions as may be specified, at the time of registration, by the Member-Secretary of the Committee or any officer authorised in this regard by the Committee.

6. *Details of the experiments conducted.* - (a) Every registered establishment shall maintain a register as per the specified format and keep complete particulars about the kind of animal to be used for conducting any experiment, the health of the animal, the nature of experiment to be performed, and the reasons necessitating the performance of such an experiment on particular species. (b) The Member-Secretary or the officer authorised by the Committee in this behalf may examine the register so maintained, and if, he is not satisfied irrespective -of the -opportunity given for improvement, he may bring the same to the notice of the Committee seeking directions in this regard.

7. Stocking of animals.— The animals shall be stocked by the breeder and the establishment in the following manner:-

(a) animal houses shall be located in a quiet atmosphere undisturbed by traffic, and the premises kept tidy, hygienic and the animals protected from drought and extremes of weather;

(b) animal cages for small animals and stables for large animals shall be such that animals can live in comfort and overcrowding is avoided;

(c) where standards have been laid down by the Indian Standards Institution, the cages, the stable, as the case may be, shall conform to those standards;

(d) animals attendants must be suitably trained and experienced in the duties allotted to them,

(e) animals shall be looked after, before and after the experiments by a trained and experienced attendant;

(f) there-shall be satisfactory arrangement for looking after the animals during off hours and on holidays,

8. Permission of the Committee required for conducting experiments. - (a) Every registered establishment before acquiring an animal or conducting any experiment on an animal/ animals shall apply for permission of the Committee or the Institutional Animals Ethics Committee recognised for the purpose by the Committee along with the details contained in the specified format to the Member Secretary of the Committee or the Institutional Animals Ethics Committee, as the case may be.

(b) The Member Secretary of the Committee or the Institutional Animals Ethics Committee, shall cause the application for permission to be brought before the Committee/ Institutional Animals Ethics Committee as the case may be, and the Committee/ Institutional Animals Ethics Committee after scrutiny of the application, if satisfied, may grant permission to the establishment stating the name of the species and the number of animals that can be acquired for carrying out the experiments.

(c) The Committee or Institutional Animals Ethics Committee, as the case may be, may, while granting permission for conducting experiments on animals, put conditions as it may deem fit to ensure that animals are not subjected to unnecessary pain or suffering before, during or after the performance of experiments on them.

(d) The Committee may require the establishments and Institutional Animals Ethics Committees and persons carrying on experiments on animals to forward to the Committee such information as it may require, on completion of experiments for which the permission has been granted.

9. Performance of experiments.- In conducting experiments on animals, regard shall be had to the following conditions, namely:

(a) experiments shall be performed in every case by or under the supervision of a person duly qualified in that behalf, that is, Degree or Diploma holders in Veterinary Science or Medicine or Laboratory Animal Science of a University or an Institution recognised by the Government for the purpose and under the responsibility of the person performing the experiment;

(b) experiments shall be performed with due care and humanity;

(c) animals intended for the performance of experiments are properly looked both before and after experiments;

(d) experiments involving operative procedure more severe than simple inoculation or superficial venesection shall be performed under the influence of anaesthetic to prevent the animal feeling pain and it shall remain so throughout the experiment. Anesthesia shall be administered by a Veterinary Surgeon trained in methods of anesthesia or a Scientist/ technician so trained for this purpose and who shall remain present near the animal till the completion of the experiment;

(e) animals which in the course of experiments under the influence of anaesthetic are so injured that their recovery would involve pain or suffering shall be destroyed humanely while still under the influence of anesthesia;

(f) when there is reason to believe that an animal is suffering abnormal or severe pain at any stage of a continuing experiment, it shall be painlessly destroyed at that stage without proceeding with the experiment;

(g) the experiment shall not be performed for the purpose of attaining or retaining manual skill except in schools, colleges and recognised training institutions;

(h) experiments shall not be performed by way of an illustration;

(i) experiments shall not be performed as a public demonstration;

(j) the substance known as Urari or Curari or any such paralysan shall riot be used or administered for the purpose of any experiment except in conjuction with anaesthetic of sufficient depth to produce loss of consciousness;

(k) no experiment the result of which is already conclusively known, shall be repeated without previous justification;

(l) there shall not be applied to the eye of an animal by way of experiment any chemical substance for the purpose of absorption through the conjunctival membrane or through the cornea calculated to only give pain;

(m) dogs held for experimental purposes shall not be debarked.

(n) where experiments are performed in any institution, the responsibility therefor is placed on the person in charge of the institution and in cases where experiments are performed outside an institution by an individual qualified in that behalf, the-experiments, are performed on his responsibility.

10. Transfer and acquisition of animals for experiment. -

(a) A breeder shall not transfer any animal by sale or otherwise to an establishment which is not registered under these' rules.

(b) An establishment shall not acquire any animal by sale or otherwise except from a registered breeder/establishment.

(c) Every establishment after acquisition of a animal or animals shall not transfer such animal or animals by sale or otherwise to any other establishment or person except to a registered breeder/establishment.

(d) The animals used for experimentation in a production/ breed improvement programme may be given out by the breeder' institution for domestic use.

(e) No animal shall be imported by a breeder or an establishment which is available in the country.

(f) A breeder or establishment shall comply, with the directions given by the Committee for the purpose of controlling and supervising experiments on animals.

11. Records.

(a) Every, establishment/Institutional Animals Ethics Committee shall maintain a record of the animals under its control and custody in the specified format..

(b) Every establishment/Institutional Animals Ethics Committee shall furnish such information, as the Committee may from time to time require in the specified format.

(c) All laboratories shall inform the exact number/ species of animals to the Member Secretary or any officer authorised in this regard by the Committee as per the specified format.

12. Contract animal experiments.- No establishment shall contract or undertake to perform contract research or experiments on contract basis on behalf of any other establishment or research or educational Institution, This shall not apply to collaborative research between academic institutions.

13. Composition of Institutional Animals Ethics Committee.- Every Institutional Animals Ethics committee shall include a biological scientist, two scientists from different biological disciplines, a veterinarian involved in the care of animal, the scientist in charge of animals facility of the establishment concerned, a scientist from, outside the institute, a non scientific socially aware member and a representative or nominee of the specialist may be co-opted while reviewing special project using hazardous agents such as radio-active substance and deadly micro organisms.

14. Power to suspend or revolve registration. -

(a) If the Committee is satisfied, on the report of the Member-Secretary of the authorised officer of the Committee made to it as a result of any inspection or information received otherwise that the rules made by it are not being complied with by any establishment or breeder or an Institutional Animals Ethics Committee, the Committee may, after giving a reasonable opportunity to the establishment or breeder or Institutional Animals Ethics Committee of being heard in the matter, revoke the registration of such establishment or breeder or Institutional Animals Ethics Committee either for a specified period or indefinitely, or may allow the establishment of- breeder or Institutional Animals Ethics Committee to carry on subject to such special conditions as the Committee may impose.

(b) The Committee may, pending the final determination, if, it is of the opinion that an establishment or breeder has prima facie failed to comply with the provisions of these Riles, suspend the registration of such establishment or the breeder.

(c) The Committee may in the event of revocation or suspension of registration of an establishment or breeder, issue such directions as it, deems fit for the care and protection of the animals which are under the custody or control of such establishment or the breeder.

(d) That in the event of suspension or revocation of a license, such establishment or breeder shall forthwith on the communication of the order cease to perform any experiment on, any animal or acquire or transfer any animal.

S.O. 732(E)—Whereas certain draft rules further to amend the Experiments on Animals (Control and Supervision) Rules, 1968, was published as required by sub-section (1) of section 17 of the Prevention of Cruelty of Animals Act, 1960 (59 of

1960) under the notification of the Government of India in the Ministry of Environment and Forests vide number S.O.44(E) dated, the 15th January, 1998, inviting objections and suggestions from all persons likely to be affected thereby before the expiry of a period of 30 days from the date on which the copies of the Gazette containing the said notification are made available to the public;

And whereas the said Gazette was made available to the public on 15th January, 1998;

And whereas the objections and suggestions received from the public on the said draft rules have been duly considered by the Committee.

Now, therefore, in exercise of the powers conferred by Section 17 of the Prevention of Cruelty of Animals Act, 1960 (59 of 1960), the Committee for control and supervision of experiments on animal hereby makes the following rules further to amend the Experiments on Animals (control and Supervision) Rules, 1968, namely:-

1. (1) These rules may be called the Experiments on Animals (controls and Supervision) (Amendment) Rules, 1998. (2) The Shall come into force on the date of their publication in the Official Gazette.

2. In the Experiments on Animals (controls and Supervision) Rules, 1968, i. in rule 2, after clause (c), the following clause shall be inserted, namely:- (d) "Animal-control authority", used with reference to an animals, includes any public or private authority, shelter or pound in possession or custody of the animal; ii. after rule 4, the following rule shall be inserted, namely:-

"4A, Restriction on sale, etc., of animals for experiments.

1. No officer, employee or agent of any animal-control authority shall sell, give, transfer, trade, supply or otherwise provide any animal coming into his or her possession to nay animal dealer, commercial kennel, pet shop, laboratory, educational institution or other scientific, biomedical or veterinary purposes.

2. No hospital, educational institution, laboratory or any person shall purchase or accept any dog or cat not purposely bred for research from any animal-control authority, commercial kennel or animal dealer for use in research product development, testing, education, biologicals production, or other scientific, biomedical, or veterinary purpose."

S.O. No. 1056 dated the 13th March 1979 - Whereas a draft of the Prevention of Cruelty to Animals (Capture of animals) Rules,1978 was published as required by clause (i) of sub-section (2) of Section 38 of Prevention of Cruelty to Animals Act, 1960 (59 of 1960), at pages 139 - 140 of the Gazette of India, Part 11, Section 3 Sub-Section (ii) dated the 13th January 1979 under the notification of the Government of India in the Ministry of Agriculture & Irrigation (Department of Agriculture) No.14 - 19/76-LDI dated the 30th December, 1978 inviting objections and suggestions from all persons likely to be affected thereby within a period of fortyfive days from the date of publication of the said notification in the Official Gazette.

And whereas the said Gazette was made available to the public on the 13th January 1979.

And whereas no objections and suggestions from the public on the said draft have been received.

Now, therefore, in exercise of the powers conferred by clause (i) of subsection (2) of Section 38 of the Prevention of Cruelty of Animals Act, 1960 (59 of 1960), the Central Government hereby makes the following rules, namely:

1. Short Title and commencement

(1) These rules may be called the Prevention of Cruelty (Capture of Animals) Rules, 1979.

2. Capture of Birds:

No bird shall be captured for the purpose of sale, export or for any other purpose except by net method.

Explanation: A bird is said to be captured by the net method if in its capture the following contrivance is used, namely, a contrivance made of spun thread which is soft, pliable and sufficiently strong, like cotton, jute or any synthetic fibre, woven in such a way as to form a mesh of suitable size so that the bird is captured without any injury being caused to it.

3. Capture of other animals: (i) No animal shall be captured for the purpose of sale, export or for any other purpose except by sack and loop method. Provided that an animal which cannot be captured by reason of its size, nature of other condition or circumstances by the sack and loop method, may be captured with the help of tranquiliser guns or by any other method which renders the animal insensible to pain before capture.

(2) Nothing in this rule shall apply to the capture of birds.

Explanation : An animal is said to be captured by the sack and loop method if in its capture the following contrivance is used, namely a strong canvass in the form of sack, not less than 92 cms. in length and 138 cms in diameter, which has a smooth rope, not less than 5.5 meter in length passing through ten or more rings of not less than 4 cms. in diameter each attached at the open end, thus forming a loop, the sack having small holes at convenient places to enable the animal to breathe during captivity, and the animal is captured by the sack being thrown on it and secured by having the loop pulled.

THE PREVENTION OF CRUELTY TO ANIMALS (REGISTRATION OF CATTLE PREMISES) RULES, 1978.

In exercise of the powers conferred by clause (i) of sub-section (2) of section 38 of the Prevention of Cruelty to Animals Act, 1960 the Central Government hereby makes the following rules, namely

1. Short Title and application:

(1) These rules may be called the Prevention of Cruelty to Animals (Registration of Cattle Premises) Rules, 1978.

(2) These rules shall apply only to cities or towns which have a population exceeding one lakh.

(3) They shall come into force on the date of their publication in the Official Gazette.

2. Definitions: In these rules, unless the context otherwise requires : (a) "cattle" means oxen, buffaloes, cows, bullocks and horses including their young ones; (b) "Certificate" means the certificate of Registration. (c) "registering authority" means such officers of the veterinary department of the State Government or of a local authority as the State Government may, by general or special order, specify in this behalf.

3. Registration of Premises: Every person owning or in charge of premises in which not less than five heads of cattle are kept for the purpose of profit, shall, in any case, where the premises are already in existence, within three months from the commencement of these rules and, in any case where, after the commencement of these rules any such premises, apply to the registering authority for the registration of such premises.

4. Application for Registration: Every application for registration shall contain full information regarding the number and types of animals kept or to be kept, the purpose for which they are being kept or are to be kept, the provision made or to be made as respects floor space, flooring, ventilation, supply of food and water, disinfection, drainage, disposal of dung or unwanted matter, boundary walls and shall also contain such other information relevant to the matter as may be specifically called for by the registering authority.

5. Certificate of Registration :

(i) If the registering authority is satisfied that, having regard to the information supplied, the welfare of the cattle is adequately secured and that they are not likely to undergo any unnecessary suffering, he shall register the premises and issue to the applicant a certificate in respect thereof.

(ii) Every certificate shall be valid for a period of three years from the date of issuer thereof, but it may be renewed from time to time for a period of three years at a time on application made by the person owning or in charge of the premises, within three months from the date of expiry of the existing certificate.

6. Inspection of Premises: Every premises registered under these rules shall be open for inspection at all reasonable times by any veterinary or public health officer of the local authority or of the State Government who may be authorised by the State Government in this behalf by general or special order.

7. *Cancellation of registration:* If any premises are not maintained in the manner required under these rules, the registering authority may, by notice in writing stating the grounds on which the notice proceeds and after giving an opportunity to the person concerned to show cause, cancel the certificate.

8. *Appeal:* An appeal shall lie from any order refusing or cancelling the registration of any premises under these rules to such officer or other authority as the State Government may specify in this behalf.

9. *Display of section 12 of the act:* If in any premises milch cattle are kept, there shall be displayed by the owner of cattle prominently in or near the premises, a copy of section 12 of the Prevention of Cruelty to Animals Act, 1960 (59 of 1960) (as reproduced below) in a language commonly understood in the locality.

"12. If any person performs upon any cow or other milch animal the operation called phooka or doom dev or permits such operation being performed upon any such animal in his possession or under his control, he shall be punishable with fine which may be extended to one thousand rupees, or with imprisonment for a term which may extend to two years, or with both, and the animal on which the operation was performed shall be forfeited to the Government."

10. *Saving:* If in any area to which these rules apply, any rule, regulation or bye-laws made under any law for the time being in force, by any local authority which contains the provisions for the registration or licensing of premises in which cattle or any type thereof 'are kept then such rule, regulation or bye-laws to the extent to which it contains provisions relating to cattle or any type thereof, as the case may be, shall to that extent be of no avail.

7

Transport of Animals, Rules

In exercise of the powers conferred by clause (h) of sub-section (2) of Section 38 of the Prevention of Cruelty to Animals Act, 1960 (59 of 1960); the Central Government hereby makes the following rules, the same having been previously published as required by the said Section, namely :

Transport of Animals Rules, 1978

1. Short Title : These rules may be called the Transport of Animals, Rules, 1978.

2. Definitions : In these rules, unless the context otherwise requires

(a) qualified veterinary surgeon means one who holds a diploma or a degree of a recognised veterinary college.

(b) "Schedule" means a schedule appended to these rules.

TRANSPORT OF DOGS AND CATS

3. Rules 4 to 14 shall apply to the transport of dogs and cats of all breeds whether by rail, road, inland, waterway, sea or air.

4. (a) A valid health certificate by a qualified veterinary surgeon to the effect that the dogs and cats are in a fit condition to travel by a rail, road, inland waterway, sea or air and are not showing any sign of infectious or contagious disease including rabies, shall accompany each consignment and the certificate shall be in the form specified in Schedule - A. (b) In the absence

of such a certificate, the carrier shall refuse to accept the consignment for transport.

5. No dog or cat in an advanced stage of pregnancy shall be transported.

6. (a) Dogs or cats to be transported in the same container shall be of the same species and breed. (b) Unweaned puppies of kittens shall not be transported with adult dogs or cats other than their dams. (c) No female dog or cat in season (cestrus) shall be transported with any male.

7. (a) Any dog or cat reported to be vicious or exhibiting a vicious disposition shall be transported individually in a cage, muzzeled and labelled to give warning to the handlers. (b) In extreme cases, the dogs and cats shall be adminsitered with sedative drugs by a qualified verterinary surgeon.

8. (1) When dogs or cats are to be transported for long distances: (a) they shall be fed and given water atleast two hours prior to their transport and shall not be packed for transport if they are hungry or thirsty. they should be exercised as late as possible before despatch. (b) they shall be given adequate water for drinking every four hours in summer or every six hours during winter. (c) they shall be fed once in twelve hours in the case of adult dogs or cats and they shall be fed once in four hours in the case of puppies and kittens in accordance with the instructions of the consignors if any. (e) adequate arrangements shall be made for their care and management during the journey.

(2) When the dogs or cats are to be transported by rail involving a journey of more than, six hours, an attendent shall accompany the dogs or cats to supply them with food and water on the way and the attendent shall have access to the dogs or cats for this purpose at all stations and no dog or cat shall be exposed to the direct blast of air during such journey.

9. Where dogs or cats are to be transported for short distance by road in a public vehicle, the following precautions are to be taken namely: (a) they shall be put in a cage and the cage containing the dogs or cats shall not be put on the roof of the

vehicle but shall be put inside the vehicle preferably near the end of the vehicle; (b) the vehicle transporting the dogs or cats shall as far as possible maintain constant speed, avoiding sudden stops and reducing effects of shocks and jolts to the minimum. (c) at least one attendant shall be present at all times during transit who shall ensure that proper transit conditions are observed and shall also replenish food and water whenever necessary.

10. Where dogs or cats are to be transported by air: (a) the cages shall be properly cleaned and disinfected before the dogs or cats are put in the cages. (b) sufficient paddy straw or saw dust or paper cuttings shall be provided for cats in the cages as resting material. (c) for international transport, the dogs or cats shall be kept in pressurized compartment with regulated temperature.

11. The size and type of crates for transport of dogs and cats shall confirm as clearly as may be to the size and type specified in Schedule - B and Schedule - C respectively.

12. All containers of dogs or cats shall be clearly labelled showing the names address and telephone number (if any) of the consignor.

13. The consignee shall be informed about the train or transport arrival or flight number and its time of arrival in advance.

14. Consignment of dogs or cats to be transported by rail or road shall be booked by the next passenger or main train or bus and should not be detained after accepting the consignment for booking.

TRANSPORT OF MONKEYS

15. Rules 16 to 23 shall apply to the transport of all types of monkeys from the trapping area to the nearest rail-head.

16. (a) A valid health certificate by a qualified veterinary surgeon to the effect that the monkeys are in a fit condition to travel from the trapping area to the nearest unit-head and are not showing any sign of infections or contagious disease

shall accompany each consignment. (b) In the absence of such a certificate, the carrier shall refuse to accept the consignment for transport. (c) The certificate shall be in a form specified in Schedule - D.

17. (1) Monkeys from one trapping area shall not be allowed to mix with monkeys from any other trapping area for preventing the dangers of cross - infection. (2) The time in transit from trapping area to the nearest rail-head shall be as short as possible and factors causing stress to monkeys shall be reduced to the minimum. (3) If the travel time is longer than six hours provision shall be made to feed and to give -water to the monkeys en route. (4) During transit, precautions shall be taken to protect the monkeys from extreme weather conditions and monkeys that die en route shall be removed at the earliest available opportunity.

18. Monkeys that are not completely weaned, that is, under 1.8 kilogram in weight, shall not be transported except when specifically permitted by the Central Government.

19. (a) Pregnant and nursing monkeys shall not be transported except when specifically permitted by the Central Government. (b) Pregnant and nursing monkeys as well as monkeys weighing more than 5 kilograms-shall be transported in compartmented cages.

20. All monkeys in the same cage shall be of the same species and of approximately the same weight and size.

21. Monkeys captured within their natural habitat shall be placed in new, sterilized or thoroughly cleaned cages and subsequent transfer, if any, shall also be new, disinfected or thoroughly cleaned cages.

22. Monkeys shall be transported from trapping area to the nearest rail-head by the fastest means of transport available and the monkeys shall not be left un-attended at any time during the journey.

23. 1. (a) Monkeys shall be transported in suitable wooden or bamboo cages, so constructed as not to allow the escape of the monkeys but permit sufficient passage of air ventilation.

(b) No nails, metallic projections or sharp edges shall be exposed on the exterior or in the interior of the cages. (c) Each cage shall be equipped with appropriate water and feed receptacles which are leak proof and capable of being cleaned and refilled during transit.

(2) The floor of the cages shall be made of bamboo reapers and the space between each reaper shall range between 20 mm and 30mm.

(3) To facilitate carriage of these cages, provision may be made for rope loops at the four top ends.

(4) The weight of any one loaded cage shall not exceed 45 kilograms.

(5) The following two sizes of cages shall be used.

a. 910 x 760 x 510 mm - to contain not more than twelve monkeys, weighing between 1.8 and 3.00 kilograms each or ten monkeys weighing between 3.1 and 5.0kilograms,each.

b. 710 x 710 x 510 mm - to contain not more than ten monkeys weighing between 1.8 and 3.00 kilograms each or eight monkeys weighing between 3.1 and 5.00 kilograms each. Provided that wooden cages as specified in Schedule - F to these rules may also be used for carrying monkeys from the trapping area to the nearest rail-head.

(6) The construction details of two types of cages shall be given in Schedule - E.

24. Rules 25 to 32 shall apply to transport of monkeys from a rail - head to another railhead or from a rail-head to nearest airport.

25. (a) Loading and unloading shall be carried out quickly and efficiently. c. Cages shall be stored in such a manner that ventilation is adequate and the monkeys are not exposed to drought and direct heat or cold. d. Monkeys found dead shall be removed as quickly as possible for suitable disposal.

26. The transport cages shall be in accordance with specifications given in rule 28.

27. (1) Due provision shall be made by the sender for a sufficient supply of food and water for the journey. (2) In case the journey is over six hours an attendant shall accompany the monkeys to supply them food, water, and such other things, on route and he shall have access to the monkeys for feeding, giving water and attention at all stations en route. (3) The food and water containers shall be checked at least every six hours and refilled, if necessary. (4) Monkeys shall not be disturbed during the night hours.

28. Not more than one cage shall be placed over the other and gunny packing shall be placed between two cages, when one is placed over the other.

29. Monkeys shall be brought to the airport sufficiently early.

30. Monkeys shall be provided with food and water immediately before loading on the aircraft.

31. (a) The cages shall be clearly labelled showing the name, address and telephone number (if any) of the consignor and the consignee in bold red letters. (b) The consignee shall be informed about the train in which the consignment of monkeys is being sent and its, arrival time in advance. (c) The consignment of monkeys to be transported shall be booked by the next passenger or main train and should not be detained after the consignment is accepted for booking.

32 (a) A valid health certificate by a qualified Veterinary Surgeon to the effect that the monkeys are in a fit condition to travel from the nearest rail-head to another railhead or from a rail-head to the nearest airport and are not showing any signs of infectious or contagious disease shall accompany each consignment. (b) In the absence of such a certificate, the carrier shall refuse to accept the consignment for transport. (c) The certificate shall be in a form specified in Schedule - D.

33. Rules 34 to 45 shall apply in relation to the transport of monkeys by air.

34. The time in transit shall be as short as possible and factors causing stress to monkeys shall be reduced to the minimum.

35. Monkeys that are not completely weaned, that is, under 1.8 kilograms in weight, shall not be transported except when specifically permitted by the Central Government.

36. Pregnant and nursing monkeys shall not be transported except when specifically permitted by the Central Government. Pregnant and nursing monkeys and monkeys weighing over 5 kilograms shall be transported in specially designed individual cages.

37. All monkeys in the some cage shall be of the same species and of approximately the same weight and size.

38. (1) In view of the dangers of infection, only monkeys of the same species shall be transported in the same cabin or compartment of the aircraft. (2) Apparently sick or disabled monkeys exhibiting external injuries or infested with parasites shall not be transported. (3) Transport of other species of animals, birds, fish food stuff or poisonous materials, such as pesticides and insecticides, in the same cabin or compartment shall not be permitted.

39. (1) At no time during transit shall the monkeys be left unattended when carried in a freighter aircraft. (2) At least one attendant shall be present at all times when the aircraft is on the ground.

40. (1) Monkeys shall be transported in suitable wooden cages, so constructed as not to allow the escape of the monkeys and shall allow sufficient passage of air for ventilation; no nails, metallic projections or sharp edges shall be exposed in the interior or on the exterior of such cages. Each cage shall be equipped with water and food receptacles which shall be leak - proof and be capable of being cleaned and refilled during transit. A suitable absorbent material such as saw dust shall be kept in the dropping trays. (2) The weight of any one loaded cage shall not exceed 45 kilograms in any case. (3) The following two sizes of cages shall be used: (a) 460 x 460 x 460 mm - to contain not more than ten monkeys weighing from 1.8 to 3.0 kilograms each or four monkeys weighing from 3.1 to 5.0 kilograms each; and (b) 760 x 530 x 460 mm - to contain not more than ten monkeys weighing from 1.8 to 3.0 kilograms

each or eight monkeys weighing from 3.1 to 5.0 kilograms each. (4) The construction details of the two types of cages shall be as given in Schedule - F. (5) The construction details of the two types of cages used for the transport of pregnant and nursing monkeys shall be as given in Schedule - G.

4 1. (a) The cages shall be clearly labelled showing the name, address and telephones number (if any) of the consignor and the consignee in bold red letters. (b) The consignee shall be informed in advance about the flight number of the freighter aircraft in which the consignment of monkeys is being sent and its arrival time. (c) The consignment of monkeys to be transported shall be booked by the next flight of the freighter aircraft and should not be detained after the consignment is accepted for booking.

42. (1) A valid health certificate by a qualified veterinary surgeon to the effect that the monkeys are fit to travel by air and are not showing any signs of infectious or contagious disease shall accompany each consignment of monkeys. (2) In the absence of such a certificate, the carrier shall refuse to accept the consignment for shipment. (3) The form of certificate under sub-rule (1) be as given in Schedule - D.

43. (1) The air shall be changed not less than twelve times per hour and droughts shall be avoided and there shall be no dead pockets of air. (2) Except when the monkeys are being fed and given water; they shall travel in semi darkness to make them quieter and less inclined to fight and thus give them better opportunities of resting.

44. The food and water containers shall be checked at every stop and refilled ; if necessary, and a sufficient stock of food shall be available on the aircraft and at likely stopping places.

Note : About 85 grams of food per monkey is required daily. Suitable foods are dry cereal grains or gram. It is recommended that whole gram made into biscuits or wheat meal bread should be fed. A minimum of 140 ml. of water shall be allowed for each monkey per day.

45. An empty cage of the usual dimensions with its sides covered except 50mm at the top to allow for ventilation shall

be provided in the freighter aircraft for housing the monkeys which fall sick or are injured during the journey.

TRANSPORT OF CATTLE

46. Rules 47 to 56 shall apply to the transport by rail of cows, bulls, bullocks, buffaloes, yaks and calves. (hereinafter in these rules referred to as cattle).

47. (a) A valid certificate by a qualified veterinary surgeon to the effect that the cattle are in a fit condition to travel by rail or road and are not suffering from any infectious or contagious or parasitic diseases and that they have been vaccinated against rinderpest and any other infectious or contagious or parasitic diseases, shall accompany each consignment. (b) In the absence of such a certificate, the carrier shall refuse to accept the consignment for transport. (c) The certificate shall be in the form specified in Schedule - E.

48. Veterinary first-aid equipment shall accompany all batches of cattle.

49. (a) Each consignment shall bear a label showing in bold red letters the name, address and telephone number (if any) of the consignor and consignee, the number and types of cattle being transported and quantity of rations and food provided. (b)The consignee shall be informed about the train or vehicle in which the consignment of cattle is being sent and its arrival time in advance. (c)The consignment of cattle shall be booked by the next train or vehicle and shall not be detained after the consignment is accepted for booking.

50. The average space provided per cattle in Railway wagon or vehicle shall not be less than two square metres.

51. (a) Suitable rope and platforms should be used for loading cattle from vehicles. (b) In case of railway wagon the dropped door of the wagon may be used as a ramp when loading or unloading is done to the platform.

52. Cattle shall be loaded after they are properly fed and given water.

53. Cattle in advanced stage of pregnancy shall not be mixed with young cattle in order to avoid stampede during transportation.

54. (1) Watering arrangements on route shall be made and sufficient quantities of water shall be carried for emergency. (2) Sufficient feed and fodder with adequate reserve shall be carried to last during the journey. (3) Adequate ventilation shall be ensured.

55. When cattle is to be transported by rail. (a) An ordinary goods wagon shall rry not more than ten adult cattle or fifteen calves on broad gauge, not more than six adult cattle or ten calves on metre guage, or not more than four adult cattle or six calves on narrow gauge. (b) every wagon carrying cattle shall have at least one attendant. (c) cattle shall be loaded parallel to the rails, facing each other. (d) rations for padding, such as straw, shall be placed on the floor to avoid injury if a cattle lies down and this shall not be less than 6 cms thick. (e) rations for the journey shall be carried in the middle of the wagon. (f) to provide adequate ventilation, upper door of one side of the wagon shall be kept open properly fixed and the upper door of the wagon shall have wire gauge closely welded mesh arrangements to prevent burning cinders from the engines entering the wagon and leading to fire outbreak. (g) cattle wagons should be attached in the middle of the train. (h) cooking shall not be allowed in the wagons nor hurricane lamps without chimneys. (i) two breast bars shall be provided on each side of the wagon, one at height of 60 to 80 cm and the other at 100 to 110 cm. (j) Cattle-in-milk shall be milked at least twice a day and the calves shall be given sufficient quantity of milk to drink. (k) As far as possible, cattle may be moved during the nights only. (1) during day time, if possible, they should be unloaded, fed, given water and rested and if in milk, milking shall be carried out.

56. When cattle are to be transported by goods vehicle the following precautions are to be taken namely : (a) Specially fitted goods vehicles with a special type of tail board and padding around the sides should be used. (b) Ordinary goods vehicles shall be provided with anti-slipping material, such as

coir matting or wooden baord on the floor and the superstructure, if low, should be raised. (c) no goods vehicle shall carry more than six cattle. (d) each goods vehicle shall be provided with one attendant. (e) while transporting, the cattle, the goods vehicle shall not be loaded with any other merchandise; and (f) to prevent cattle being frightened or injured, they should preferably, face the engine.

TRANSPORT OF EQUINES

57. Rules 57 to 63 shall apply to the transport by rail, road or sea or horses, mules and donkeys (hereinafter-in these rules referred to as 'equines')

58. (a) A valid certificate by a qualified veterinary surgeon to the effect that the equines are in a fit condition to travel by rail; road or sea and are not suffering from any infectious or contagious disease or diseases shall accompany each consignment. (b)In the absence of such a certificate, the carrier shall refuse to accept the consignment for transport. (c)The certificates shall be in a form specified in Schedule - 1.

59. (a) Each consignment shall bear a label showing in bold red letters the name address and telephone number (if any) of the consignor and consignee the number and type of equines being transported and quantity of rations and food provided. (b) The consignee shall be informed in advance about the train or vehicle or ship in which the consignment of equines is being sent and its arrival time. (c) The consignment of equines shall be booked by the next train or vehicle or ship and shall be accepted for booking.

60. (a) Pregnant and young equines shall not be mixed with other animals. (b) Different species of equines shall be kept separately. (c) Equines shall be loaded after being fed and given water adequately, watering arrangements shall be made enroute and sufficient food carried to last during the journey. (d) Veterinary first-aid equipment shall accompany all batches of equines. (e) Adequate ventilation shall be ensured. (f) Suitable ramps and platforms, improvised where not available, shall be used for loading and unloading equines.

61. For the transport of equines by rail, the following precautions shall be taken : (a) Equines shall be transported by passenger or mixed trains only; (b)Ordinary goods wagon when used for transportation shall carry not more than eight to ten horses or ten mules or ten donkeys on braod guage and not more than six horses or eight donkeys on metre-gauge (c) in extreme hot, water shall be sprinkled over the wagons containing equines by the railway authorities to bring down temperature. Ice slabs in specially made containers may be placed inside the wagan, if recommended by a qualified veterinary surgeon; (d) every wagon shall have two attendants if the equines are more than two in number; (e) equines shall be loaded parallel to the rails, facing each other; (f) material for padding, such as paddy, straw, shall be placed on the floor to avoid injury if an animal lies down and this shall not be less than 6 cm thick; (g) to provide adequate ventilation, upper door of the side of the wagon shall be kept open and properly fixed and the upper door of the wagon shall have wire guage closely welded mesh arrangements to prevent burning cinders from the engines entering the wagon and leading to fire break out; (h) two breast bars shall be provided on each side of the wagon, one at a height of 50 to 80 cm and the other at 110 cm.

62. For the tranport of equines by goods-vehicles, the following precautions shall be taken, namely : (a) Specially fitted vehicles with a special type of tail-board and padding around the sides shall be used ; (b) ordinary goods vehicles shall be provided with antislipping material on the floor and the super structure, if low, should be raised; (c) bamboo poles of at least 8 cm diameter between each animal and two stout batons at the back shall be provided to prevent the animal from falling; (d) to prevent horses from being frightened or injured their heads should face left away from the passing traffic; (e) each vehicle shall not carry more than four to six equines; (f) each vehicle shall be provided with one attendant; (g) these vehicles shall be driven at a speed not more than 35 kilometers per hour;

63. For the transport of equines by sea the following precautions shall be taken, namely: (a) horses may normally

be accommodated in single stalls and mules in pens, each pen holding four to five mules; (b) ample ventilation shall be ensured by keeping portholes and providing permanent air trunks or electric blowers on all decks, and exhaust fans shall be installed to blow out foul air; (c) all standings shall be athwart the ship with heads facing inwards; (d) to avoid distress specially during hot weather, the ship may go underway immediately after embarking and disembarking shall be done as early as possible after anchoring. (e) colts and fillies shall be kept on the exposed decks; (f) a pharmacy and spare stalls for five per cent of equines shall be available; (g) passage between two rows of pens shall not be less than 1.5 metres.

Transport of Sheep and Goats

64. Rules 65 to 75 shall apply to the transport of sheep and goats by rail or road involving journeys of more than six hours.

65. (a) A valid health certificate by a qualified veterinary surgeon to the effect that the sheep and goats are in a fit condition to travel by rail or road and are not suffering from infectious or contagious or parasitic disease shall accompany each consignment. (b) In the absence of such a certificate, the carrier shall refuse to accept the consignment for transport. (c) The certificate shall be in a form specified in Schedule-J

66. (a) Each consignment shall bear a label showing in bold red letters the name, address and telephone number (if any) of the consignor and consignee the number and type of sheep or goats being transported and quanity of rations and food provided. (b) The consignee shall be informed in advance about the train or vehicle in which the consignment of sheep or goats are being sent and its arrival time. (c) The consignment of sheep or gaots shall be booked by the next train or vehicle and shall not be detained after the consignment is accepted for booking.

67. (a) First-aid equipment shall accompany the sheep or goats in transit. (b) Suitable romps shall be provided for loading and unloading the sheep or goats. (c) In the case of a railway

wagon, when the loading or unloading is done on the plot form the dropped door of the wagon shall be used as a ramp.

68. Sheep and goats shall be transported seperately; but if the lots are small special partition shall be provided to separate them.

69. Rams and male young stock shall not be mixed with female stock in the same compartment.

70. Sufficient food and fodder shall be carried to last during the journey and watering facility shall be provided at regular intervals.

71. Material for padding, such as straw, shall be placed on the floor to avoid injury if an animal lies down, and this shall be not less than 5 cm. thick

72. The animals shall not be fettered unless there is a risk of their jumping out and their legs shall not be tied down.

73. The space required for a goat shall be the same as that for a woolled sheep and the approximate space required for a sheep in a goods vehicle or a railway wagon shall be as under:-

APPROXIMATE WEIGHT OF ANIMAL IN KILOGRAM

Space Required in Square metres

Woolled Shorn

Not more than 20 0.18 0.16

More than 20 but not more than 25 0.20 0.18

More than 25 but not more than 30 0.23 0.22

More than 30 0.28 0.26

74. (a) No railway wagon shall accommodate more than the following number of sheep or goats:

(b) Adequate ventilation shall be provided in every wagon. Upper door of one side of wagon shall be kept open and properly fixed and the upper door of the wagon shall have wire guage closely welded mesh arrangements to prevent burning cinders from the engines entering the wagon and leading to fire breakout.

Broad gauge Metre gauge Narrow gauge					
(1)	(2)	(3)	(4)	(5)	
Area of Area of Area of Area of wagon wagon wagon wagon	**Area of Area of Area of Area of Wagon**	**Area of Area of Area of Area of Wagon**	**Area of Wagon**		
Less than 21.1 Less than 12.5 Square	21.1	Less than	12.5		
21.1	Square Metres And above	12.5	Square Metres and above		
70	100	50	60	25	

75. (1) Goods vehicles of capacity of 5 or 4 1/2.tons, which are generally used for transporting animals, shall carry not more than forty sheep or goats.

(2) In the case of large goods vehicles and wagons, partition shall be provided at every two or three metres across the width to prevent the crowding and trapping of sheep and goats.

(3) In the case of ewes, goats or lambs or kids under six weeks of age, separate panels shall be provided.

S.O.269 (E) - Whereas certain draft rules further to amend the Transport of Animals Rules, 1978 were published as required by sub-section (1) of section 38 of the Prevention of Cruelty to Animals Act, 1960 (59 of 1960) under the notification of the Government of India in the Ministry of Social Justice & Empowerment number S.O. 1164 (E) dated 26th December 2000 in the Gazette of India. Extraordinary, Part 11, Section 3. Sub Section (ii) dated the 27th December, 2000 inviting objections and suggestions from all persons likely to be affected thereby, before the expiry of the period of sixty days from the date on which copies of the Gazette containing the said notification are made available to the public.

And, whereas copies of the said Gazette were made available to the public on the 1st January 2001.

And, whereas no objection or suggestion has been received from the public in respect of the said draft rules by the Central Government.

Now, therefore in exercise of the ; owers conferred by sub-section (1) and (2) of section 38 of the Prevention of Cruelty to Animals Act 1960 (59 of 1960), the Central Government hereby makes the following rules further to amend the Transport of Animals Rules 1978, namely

1. (1) These rules may be called the Transport of Animals (Amendment) Rules, 2001. (2) They shall come into force on the date of their publication in the Official Gazette.

2. In the Transport of Animal Rules 1978 (hereinafter referred to as the said rules), after chapter VI, the following chapters shall be inserted, namely :

TRANSPORT OF POULTRY BY RAIL, ROAD AND AIR

76. Definition - In this Chapter unless the context otherwise requires, "Poultry" includes day old chicks and turkey poults, chickens, quails, guinea fowls, ducks, geese and turkeys.

77. General requirement - In transport of poultry by rail, road or air -

(a) the container shall be properly cleaned and sterilised before the poultry is placed in them

(b) poultry shall not be exposed to the sunlight, rain and direct blast of air during transport.

(c) poultry shall not be transported when the temperature exceeds 25 degree Celsius or when the temperature falls below 15 degree Celsius.

78. Day-old chicks and turkey poults - In transport of day old chicks and poultry by rail, road and air (a) chicks and poults shall be packed and dispatched immediately after hatching and shall not be stored in boxes for any length of time before dispatch.

Note : In the said transport endeavour shall be made by the consignor or his agent so that consignments shall arrive at destination within the shortest possible time after being taken out of the incubator. Seventy two hours shall normally be regarded as the maximum period to be taken trom incubator to brooder in winter and 48 hours in summer;

(b) chicks or poults shall not be fed or watered before and during transportation.

(c) every effort shall be made to ensure that chicks and poults arrive as quickly as possible at the dispatching site

(d) personal attention shall be given by the consignor or the forwarding agent to ensure that all consignments are kept out of direct sunlight, rain and heat;

(e) care shall be taken to carry the boxes in a level position so that chicks are not in danger of falling over on to their backs an' 11 The putting up of other merchandise over and around chick boxes shall be avoided.

79. Poultry other than day-old chicks and turkey poults

In transport of poultry other than day old chicks and turkey poult by rail, road or air

(a) the poultry to be transported shall be healthy and in good condition and shall be examined and certified by a veterinary doctor for freedom from infectious diseases and fitness to undertake the journey.

(b) poultry transported in the same container shall be of the same species and of the same age group

(c) poultry shall be properly fed and watered before it is placed in containers for transportation and extra feed and water shall be provided in suitable troughs fixed in the containers.

(d) arrangements shall be made for watering and feeding during transportation and during hot weather, watering shall be ensured every six hours;

(e) male stock shall not be transported with female stock in the same container

80. Road Travel - In transport of poultry by road the container shall not be placed one on the top of the other and shall be covered properly in order to provide light, ventilation and to protect from rain, heat and cold air.

81. Rail Travel - In transport of poultry by rail -

(a) in case the journey is for more than twelve hours, an attendant shall accompany the consignment:

(b) poultry shall not be exposed to rain or direct blast of air;

(c) as far as possible poultry shall be transported in wagons having adequate facilities for ventilation and no other merchandise which may result in mortality of birds shall be loaded in the same wagon;

82. Air travel - In transport of poultry by air or for international transport the containers carrying poultry shall be kept in pressurised compartments with regulated temperature and the container shall preferably be kept near the door and shall be unloaded immediately on arrival.

83. Containers for transportation - In transport of poultry by rail, road or air -

(a) containers used to transport poultry shall be make of such material which shall not collapse or crumble and they shall be well ventilated and designed to protect the health of poultry by giving it adequate space and safety.

(b) the containers shall be so designed as to render impossible for birds to crowd into the corners during transportation, and to avoid the danger of boxes being stocked so close together as to interfere with ventilation.

(c) all the containers shall be clearly labelled showing the name, address and telephone number of the consignor and the consignee.

(d) the minimum floor space per bird and the dimension of the containers for transporting poultry shall be a specified in the Table below, namely :

TABLE

S.No.	Kind of Poultry	Minimum	Demension			
		Floor space cm²	Length cm	Width cm	Height cm	Number in a container
i.	Month old chickens	75	60	30	18	24
ii.	Three month old chickens	230	55	50	35	12
iii.	Adult sock (excluding geese and turkeys)	480	115	50	45	12
iv.	Geese and turkeys	900	120	75	75	10 youngs
		1300	75	35	75	2 growing
		1900	55	35	75	1 grown up
v.	Chicks	-	60	45	12	80
vi.	Poult	-	60	45	12	60

84. Special requirement of containers for chicks and poults - In transport of poultry by road, rail or air –

(a) wire mesh or a net of any material shall not be used as a bottom for the containers.

(b) the container shall be properly secured to avoid pilferage

(c) the following instruction shall be printed on a label and fixed to the lid or printed directly on sides, namely "Care in Transit".

(d) the consignee shall be informed about the train, transport or flight number and its time of arrival well in advance

(e) poultry shall not be transported continuously for more than 6 hours and whole batch shall be inspected at every 6 hours interval.

(f) the transportation shall not remain stationary for more than 30 min and during this period, it shall be parked in shade and arrangements shall be made for feeding and watering

(g) all precautions against fire shall be taken and provision of fire extinguishers in transport shall be provided.

TRANSPORT OF PIGS BY RAIL OR ROAD

85. DEFINITION - In this chapter, unless context otherwise requires, "pigs" includes piglets, hogs, hoglets and animals of pigs family,

86. Duration of travel - Rules 87 to 95 shall apply to the transport of pigs by rail or road involving journeys of more than six hours.

87. Health Certificate -

(1) A valid health certificate by a veterinary doctor to the effect that the pigs are in a fit condition to travel by rail or road and are not suffering from infectious or contagious or parasitic disease shall accompany each consignment in the transport of pigs by rail or road.

(2) In the absence of a certificate under sub-rule (1), the carrier shall refuse to accept the consignment for transport.

(3) The certificate under sub rule (1) shall be in a form specified in Schedule K

88. Identification of consignor and consignee - For the purpose of this Chapter -

(a) each consignment shall bear a label showing in bold red letters the name, address and telephone number (if any) of the consignor and consignee, the number and type of pigs being transported and quantity of rations and food provided to them.

(b) the consignee shall be informed in advance about the train or vehicle in which the consignment of pigs is being sent and its arrival time.

(c) the consignment of pigs shall be booked by the next train or vehicle and shall not be detained after the consignment is accepted for booking.

89. First aid - In transport of pigs by rail or road.

(a) first-aid equipment shall accompany the pigs;

(b) suitable ramps shall be provided for loading and I unloading the pigs;

(c) in the case of a railway wagon, when the loading or unloading is done on the platform the dropped door of the wagon shall be u~ed as a ramp.

90. Group of pigs - In transport of pigs by rail or road, male young stock shall not be mixed with female stock in the same compartment.

91. Facility of food and water - In transport of pigs by rail or road, sufficient food and fodder shall be carried to last during the journey and watering facility shall be provided at regular intervals.

92. Padding of floor during travel - In transport of pigs by rail or road, material for padding, such as straw, shall be placed on the floor to avoid injury if an animal lies down, and this shall be not less than 5 cm thick.

93. Ban on fettering - In transport of pigs by rail or road, the animals shall not be fettered unless there is a risk of their jumping out and their legs shall not be tied down.

94. Space requirement during rail travel - In transport of pigs by rail: (a) no railway wagon shall accommodate more than the number of pigs as specified in the Table below :

TABLE

Broad gauge (1)		**Metre gauge (2)**		**Narrow gauge (3)**
Area of Wagon	Area of Wagon	Area of Wagon	Area of Wagon	
Less than 21.1 squares Metres	More than 21.1 Square Metres	Less than 12.5 Square Meter	More than 12.5 Square Meter	
Number of Pigs 35	Number of Pigs 50	Number of Pigs 25	Number of Pigs 30	not allowed

(b) adequate ventilation shall be provided in every wagon and the upper door of one side of wagon shall be kept open and properly fixed and the upper door of the wagon shall have wire gauge closely welded mesh arrangements to prevent burning cinders from the engines entering the wagon and leading to fire breakout.

95. Space requirement during road travel - In transport of pigs by road -

(a) goods vehicles of capacity of 5 or 4.5 tons, which are generally used for transportation of animals, shall car not more than twenty pigs.

(b) in the case of large goods vehicles and containers, Explanation : For the purpose of this rule the certificate partition shall be provided at every two or three metres shall be issued in such form as may be specified for this across the width to prevent the crowding and trapping purpose by the Central Government of pigs

(c) in the case of pigs under six weeks of age, separate panels shall be provided.

MISCELLANEOUS

96. Issue of certificate before transportation -

(1) A valid certificate issued by an officer or any person or Animal Welfare Organisation duly recognised and authorised for this purpose by the Animal Welfare Board of India or the Central Government shall be procured by any person making transport of any animal before transportation of such animal verifying that all the relevant Central and State Acts, rules and orders pertaining to the said animals including the rules relating to transport of such animals have been duly complied with and that the animal is not being transported for any purpose contrary to the provision of any law.

(2) In the absence of such certificate, the carrier shall refuse to accept the consignment for transport.

97. Cancellation of permit or authorisation for transport -

(1) In the event of contravention or non compliance of any of the rules contained in these rule for transport of animals, if it is pointed out in writing by any officer or persons or Animal Welfare Organisations authorised for this purpose by the Animal Welfare Board of India or the Central Government, then, any permit or authorisation issued for such transport shall be immediately cancelled by the concerned authority and it shall be the duty of the police to stop the further transport even from the intermediary station and proceed against the said offenders and deal with the animal in accordance with law.

(2) The custody of the animals immediately after unloading from the rail wagons, truck or any other vehicle shall be given to the authorised Animal Welfare Organisation if available, till the competent authority or the magistrate having jurisdiction decides about their care and upkeep.

98. General conditions of transport -

(1) Animals to be transported shall be healthy and in good condition and such animals shall be examined by a veterinary doctor for freedom from infectious diseases and their fitness to undertake the journey; provided that the nature and duration of the proposed journey shall be taken into account while deciding upon the degree of fitness.

(2) An animal which is unfit for transport shall not be transported and the animals who are new born, diseased, blind emaciated, lame, fatigued or having given birth during the preceding seventy two hours or likely to give birth during transport shall not be transported.

(3) Pregnant and very young animals shall not be mixed with other animals during transport.

(4) Different classes of animals shall be kept separately during transport.

(5) Diseased animals, whenever transported for treatment, shall not be mixed with other animals

(6) Troublesome animals shall be given tranquilisers before loading during transport.

(7) Animals shall be transported in their on-farm social groups (established atleast one week prior to journey).

APPLICATION OF FINES RULES, 1978.

In exercise of the powers conferred by clause (K) o f sub-section (2) of Section 38 of the Prevention of Cruelty to Animals Act, 1960 (59 of 1960), the Central Government hereby makes the following rules, the some having been previously published as required by the said Section, namely

1. Short Title: These rules may be called the Prevention of Cruelty to Animals (Application of Fines) Rules, 1978.

2. Definitions:

In these rules, unless the context otherwise requires

(a) "Act" means the Prevention of Cruelty to Animals Act, 1960 (59 of 1960)

(b) "Board" means the Animal Welfare Board of India established under the Act

(c) "Fines" means fines levied under the Act.

3. Fines, after deducting cost of collection, to be made over to- Board

(1) . Fines levied and realised under the Act shall, subject to any deductions relating to the cost of collection, be made over by the State Government to the Board as soon as may be after due appropriation by law (State Legislature) in this behalf.

4. Application of fines made over to Board:

(1) Fines made over by any State Government to the Board shall be applied exclusively for the following purposes, namely:-

(i) the grant of financial assistance to societies dealing with the Prevention of Cruelty to Animals or organisation actively interested in animal welfare work which are for the time being recognised by the Board.

(ii) the maintenance of infirmaries, pinjrapoles and veterinary hospitals.

(2) Fines realised in one State and made over to the Board shall be utilised only for the benefit of such societies or other organisations within the jurisdiction of the State and not otherwise.

5. Principles to govern application of fines:

In applying the fines for the benefit of societies or other organisations in any State, the Board shall have due regard to the following principles, namely:-

(i) Financial assistance shall first be given to societies dealing with the prevention of cruelty to animals within the jurisdication of the state which are for the time being recognized by the Board.

(ii) In granting fiancial assistance to such societies, due regard shall be had to the amounts they had been receiving from the State Government prior fo the coming into force of these rules, and consistently with the amount of fines at its disposal and having regard to the revenues of the Societies concerned, the objects for which assistance is to be given and other relevant matters, the Board shall make every endeavour to ensure that there is no diminution in the amounts such societies had been receiving earlier.

(iii) If after the grant of financial assistance to the societies earlier referred to in this rule, there is any unspent balance, it may be applied by the Board at its discretion for the benefit of any other organisation actively interested in animal welfare work including infirmaries, pinjrapoles and veterninary hospitals.

PRERFORMING ANIMALS RULES, 1973

In exercise of the powers conferred by section 38 read with section 37 of the Prevention of Cruelty to Animals Act, 1960 (59 of 1960), the Central Government hereby makes the following rules, namely:

1. Short Title and commencement:

1. These rules may be called the Performing Animals Rules, 1973.

2. They shall come into force in any State on such date as the State Government may, by notification in the Official Gazette, appoint.

2. Definitions : In these rules, unless the context otherwise requires

a. "Act" means the Prevention of Cruelty to Animals Act, 1960.

b. "performing animal" means any animal which is used at, or for the purpose of any entertainment to which the public are admitted through sale of tickets.

c. "prescribed authority" means the State Government or such other authority as the State Government may, by general or special order, specify in this behalf.

d. "schedule" means a schedule appended to these rules.

3. Application for registration :

i. Every application by a person desirous of exhibiting or training any performing animal for registration under the Act shall be in the form and shall contain the particulars set out in the first Schedule.

ii. Every such application shall be made to the prescribed authority within whose jurisdiction the applicant ordinarily resides and, if he has no fixed place of residence, the application shall be made to such authority as the Central Government may by order specify in this behalf.

3. Fee and Registration :

Every application for registration shall be accompanied by a fee of rupees twentyfive which may be paid either in cash or in such other manner as may be specified by the prescribed authority.

4. Form of Certificate of Registration

i. The certificate of registration to be issued by the prescribed authority shall be in the form set out in the Second Schedule.

ii. Every registration shall be given a serial number according to the order in which it is made, and the serial number shall be inserted in the certificate of registration issued to the applicant.

3. Register :

Every person to whom a certificate of registration is issued under these rules shall have his name entered in a register which shall be kept in the form set out in the Third Schedule.

4. Inspection of Register

The register kept under these rules shall be open to inspection during office hours on any working day on payment of a fee of two rupees and any person may take extract therefrom or may require the prescribed authority to issue to him a certified copy of any entry therein on payment of a fee of five rupees.

5. Application for variation of entries in register :

Every application under sub-section (5) of section 23 of the Act for the variation of any particulars entered in the register shall be in the form set out in the Fourth Schedule and when any particulars are varied the existing certificate of registration shall be cancelled and a new certificate issued to the applicant.

6. Issue of duplicate copies of certificates

Any person whose name is registered under these rules may, on proof by him that the original certificate of registration has been lost or destroyed and on payment of a fee of rupees five, be given a duplicate copy of the certificate of registration which for the purpose of these rules shall have the same effect as the original certificate of registration.

7. Copies of certificates etc. to be sent to the Animal Welfare Board of India :

The prescribed authority shall cause a copy of every certificate of registration or duplicate thereof or a new certificate issued under these rules to be sent to the Animal Welfare Board of India established under the Act, as soon as may be after it is issued.

FIRST SCHEDULE

(SEE RULE 3)

Form of Application

I, the undersigned, do hereby apply for registration under the Performing Animal Rules, 1973 and do hereby declare the following particulars to be true and complete to the best of my knowledge and belief.

Signature ....

Date ....

Address to which certificate of

registration is to be sent.

....

PARTICULARS

1. Full name of applicant(in block letters)

2. State name (if any used in India)

3. Nationality

4. Either (a) address of fixed place of residence in India, or (b) permanent postal address in India to which letters addressed to the applicant may be forwarded.

1. Address or addresses (if any) in India, other than temporary addresses while on tour, at which applicant trains or intends to train performing animals. (If none, write, "None".)

2. State whether previously registered under the Performing Animals Rules, 1973. If so, state the number and date of certificate of registration.

3. (i) Kinds of performing animals proposed to be To be trained To be exhibited Kind Number Kind Number; (a) trained, (b) exhibited, Stating number of each kind Kind Number; (ii) Trained animals already available for being exhibited.

8. Describe briefly the general nature* of the performance or performances in which the performing animals are to be exhibited or for which they are to be trained, mentioning any apparatus which is used for the purpose of the performance.

* The description must be sufficient to give a general idea of what is done by the animals taking part in the performance, and should state the approximate duration of the performance, the number of times for which it is usually to be given in one and the same day, and the number of animals of each kind taking part in the performance. It need not give details which would divulge any professional secret.

SECOND SCHEDULE

(See Rule 5)

Certificate of Registration

This is to certify that the person to whom the under- Serial Number of Entry

mentioned particulars relate has this day been registered in Register

under the performing Animals Rules, 1975 with the

registration authority for the

Name of the place:

Date: Signature of Clerk or registration authority

PARTICULARS

of er tor	Nationality	Either (a) Address of fixed place of residence in India or (b) Pemanent postal address in India to which letters addressed to the trainer or exhibiter may be forwarded	Address or addresses at which the performing animals are to be trained	Particulars of any previous registration	Kinds of performing animals		Description of general nature of performance	Date of Registration	Particulars of any order of Court made under section 24 of the Prevention of Cruelty to Animals Act, 1960
					to be trained	To be exhibited			
					Kind No.	Kind No.			
	2	3	4	5	6	7	8	9	10

THIRD SCHEDULE

(SEE RULE 6)

Form of Register

Serial Number	Name of trainer or exhibitor	Nationality	Either (a) Address of fixed place of residence in India or (b) Permanent postal address in India to which letters addressed to the trainer or exhibitor may be forwarded	Address or Addresses at which the performing animals are to be trained	Particulars of any previous registration	K[illegible] of performing Animals		Description of general nature of performance	Date of Registration	Particulars of any order of Court made under section 24 of the Prevention of Cruelty to Animals Act, 1960
						to be trained Kind No.	to be exhibited Kind No.			
1	2	3	4	5	6	7	8	9	10	11

THE PREVENTION OF CRUELTY TO ANIMALS (LICENSING OF FARRIERS) RULES, 1965.

In exercise of the powers conferred by clause (f) of subsection (2) of section 38 of the Prevention of Cruelty to Animals Act, 1960 (59 of 1960), the Central Government hereby makes the following rules, the same having been previously published as required by subsection (1) of that section, namely

The Prevention of Cruelty to Animals (Licensing of Farriers) Rules, 1965

1. Short title and commencement:

1. These rules may be called the Prevention of Cruelty to Animals (Licensing of Farriers) Rules, 1965.

2. They shall come into force in any State on such date as the State Government may, by notification in the official Gazette, appoint, and different dates may be appointed for different areas of the State.

1. Definitions:

In these rules, unless the context otherwise requires

a. "cattle" means buffaloes, bullocks, horses, mules, or donkeys and includes other animals used for draught, pack or carriage purpose, which require shoeing;

b. "farrier" means a person who carries on the business of shoeing cattle

c. "licence" means a licence granted under these rules;

d. "licensing authority" means such officer of the veterinary department of the State or a local authority or any organiscition for the welfare of animals as the State Government may, by general or special order, specify in this behalf.

3 Farriers to be licenced :

No person shall, after the commencement of these rules, begin to carry on the business of a farrier, and no person carrying on the business of a farrier at the commencement of these rules, shall, after the expiration of three months from such commencement, continue to carry on such business, except under a licence.

4. Persons entitled to apply for licence Every person who

i. has completed the age of eighteen years , and

ii. has undergone any such training in the business of shoeing cattle as may be approved by the licensing authority;* or

iii. has been carrying on the business of a farrier for not less than two years before the commencement of these rules shall be entitled to a licence.

4. Application for licence :

Every person who at the commencement of these rules is carrying on the business of a farrier and who intends to carry on such business after such commencement and every person who intends to begin such business after such commencement shall apply in writing to the licensing authority for a licence giving his name, place of residence, place of business. his qualifications for the licence and such other particulars as the licensing authority may require

5. Grant of licence :

The licensing authority shall after satisfying himself as to whether the applicant is a fit and proper person to be granted a licence and whether he has equipped himself or has made arrangements for equipping himself with proper tools and other implements for the purpose of his business, grant to, every applicant who is duly qualified in this behalf a licence in the form prescribed in the Annexure to these rules.

Explanation : The tools and other implements which a person carrying on or intending to carry on the business of a farrier shall ordinarily have in his possession are the following, namely

1 Driving hammer with claws.

2 Hand hammer.

3 Drawing knife.

4 Scorcher knife.

5 Pincers.

6 Buffer.

7 Rasp.

8 Chisel for cutting bar iron.

9 Punch for making nail holes.

10 Nails for shoeing.

11 Twitch.

12 Wooden plank for finishing work.

13 Iron anvil.

14 Good quality wrought iron for shoes.

6. Term of licence and renewal thereof :

1. A licence shall be valid for a period of two years from the years from the date of its grant, but it may be renewed from time to time on application made by the licence stating the period from which the licence is to be renewed: Provided that no licence shall be renewed for a period exceeding two years at a time.

2. The renewal of a licence shall be made by inscribing, in the columns provided for the purpose in the licence, the date of renewal, the date of expiry of the renewed licence and the signature of the licensing authority.

8. Issue of duplicate licence :

If a licence is defaced, lost or destroyed the licensing authority may after making such inquiry into the matter as he thinks fit, issue a duplicate.

9. Farrier to exercise reasonable care and skill :

Every licence under these rules shall exercise a reasonable degree of care and skill in the shoeing of cattle.

10. Cancellation of licence:

1. It shall be lawful for ' the licensing authority to enter the place of business of any licence during normal working hours for the purpose of inspection; and if, in the opinion of the licensing authority the licence is unable to exercise a reasonable degree of care and skill in the shoeing of cattle or is not properly equipped for the purposes of his business, he may, after giving the licence a reasonable opportunity of being heard, cancel the licence.

2. A licence may also be cancelled if the licensing authority is satisfied, after giving the licence a reasonable opportunity of being heard, that there has been a breach of any of the conditions of the licence.

"10A.An appeal shall lie from any order refusing or canceling a licence under these rules to such authority as the State Government may, by notification in the official Gazette, specify for the purpose."

8. Issue of fresh licence after cancellation:

A person whose licence has been cancelled under rule 10 may be granted a fresh licence on application made in this behalf if the licensing authority is satisfied that having regard to the circumstances obtaining at the time of such application, there is no reason why the applicant should not be granted a fresh licence.

9. Fees :

1. The fees payable on every application for a licence shall be one rupee and that on every application for renewal of the licence or for a duplicate thereof shall be fifty paise.

2. Such fees may be paid either in cash or by affixing non-judicial stamps of equivalent value to the application.

8. Maintenance of register

The licensing authority shall maintain a register containing full particulars relating to every licence o Inserted by the Licensing of Farriers (Amendment) Rules, 1966 - vide Government of India, Ministry of Food, Agriculture, Community Development and co-operation (Department of Agriculture) Notification No. 1913/65-LD, dated the 8th March, 1966

Farrier's Licence

Licence No ....

1. Name of Licence.

2. Place of residence and full postal address.

1. Place of business.

4. Duration of Licence.

From..............................To ....

CONDITIONS OF LICENCE

1. This licence is valid for two years only from the date of its grant, unless renewed, on application made under rule 7 of the Prevention of Cruelty to Animals (Licensing of Farriers) Rules, 1965, within one month before the date of expiry of the original or earlier licence.

2. During the continuance of the licence, the licence shall be bound to produce for inspection during normal workings hours and at his place of business all the tools and other implements in his possession and kept for the purpose of his business if a demand for the production of the same is made by the licensing authority.

3. The licence shall afford all reasonable facilities for the purpose of enabling the licensing authority to inspect the place of business of the licence and the manner in which he is carrying on the business.

RENEWAL ENDORSEMENT

Date of Renewal	Date of Expiry	Signature of licensing authority	Remarks
	2	3	4

THE PREVENTION OF CRUELTY TO DRAUGHT AND PACK ANIMALS RULES

In exercise of the powers conferred by sub-section (2) of section 38'of the Prevention of Cruelty to Animals Act, 1960 (59 of 1960), the Central Government hereby makes the following rules, the same having been previously published as required by sub-section (i) of that section, namely

The Prevention of Cruelty to Draught and Pack Animals Rules, 1965

1. Short title and commencement:

(1)These rules may be called the Prevention of Cruelty to Drought and Pack Animals Rules, 1965.

1. They shall come into force in any State on such date as the State Government may, by notification in the official Gazette, appoint.

2. Definitions

1. In these rules, unless the context otherwise requires

a. "large bullock" or "largo buffalo" respectively means a bullock or buffalo, the weight of which exceeds 350 kilograms;

b. "medium bullock" or "medium buffalo" respectively means a bullock or buffalo, the weight of which exceeds 250 kilograms, but does not exceed 350 kilograms"small bullock" or

c. "small buffalo" respectively means a bullock or buffalo, the weight of which does not exceed 250 kilograms ;

d. "street" includes any way, road, lane, square, alley or passage, whether a throughfare or not over which the public have a right of way; "vehicle" means a wheeled conveyance of any description which is capable of being used as such on any street.

1. For the purposes of clauses (a), (b) and (c) of sub-rule (1), the weight of an animal shall be determined by applying any of the following formulae, namely:

$$\frac{\text{length x Girth 2 in cms.}}{10838} = \text{Weight of animal in kgms}$$

or

$$\frac{9(\text{length in cms. x Girth in cms}^2)}{1{,}00{,}000}$$

3.Maximum loads for draught animals:

1. No person shall cause any animal specified in column 1 of the table below to draw a vehicle of the kind described in the corresponding entry in column 2 thereof if it carries a load in excess of the weight specified in the corresponding entry in column 3 thereof.

1. Where the vehicle to be drawn is a four-wheeled vehicle, weight specified in column 3 of the said table shall, in each case, be read as being one and a quarter times and, if the four-wheeled vehicle is one fitted with pneumatic tyres, as being one and a half times, as much as the weight so specified.

2. Where the vehicle, whether two-wheeled or four-wheeled is to be drawn by two animals of either species referred to in each of the entries in column 1 ofmthe said table, the weight specified in the corresponding entry in column 3 thereof shall be read as being twice, and, if the vehicle is one fitted with pneumatic tyres, as being two and a half times as much as the weight so specified.

S.No.	1	2	3
	Small bullock or small buffalo	Two-wheeled vehicle	
		a) if fitted with ball bearing	1000 kilograms
		b)if fitted with pneumatic tyres	750 kilograms
		c)if not fitted with pneumatic tyres	500 kilograms
2.	Medium bullock or medium buffalo	Two-wheeled vehicle	
		a) if fitted with ball bearing	1400 kilograms
		b)if fitted with pneumatic tyres	1050 kilograms
		c)if not fitted with pneumatic tyres	900 kilograms
3.	Large bullock or large buffalo	Tow-wheeled -vehicle	
		a) if fitted with ball bearing	1800 kilograms
		b)if fitted with pneumatic tyres	1350 kilograms
		c)if not fitted with pneumatic tyres	900 kilograms
4.	Horse or mule	Two- wheeled vehicle	
		a)if fitted with pneumatic tyres	750 kilograms
		b)if not fitted with pneumatic tyres	500 kilograms
5.	Pony	Two -Wheeled vehicle	
		a)if fitted with pneumatic tyres	600 kilograms
		b)if not fitted with pneumatic tyres	400 kilograms
6.	Camel	Two-Wheeled Vehicle	1000 kilograms

3. Where the route by which a vehicle is to be drawn involves an ascent for not less than one kilometer and the gradient is more than three meters in a distance of thirty meters, the weight specified in column 3 of the said table shall, in each case, be read as being one-half of what is so specified.

Explanation 1: The weights specified in this rule shall be inclusive or the weight of the vehicle.

Explanation 2: In calculating any weight for the purpose of this rule, fractions shall be disregarded.

4. Maximum load for certain pack animals:

No person shall cause any animal specified in column 1 of the table below to carry any load in excess of the weight specified in the corresponding entry in column 2 thereof.

S.No.	1	2
1	Small bullock or buffalo	100 kilograms
2	Medium bullock or buffalo	150 kilograms
3	Large bullock or buffalo	175 kilograms
4	Pony	70 kilograms
5	Mule	200 kilograms
6	Donkey	50 kilograms
7	7. Camel	250 kilograms

5. Maximum number of passengers for animal drawn vehicles : No person in charge of any vehicle drawn by any animal referred to in column I of the table under sub-rule (1) or rule 3 shall allow more than four persons, excluding the driver and children below 6 years of age, to ride on the vehicle.

6. General Conditions for use of draught and pack animals: No person shall use or cause to be used any animal for drawing any vehicle or carrying any load

1. for more than nine hours in a day in the aggregate.

2. for more than five hours continuously without a break for rest for the animal

3. in any area where the temperature exceeds 37'C (99'F) during the period between12.00 noon and 3.00 p.m.

7. Animals to be disengaged after work:

No person shall continue to keep or cause to be kept in harness any animal used for the purpose of drawing vehicles, after it is no longer needed for such purpose.

8. Use of Spiked bits prohibited: No person shall, for the purpose of driving or riding an animal or causing it to draw any vehicle or for otherwise controlling it, use any spiked stick or bit, harness or yoke with spikes, knobs or -projections or any other sharp tackle or equipment which causes or is likely to cause bruises, swellings, abrasions or severe pain to the animal.

9. Saddling of horses : No person shall cause a horse to be saddled in such a way that the harness rests directly on the animal's withers without there being sufficient clearance between the arch of the saddle and the withers.

10. Certificates regarding unladen weight of vehicles, etc.

1. For the purpose of these rules, the Board may authorise any organisation established for the purpose of preventing cruelty to animals or for promoting their welfare to issue to the owner of any vehicle which may be brought before it for examination, a certificate as to its unladen weight, and any certificate so issued may be accepted as evidence of the weight of such vehicle.

1. Nothing contained in this rule shall be construed as being in derogation of any right conferred by any law for the time being in force authorising any local authority to determine the unladen weight of any vehicle and to grant the necessary certificate-or stamp the vehicle in this behalf.

11. Powers of police officers and. other authorised persons:

1. If any police officer above the rank of a constable or any other person authorised in this behalf by the State Government or by the Board by general or special order has reason to believe that an offence against rule 3 or 4, has been or is being committed in respect of any animal referred to therein, he may, in any case where a weigh bridge is available within a reasonable distance, require the owner or other person in charge of such animal to take the animal or the vehicle or both to the weigh bridge for the purpose of determining the weight. of the load which the animal has been or is drawing or carrying.

2. If the owner or other person in charge of the aforesaid animal refuses to comply with the demand of the police officer or other person as so authorised, it shall be lawful for such police officer or other person to take the animal or the vehicle or both to the weight bridge for the purpose aforesaid:

3. As soon as any weight is determined under this rule, the owner or other person in charge of the said animal shall be given a statement in writing signed by the police officer or the person authorised as aforesaid, as the case may be, as to the weight so determined and any other information relevant for the purpose.

12. Application of rules where local bye-laws etc. exist:

If there is in force in any area to which these rules extend, any rule, regulation or bye-law made under any law for the time being in force by any local authority in respect of any of the matters for which provision is made in these rules, such rule, regulation or bye-law shall, to the extent to which

a. It contains provisions less irksome to the animal than those contained in these rules, prevail,

b. It contains provisions more irksome to the animal than those contained in these rules, be of no effect.

(Notified in the Gazette of India, Part 11, Section 3, Sub-section (ii), vide Government of India, Ministry of Food and Agriculture, No. 9-18/62-LD. Dated 23rd March, 1965.)

MINISTRY OF SOCIAL JUSTICE AND EMPOWERMENT

Notification

New Delhi, the 14th October, 1998

G.S.R. 619(E).— Whereas the High Court of Delhi in C.W.P No. 890/91 by its order dated 21st August, 1997 directed that "the Central Government may take up the notification dated 2-3-1991 for consideration afresh" and "take into consideration such material as may be available with it or it may choose to collect through any of the authentic agencies or such other agency or committee of experts as it may choose to appoint";

Whereas in pursuance of the order of the Hon'ble High Court of Delhi, the Central Government constituted a Committee under the Chairmanship of Additional Inspector General of Forests (Wildlife) to have a fresh tool at the notification G S P No.252 dated 2-3-1991 in the light of the additional material available with any authenticated agencies such other agency persons;

Whereas the said Committee submitted its report to the Central Government;

Whereas the Central Government has taken into consideration the report of the said Committee;

Now, therefore, in exercise of the powers conferred by section 22 of the Prevention of Cruelty of Animals Act, 1960 (59 of 1960), and in supersession of the Notification of the Government of India in the erstwhile Ministry of Environment and Forests G.S.R. No. 252 dated 2-3-1991 and G.S.R. No. 485 dated 7-8-1991, except as respects things done or omitted to be done before such supersession, the Central Government hereby specifies that the following animals shall not be exhibited on trained as a performing animals, with effect from the date of publication of this notification, namely : 1. Bears 2. Monkeys 3. Tigers 4.Panthers 5. Lions

BIBLIOGRAPHY

Ausubel, F.M.: *Current Protocols in Molecular Biology*, New York, John Wiley and Sons, 1989.

Bernauer, Thomas: *Genes, Trade, and Regulation: The Seeds of Conflict in Food Biotechnology*, Princeton, Princeton University. 2003.

Brandwein, P.F.: *Sourcebook for the Biological Sciences*, San Diego, Harcourt Brace JOvanovich, 1986.

Broach, J.R.: *The Molecular Biology of the Yeast*, Cold Spring Harbor, Cold Spring Harbor Laboratory, 1981.

Chrispeels, Maarten : *Plants, Genes and Crop Biotechnology*, Sudbury MA, Jones and Barlett Publishers, 2003.

Costanza, R.: *Ecological Economics*, Columbia Uni. Press., New York, 1991.

Cox, Earl D. : *Beyond Humanity: Cyber Evolution and Future Minds*, Roackland, Charles River Media, 1996.

Daubenmire, F.: *Plants and Environment*, New York, Wiley, 1947.

David Sadava: *Plants, Genes and Crop Biotechnology*, Sudbury MA, Jones and Barlett Publishers, 2003.

Dodds, John H.: *Plant Genetic Engineering*, New York, Cambridge University Press, 1985.

Dusenbery, David B.: *Life at a Small Scale: the Behavior of Microbes*, New York, Scientific American Library, 1996.

E. Dereniak and D. Crowe, *Optical Radiation Detectord*, John Wiley and Sons, 1984.

Fransman M, Junne G, Roobeek A: *The Biotechnology Revolution?*, Oxford, Blackwell, 1995.

Jameson, J. L.: *Principles of Molecular Medicine*, Totowa, Humana Press, 1998.

Goodman, D.C.: *From Farming to Biotechnology: A Theory of Agro-industrial Development*, Oxford, Blackwell, 1987.

Lodish, H.: *Molecular Cell Biology*, New York, Freeman, 2000.

Maarten, C.: *Plants, Genes and Crop Biotechnology*, Sudbury MA, Jones and Barlett Publishers, 2003.

Murray, David: *Seeds of Concern: The Genetic Manipulation of Plants*, Sydney, University of New South Wales, 2003.

Postman, Neil: *Technopoly: The Surrender of Culture to Technology*, New York, Vintage Books, 1992.

Raff, K. Roberts, and J. Watson, *Molecular Biology of the Cell*, New York: Garland Publishing, 1989.

Sheldon, J.K.: *Practical Environmental Bioremediation*, Lewis Publishers, Boca Raton, 1992.

Shetty, Kalidas: *Food Biotechnology*, New York, Dekker/CRC Press, 2005.

Slater, R.J.: *Experiments in Molecular Biology*, Clifton, Humana Press, 1986.

Teich, M.: *Fundamentals of Photonics*, New York: Wiley, 1991.

Walden, Richard: *Genetic Transformation in Plants*, England, Open University Press, 1988.

Wood, E.J. Ferguson: *Marine Microbial Ecology*, London, Chapman and Hall, 1965.

INDEX

□□□